Creating Keepsakes

SCRAPBOOK | MAGAZINE

A TREASURY OF FAVORITES

W9-CCQ-644

Scrapbooking
EVERYDAY
MOMENTS

Presenting over 775 of the best designs and ideas
from *Creating Keepsakes* publications, to help scrappers
capture the silly and endearing moments of "real life."

PRODUCED EXCLUSIVELY FOR LEISURE ARTS

Founding Editor	Lisa Bearnson
Co-founder	Don Lambson
Editor-in-Chief	Tracy White
Special Projects Editor	Leslie Miller
Copy Editor	Kim Sandoval
Editorial Assistants	Joannie McBride, Fred Brewer
Administrative Assistant	Michelle Bradshaw
Art Director	Brian Tippetts
Designer	Blue Sky Studios
Production Designers	Just Scan Me!, Exposure Graphics
Publisher	Mark Seastrand
Media Relations	Alicia Bremer, 801/364-2030
Web Site Manager	Emily Johnson
Assistant Web Site Editor	Sarah Wilcox
Production Manager	Gary Whitehead
Business Sales Manager	Tara Schofield
Business Sales Assistants	Jacque Jensen, Melanie Cain
Advertising Sales Manager	Becky Lowder
Wholesale Accounts	800/815-3538

Donna Hair, stores A–G,
and outside of U.S., ext. 235

Victoria James, stores H–R, ext. 226

Kristin Schaefer, stores S–Z
(except "Scr"), ext. 250

Sherrie Burt, stores starting with "Scr,"
ext. 244

Kim Biehn, distributor accounts, ext. 251

PRIMEDIA
Consumer Magazine & Internet Group

Vice President, Group Publisher	David O'Neil
Circulation Director	Lisa Harris
Associate Circulation Director	Darcy Cruwys
Circulation Manager	Sara Gunn
Promotions Manager	Stephanie Michas
Business Manager	Laurie Halvorsen

PRIMEDIA, Inc.

Chairman	Dean Nelson
President & CEO	Kelly Conlin
Vice-Chairman	Beverly C. Chell

PRIMEDIA Enthusiast Media

EVP Consumer Marketing/Circulation	Steve Aster
SVP/Chief Financial Officer	Kevin Neary
SVP, Mfg., Production & Distribution	Kevin Mullan
SVP/Chief Information Officer	Debra C. Robinson
VP, Consumer Marketing	Bobbi Gutman
VP, Manufacturing	Gregory A. Catsaros
VP, Single Copy Sales	Thomas L. Fogarty
VP, Manufacturing Budgets & Operations	Lilia Golia
VP, Human Resources	Kathleen P. Malinowski
VP, Business Development	Albert Messina
VP, Database / e-Commerce	Suti Prakash

PRIMEDIA Outdoor Recreation and Enthusiast Group

SVP, Group Publishing Director	Brent Diamond
SVP, Marketing and Internet Operations	Stephen H. Bender
VP, Marketing and Internet Operations	Dave Evans

SUBSCRIPTIONS

To subscribe to *Creating Keepsakes* magazine or to change the address of your current subscription, call or write:

Phone: 888/247-5282
International: 760/745-2809
Fax: 760/745-7200

Subscriber Services
Creating Keepsakes
P.O. Box 469007
Escondido, CA 92046-9007

Some back issues of *Creating Keepsakes* magazine are available for $5 each, payable in advance.

CORPORATE OFFICES

Creating Keepsakes is located at 14901 Heritagecrest Way, Bluffdale, UT 84065. Phone: 801/984-2070. Fax: 801/984-2080. Home page: *www.creatingkeepsakes.com*.

Scrapbooking Everyday Moments
Hardcover ISBN 1-57486-460-2
Softcover ISBN 1-57486-461-0
Library of Congress Control Number 2004113013

Published by Leisure Arts, Inc., 5701 Ranch Drive, Little Rock, Arkansas 72223. 501-868-8800. *www.leisurearts.com*. Printed in the United States of America.

Special Projects Director: Susan Frantz Wiles
Vice President and Editor-in-Chief: Sandra Graham Case
Executive Director of Publications: Cheryl Nodine Gunnells
Senior Publications Director: Susan White Sullivan
Senior Design Director: Cyndi Hansen
Senior Art Operations Director: Jeff Curtis
Art Imaging Director: Mark Hawkins
Director of Retail Marketing: Stephen Wilson
Director of Designer Relations: Debra Nettles
Graphic Design Supervisor: Amy Vaughn
Graphic Artist: Katherine Atchison
Associate Editor: Susan McManus Johnson
Editorial Assistants: JoAnn Forrest, Merrilee Gasaway, Amy Hansen, April Hansen, and Janie Wright
Imaging Technicians: Stephanie Johnson and Mark Potter
Publishing Systems Administrator: Becky Riddle
Publishing Systems Assistants: Clint Hanson, John Rose, and Chris Wertenberger

Publisher: Rick Barton
Vice President, Finance: Tom Siebenmorgen
Director of Corporate Planning and Development: Laticia Mull Dittrich
Vice President, Retail Marketing: Bob Humphrey
Vice President, Sales: Ray Shelgosh
Vice President, National Accounts: Pam Stebbins
Director of Sales and Services: Margaret Reinold
Vice President, Operations: Jim Dittrich
Comptroller, Operations: Rob Thieme
Retail Customer Service Manager: Stan Raynor
Print Production Manager: Fred F. Pruss

Preserving the Everyday Moments

During a recent media interview I was asked "Why should I scrapbook?" Quickly I replied that "scrapbooking is a creative, artistic way to document and preserve your memories." But later as I was driving home from my office I began to think more deeply about the answer to that simple question. Scrapbooking does more than simply help us preserve the events that make up our lives. Scrapbooking has the potential to reveal the real memories behind those events. Scrapbooking can expose the details of our lives that may otherwise be lost in the rush of everyday life.

Each day you are faced with moments worth remembering—from the mess your two-year-old made while you were in the shower, to the tender hug you shared with your significant other after a rough day at work. At *Creating Keepsakes* scrapbook magazine, we work to provide you with a variety of ways to include those details that make up your everyday life. In this volume we've gathered some of our favorite articles from the past three years. These articles will touch your heart and inspire you to preserve your own everyday moments. ♥

Sincerely,

Tracy

Tracy White
Editor-in-Chief
Creating Keepsakes Magazine

CREATING Keepsakes

contents

SCRAPBOOKING EVERYDAY MOMENTS

MICHELLE TARDIE

THE DiRT EATERS MOTTO

yuCK!

It doesn't taste good!
These were the first words out of Makayla's mouth after she had eaten a handful of dirt from my planter. I couldn't help but laugh, she honestly was proud of the fact she was a little dirt eater and was smiling about it after the initial taste had been washed out of her mouth. When I asked her why she had decided to eat dirt she said "I don't know" typical response from my little 3 year old Boo Boo McGoo.
I love this little face even if it is covered in dirt. September of 2003

18

Family Time

Field Trips   Eating out

Saturdays

Love

TAMMY LOMBARDI

Every saturday when Sam gets home from work we take a family drive around town. We usually start at a local sandwich shop and drive around while eating our lunch. "Take-out" has become a big thing with us! Lately we have stopped by Nana and Poppy Farmer's to say hi and visit. Then we pick a place to take the kids for some fun.....the mall, a park, or on this particular day- a strawberry field to pick some berries. No matter what we do or where we go we always have fun just being together as a family! These simple times are the memories I'll always cherish.   February 15, 2003

158

LESLIE LIGHTFOOT

174

MARY LARSON

256

"Do not trust your memory;

it is a net full of holes;

the most beautiful prizes

slip through it."

—GEORGES DUHAMEL

ordinary moments

Life is full of moments that seem ordinary . . . they're just another part of another day. Yet, when children grow up and leave home, many favorite memories spring from those "ordinary moments." Be sure to capture these moments on film—you're sure to find some treasures:

- Watching a movie and eating freshly made popcorn
- Sleeping in the early hours of the morning
- Holding hands
- Eating meals together
- Cheering one another on at sporting events
- Reading stories

- Working around the house or in the yard
- Walking in the front door
- Sitting on the front porch
- Riding bikes or taking a walk after dinner
- Practicing an instrument
- Playing games in the yard
- Finishing homework

- Getting the mail or newspaper
- Traveling in the car
- Baking sweets in the kitchen
- Visiting a favorite restaurant
- Enjoying a homemade breakfast in bed
- Playing with the family pet
- Sharing toys
- Lending a helping hand

ARTICLE BY CATHERINE SCOTT

A Good Laugh

Scrapbook the silly, "not so serious" stuff
that reflects more about you and others

BY JULIE SCATTAREGIA

PHOTO • CORBIS

PHOTO © JOHN MADERE / CORBIS

W e've all heard that "Laughter is the best medicine." And, it's no surprise! A good belly laugh can reduce stress, lift depression and increase creativity.

Sure, other things can give us a healthy boost. Take, for instance, the new high-energy drink I recently read about. It sounded great until I read the ingredients: dandelion innards and fiddlehead ferns mixed with seaweed and other algae I normally pick out of my swimsuit at the beach. So, given the choice between a weed-infested tonic and a good guffaw,

there's no doubt which I would choose. Laughing is much more fun. And I guarantee it tastes better!

I love to laugh. Don't you? While many of my scrapbook layouts are serious in nature, I also create layouts that detail the "not so serious yet just as important" moments in life. What a great way to instill a sense of humor in your kids, show people your vulnerable yet goofy side, and relive your hilarious stories. The silly stuff in life is still from the heart! Here's how to include it in your scrapbook.

DRAW FROM PERSONAL EXPERIENCES

Nothing beats real life for humorous material! Take a look at humor diva Erma Bombeck. She was a brilliant writer who focused on the strange, funny, everyday details of life. We all experience them.

Ever had one of those "It could only happen to me!" moments? Been there, done that. Take, for instance, the time I decided to get fake nails on my short, stubby fingers. I admired my long, lanky fingers all the way home. A few hours later, while trimming cardstock, wham! I accidentally slammed the blade across three of my beautiful new nails! In disgust, I yanked off the rest of the nails. (Do not try this at home. It's entirely too painful.)

Take a few minutes to think about the humorous things that have happened to you over the years. Write them down. Interestingly enough, one story may trigger the thought of another, then another. I'm not suggesting that you create a layout about every humorous incident, but perhaps you'll find groupings that could tell a significant story.

For example, I grew up in the '70s. What was so funny about this decade? What wasn't? I couldn't resist creating a layout about my life in the '70s (see below). It's a piece of my childhood nostalgia with a twist of humor. I can only imagine my kids' reactions when we look at this layout years from now. No doubt they'll have the same reaction as we do to past generations.

PAGE IDEAS

Scrapbook ideas like the following that draw from your personal experience:

- Share a funny experience that happened on your way somewhere.
- Tell about any unexpected surprises on your wedding day.
- Record humorous details about events such as a pregnancy, a vacation or your first day on the job.

Playfully highlight what was hip—or not—about a decade you've experienced.

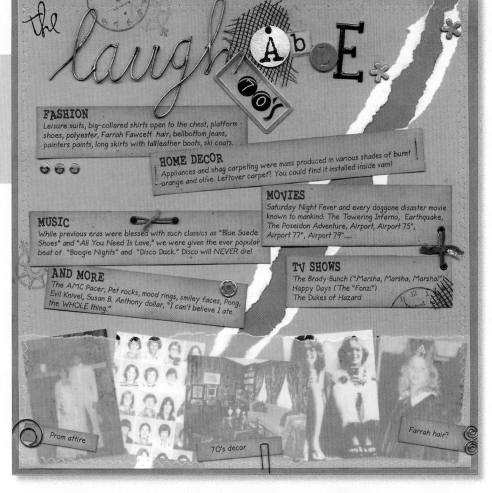

Page by Julie Scattaregia. **Supplies** *Patterned paper:* Close To My Heart; *Computer fonts:* CK Corral, "Fresh Fonts" CD; CK Neat Print, "Special Occasions" CD, Creating Keepsakes; *Bubble letters:* Li'l Davis Designs; *Eyelets, rub-ons, mini brads and metal letters:* Making Memories; *Metal word ("laugh"):* Sonnets, Creative Imaginations; *Rubber stamps:* Inkadinkado and Stampabilities; *Stamping ink:* Ranger Industries; *Conchos:* Scrapworks; *Mesh:* Stampendous!; *Clips:* 7 Gypsies.

LISTEN TO CHILDREN

"Knock knock."

"Who's there?"

"Euripides."

"Euripides who?"

"Euripides pants, you buy me a new pair!"

This happens to be the favorite knock-knock joke around our house. It usually gets converted into sillier punch lines like, "You rip 'em, you get me more." Not quite the same impact, but you should hear the raucous ha-ha's coming from our kids. Whether it's knock-knock jokes or eye-opening questions, kids really do say the darndest things!

The layout below was inspired by a conversation I had with my then three-year-old boy and five-year-old girl. Who would have imagined such a strong reaction to changing the color of my hair? Still, their reactions were priceless and I couldn't resist creating a layout on the topic.

Over the years, I've written down a lot of the silly and sweet things my kids have said or done. I decided to combine some of the humorous entries into a mini album (see pages 11–13). It's a work in progress that's been pure fun.

You'll notice the album contains only a few pictures. Capturing these moments didn't require a camera. Instead, it required only a great memory or a pencil. I chose the latter. If you haven't already, begin recording the funny things you hear kids say. Children love to read about themselves. What you write becomes magical to them, and laughing together is binding.

Share what happened when you experimented with a new look.

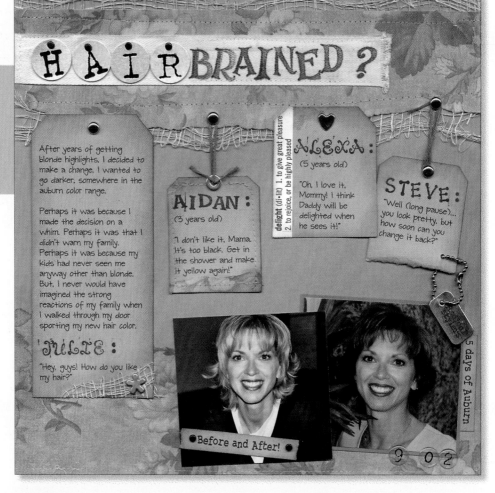

Page by Julie Scattaregia. **Supplies** *Patterned paper:* Daisy D's; *Computer font:* CK Journaling, "The Best of Creative Lettering" CD Combo, *Creating Keepsakes; Brads:* Creative Imaginations; *Bubble numbers:* Li'l Davis Designs; *Heart brad, flower brad, mini brads and metal letters:* Making Memories; *Rubber stamps:* Stamp Craft (small) and Stampin' Up! (large); *Fibers:* On The Surface; *Metal tag and chain:* From a hairbrush; *Other:* Twill and ribbon.

PAGE IDEAS
Scrapbook ideas like the following that come from listening to your children:

- List your child's favorite jokes and how your child likes to tell them.

- Record some of the funniest questions asked by your child. When my daughter was two, she asked, "Mom, do rabbits have knees?"

- Use funny or mixed-up phrases. Ask my son what his favorite soda is, and he'll answer, "Root beard."

- Have fun with children's exaggerations. For example, "I told him to stop 20 million, gazillion times and he still wouldn't!"

Charm others with a mini book that offers humorous takes on life.

Supplies *Album:* Canson; *Metal message, keyhole and chain:* Li'l Davis Designs; *Eyelet charms:* Making Memories; *Ribbons:* K & Company (green) and C.M. Offray & Son (all others); *Other:* Elastic. *Idea to note:* Julie tied elastic to the metal keyhole to create a closure for her album.

Start a laughter album with a "Thanks for all the smiles" layout.

Pages by Julie Scattaregia. **Supplies** *Patterned papers:* me & my BIG ideas; *Rubber stamps:* Postmodern Design (diamond), PSX Design ("Laugh") and Stampendous! ("Thank You"); *Stamping ink:* Close To My Heart; *Brad, mini brads, photo corners and page pebble:* Making Memories; *Ribbon:* C.M. Offray & Son; *Label:* Dymo.

For a fresh twist, document kids' funny takes on song lyrics.

Pages by Julie Scattaregia. **Supplies** *Patterned papers:* me & my BIG ideas; *Computer font:* Times New Roman, Corel WordPerfect; *Square brads:* Making Memories; *Chalk:* Craf-T Products; *Tags:* DMD Inc.; *Fibers:* Winklash; *Label:* Dymo.

Kids say the darndest things! Record their gems for posterity.

Pages by Julie Scattaregia. **Supplies** *Patterned papers and poemstone:* Sonnets, Creative Imaginations; *Rub-ons:* Making Memories.

THE WORLD OUTSIDE YOUR DOOR

Be receptive to the world around you. My in-laws love to share humorous stories about my husband, Steve, when he was a child. They're still connected at a deep emotional level. The stories come straight from the heart.

When I asked, my father-in-law enthusiastically agreed to write down each story with wonderful detail. I

created a layout that would give these stories permanence (see below).
Not only is this a special way to pass down pieces of my husband's childhood, it gives my kids ammunition. Turns out Daddy was quite the rascal!

PAGE IDEAS

Interact with the world outside your door, and scrapbook ideas like the following:

- Record today's "hot" phrases and lingo. Need help? Grab any teenager and have a five-minute conversation. You'll quickly find out!

- Eavesdrop. Listening to the people around you can spark an idea for a page layout.

- Get ideas from books, movies or TV.

Pages by Julie Scattaregia. **Supplies** *Patterned papers:* 7 Gypsies, Karen Foster Design, Li'l Davis Designs; *Computer font:* Franklin Gothic Medium, Corel WordPerfect; *Stickers:* David Walker; *Bookplate, metal key, safety pin and bubble letters, frames and numbers:* Li'l Davis Designs; *Eyelets, mini brads and key tag:* Making Memories; *Rubber stamps:* Inkadinkado, Limited Edition Rubber Stamps and Stampabilities; *Stamping ink:* Close To My Heart (black) and Ranger Industries (sepia); *Nickel clock and tags:* 7 Gypsies; *Scrabble letters:* EK Success; *Word accent:* K & Company; *Charms:* Giraffe Crafts; *Heart button:* Theresa's Hand Dyed Buttons; *Lace and ribbon:* C.M. Offray & Son; *Stamp stickers:* me & my BIG ideas; *Embroidery floss:* DMC; *Other:* Ticket stub and circle clip.

Gather humorous stories about a loved one and incorporate them on a layout.

LISTEN TO YOURSELF

I'm sure you've had uncontrollable laughing spells over the silliest little things. No matter what you do, you just can't stop laughing. When you're finally somewhat under control, your insides feel like a punching bag, your mascara is somewhere near your chin, and you're completely exhausted. Now, I call THAT a successful day!

So, what is it that makes you laugh? Do you laugh easily? How would you describe your sense of humor? Pay attention to those things that make you laugh. Comedy dies quickly under the microscope, so don't overanalyze. Simply pay attention to those things that make you laugh. Create a page about your humor or something "typical" you and others can chuckle over (see below).

PAGE IDEAS

Scrapbook what "cracks" you or others up. Here are a few ideas:

• Confess your quirks or strange habits. Not sure what they are? Ask family members!

• Consider which humorous books and comedies are your favorites. Tell why.

Admit an idiosyncrasy and how you've adapted.

Pages by Erin Lincoln. **Supplies** *Metal letters, snaps and eyelets:* Making Memories; *Computer font:* Copper Lt BK, Corel WordPerfect; *Transparency:* Magic Scraps; *Photo clip art:* Holy Cow Graphics; *Other:* Map.

ONE FINAL THOUGHT

Humor is subjective. What's hilarious to you may barely crack a lip twitch with the next person But really, who cares? This is your life. Your moments. Your stories. You're doing this for you and those you love. If it tickles your funny bone, you're on to something. Said Ella Wilcox, "Laugh and the world laughs with you." And if they don't, just toss them one of those dandelion/seaweed concoctions. At least you'll get a laugh out of it! ♥

caught ya!

by Lanna Carter

9 layouts that are sure to bring a smile

Kids and mischief?

They just seem to go together. When we asked for "Caught Ya" pages, layouts about kids just poured in. The demographic that was notably missing? Adults. Either we're too embarrassed about our own "moments" or we have so much fun photographing our kids' devious deeds that we forget to capture our own.

So, here's my challenge to you. After you peruse these nine layouts, use them as inspiration for a layout about your own crazy or outlandish feats.

PHOTO © SKYLAR NIELSEN

Static

by Tarri Botwinski • Grand Rapids, MI

Quinn
Jumps
& Jumps
& Jumps!!
Quinn's
Hair
is still
Jumping!

static

Quinn was fascinated by the trampoline! She would not stop jumping! The more she jumped, the more her hair stood on end!! It wasn't long before everyone was watching and giggling! She had no idea they were giggling about her hair, she thought the were giggling about her jumping - which made her jump even more - which made her hair stand up even more!

JOURNALING: "Quinn was fascinated by the trampoline. She would not stop jumping. The more she jumped, the more her hair stood on end! It wasn't long before everyone was watching and giggling! She had no idea they were giggling about her hair; she thought they were giggling about her jumping—which made her jump even more, which made her hair stand up even more!"

Supplies *Patterned paper:* Colors By Design; *Eyelets:* Making Memories; *Stamping ink:* Close To My Heart; *Computer font:* Kayleigh, downloaded from the Internet; *Letter stickers:* SEI; *Other:* Netting.

I'm Not in Here, Mommy!

by Christine Brown • Hanover, MN

Supplies *Patterned papers:* Karen Foster Design and 7 Gypsies; *Computer font:* AmeriType, downloaded from the Internet; *Letter stickers:* Li'l Davis Designs (black) and Creative Imaginations (bits and baubles); *Other:* Twill tape and Rollabind binders. *Idea to note:* Christine scanned a Nestle image from 7 Gypsies paper. She opened a picture of her son in Photoshop, then converted the photo to a black-and-white outline with the stamped image filter. Using the cloning tool, she erased the boy in the Nestle logo, then layered her son's outline in its place. Christine alternated the two "logos" for her bottom border.

JOURNALING: "Grant, Grant, Grant . . . aren't you something? You sure LOVE your sugar! . . . As I came downstairs to check on you, all I heard was a little voice from the kitchen peeping, 'I'm not in here, Mommy! Don't come in!'

"I chuckled to myself at your naiveté. There you sat at the kitchen counter, Nestle's Quick canister in front of you, fingers and face and counter smeared in a chocolate mess, with a devious grin on your face as wide as the Grand Canyon.

"When I asked you what you were doing, you replied, 'Nothing!' Ha! Nothing? It looks like something to me! But how could I be mad? I knew that you must've worked hard for your prize because that canister is not easy to open. You earned your right! And anyway, who says that milk is required to enjoy Nestle's Quick?"

What Mess? This Is Art

by Maureen Spell • Carlsbad, NM

Says Maureen, "I wasn't too happy when I found my youngest daughter covered in black paint, but I couldn't resist pulling out the camera and taking pictures of her and her mess!"

Supplies *Patterned paper:* Doodlebug Design; *Letter stickers:* Shotz, Creative Imaginations; Doodlebug Design; *Stamping ink:* All Night Media; *Computer font:* Script MT Bold, downloaded from the Internet; *Square clip and bookplate:* Making Memories; *Bow:* Scrappers; *Frame:* My Mind's Eye.

The Dirt Eater's Motto

by Michelle Tardie • Richmond, VA

JOURNALING: " 'Yuck! It doesn't taste good!' These were the first words out of Makayla's mouth after she had eaten a handful of dirt from my planter. I couldn't help but laugh. She was honestly proud of the fact that she was a little dirt eater, and was smiling about it after the initial taste had been washed out of her mouth. When I asked why she had decided to eat dirt, she said, 'I don't know'—a typical response from my little three-year-old Boo Boo McGoo.

"I love this little face even if it is covered in dirt."

Supplies *Patterned papers:* KI Memories; *Tile stickers:* EK Success; *Letter stickers:* Life's Journey, K & Company; me & my BIG ideas; *Eyelet:* Creative Imaginations; *Computer fonts:* CK Fraternity, Becky Higgins' "Creative Clips & Fonts" CD, *Creating Keepsakes*; Fat Finger, downloaded from www.scrapvillage.com; *Mesh:* Magic Mesh, Avant Card; *Brads:* Boxer Scrapbook Productions; *Bookplate:* Nunn Designs; *Frame:* Polly & Friends, Leeco Industries.

Supplies *Patterned paper:* Chatterbox; *Letters:* This & That; *Twill tape:* Wrights; *Computer fonts:* 39 Smooth, downloaded from the Internet; 2Peas Jack Frost, downloaded from *www.twopeasinabucket.com*; *Brads:* HyGlo, American Pin & Fastener. *Idea to note:* Candi ran twill tape through her printer for a customized border.

Monkey

by Candi Gershon • Fishers, IN

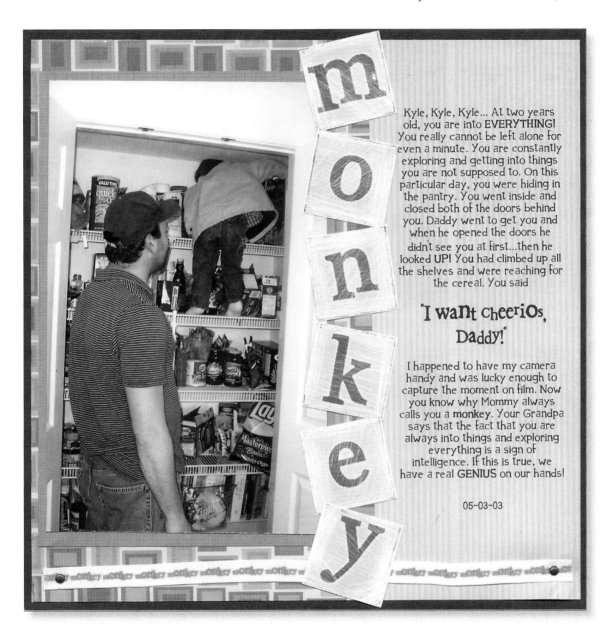

Kyle, Kyle, Kyle... At two years old, you are into EVERYTHING! You really cannot be left alone for even a minute. You are constantly exploring and getting into things you are not supposed to. On this particular day, you were hiding in the pantry. You went inside and closed both of the doors behind you. Daddy went to get you and when he opened the doors he didn't see you at first...then he looked UP! You had climbed up all the shelves and were reaching for the cereal. You said

"I want cheerios, Daddy!"

I happened to have my camera handy and was lucky enough to capture the moment on film. Now you know why Mommy always calls you a monkey. Your Grandpa says that the fact that you are always into things and exploring everything is a sign of intelligence. If this is true, we have a real GENIUS on our hands!

05-03-03

JOURNALING: "Kyle, Kyle, Kyle. At two years old, you are into EVERYTHING! You really cannot be left alone for even a minute. . . . On this particular day, you were hiding in the pantry. You went inside and closed both of the doors behind you. Daddy went to get you, and when he opened the doors he didn't see you at first, then he looked UP! You had climbed up all the shelves and were reaching for the cereal. You said, 'I want Cheerios, Daddy!'

"I happened to have my camera handy and was lucky enough to capture the moment on film. Now you know why Mommy always calls you a monkey. Your grandpa says that the fact you are always into things and exploring everything is a sign of intelligence. If this is true, we have a real GENIUS on our hands!"

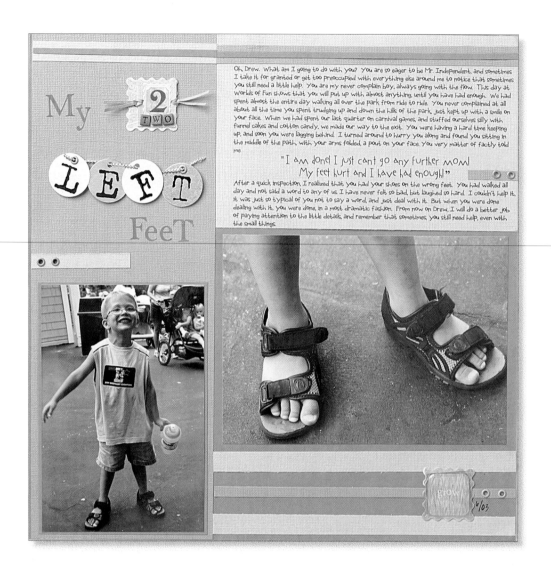

The photo layout includes the handwritten journaling:

Oh, Drew. What am I going to do with you? You are so eager to be Mr. Independent, and sometimes I take it for granted or get too preoccupied with everything else around me to notice that sometimes you still need a little help. You are my never complain boy, always going with the flow. This day at Worlds of Fun shows that you will put up with almost anything, until you have had enough. We had spent almost the entire day walking all over the park from ride to ride. You never complained at all about all the time you spent trudging up and down the hills of the park, just kept up with a smile on your face. When we had spent our last quarter on carnival games, and stuffed ourselves silly with funnel cakes and cotton candy, we made our way to the exit. You were having a hard time keeping up, and soon you were lagging behind. I turned around to hurry you along and found you sitting in the middle of the path, with your arms folded, a pout on your face. You very matter of factly told me

"I am done! I just can't go any further Mom! My feet hurt and I have had enough!"

After a quick inspection, I realized that you had your shoes on the wrong feet. You had walked all day and not said a word to any of us. I have never felt so bad, but laughed so hard. I couldn't help it, it was just so typical of you not to say a word, and just deal with it. But when you were done dealing with it, you were done, in a most dramatic fashion. From now on Drew, I will do a better job of paying attention to the little details, and remember that sometimes, you still need help, even with the small things.

My Two Left Feet

by Miley Johnson • Omaha, NE

Supplies *Textured cardstock:* Bazzill Basics; *Metal tiles, chain, metal letters and eyelets:* Making Memories; *Computer font:* 2Peas Tadpole and 2Peas Tuxedo, downloaded from *www.twopeasinabucket.com*; *Stamp and poemstone:* Sonnets, Creative Imaginations.

JOURNALING: "You are so eager to be Mr. Independent, and sometimes I take it for granted or get too preoccupied to notice that sometimes you still need a little help. This day at Worlds of Fun shows that you will put up with almost anything, until you have had enough.

"We had spent almost the entire day walking all over the park from ride to ride. You never complained about all the time you spent trudging up and down the hills of the park, just kept up with a smile on your face. When we had spent our last quarter on carnival games and stuffed ourselves silly with funnel cakes and cotton candy, we made our way to the exit.

"You were having a hard time keeping up, and soon you were lagging behind. I turned around to hurry you along and found you sitting in the middle of the path, your arms folded, a pout on your face. You very matter-of-factly told me, 'I am done! I just can't go any further, Mom! My feet hurt and I have had enough!'

"After a quick inspection, I realized that you had your shoes on the wrong feet. You had walked all day and not said a word to any of us. I have never felt so bad, but laughed so hard. I couldn't help it . . . it was just so typical of you not to say a word and just deal with it. But when you were done dealing with it, you were done, in a most dramatic fashion.

"From now on, Drew, I will do a better job of paying attention to the little details. And remember that sometimes you still need help, even with the small things."

Supplies *Corrugated paper:* DMD, Inc.; *Embossing powder and stamping ink:* Ranger Industries; *Pens:* Zig Writer and Gel Pen, EK Success; Slick Writer, American Crafts; *Chain:* The Dollar Store; *Tag:* Avery; *Fabric and burlap:* Wal-Mart; *Other:* Brads. *Ideas to note:* To create her circle tag, Kendra cut out a circle, rubbed the edges with embossing ink, then dipped the circle in embossing powder and heated it. She wrote her journaling on a transparency and attached it to the journaling block with brads.

When There's a Wail, There's a Way

by Kendra McCracken • Bolivar, MO

JOURNALING: "Will approaches every situation asking, 'What thrills are present?' The boy has NO FEAR. Every day that we went to the site where Shawn was building our barn-house, Will tried to climb the ladder. And every day when he tried, we told him no. And every day, when we told him no, he cried.

"One day, we decided to see just how far he would climb. Shawn got behind him and held on. Will climbed all the way to the 2nd floor. He may have no fear, but when I think of the future, I have enough for both of us."

Supplies *Textured cardstock:* Bazzill Basics; *Letter stickers:* Sonnets, Creative Imaginations; *Computer font:* Garamond, Microsoft Word; *Mesh:* Magic Mesh, Avant Card; *Brads:* Making Memories; *Ribbon:* C.M. Offray & Son; *Other:* Buttons.

The Toilet Paper Incident

by Shari Schwalbe • Coral Springs, FL

JOURNALING: "Ian always loved playing in the bathroom while I took a shower, but it became much more exciting the day he discovered toilet paper! And he didn't just pull the toilet paper either. He spun the dispenser so that all of the toilet paper unraveled at high speed.

"Ian was so intrigued by this new toy that he unraveled the entire roll. Of course, I thought it was much more important to grab the camera than to save that one roll of toilet paper. Eric and I quickly learned to keep the toilet paper on the counter instead of on the dispenser."

Trouble Strikes Again

by Ursula Page • Virginia Beach, VA

Supplies *Patterned paper:* Chatterbox; *Stickers:* Shotz and Flea Market, Creative Imaginations; *Circle letters:* Paper Pizazz; *Computer fonts:* Arial, Microsoft Word; Typical Writer, downloaded from the Internet; 2Peas Think Small and 2Peas Billboard, downloaded from *www.two-peasinabucket.com*; *Raised squares:* Making Memories; *Ribbon:* C.M. Offray & Son; *Transparency:* Scraps Ahoy. *Idea to note:* Ursula raised portions of her title with pop dots.

JOURNALING: "It was a quiet Saturday morning, so I decided to leave Chris with the kids and head to Target for some childfree shopping. After a blissful hour of shopping in peace, I headed home. I rang the doorbell and surprisingly, no one came to the door. I dropped my bags, used my key and headed inside.

"I then heard Sterling's voice from the back of the house saying, 'Mommy, you gotta come here!' A little hesitant, I ventured to the back to find Chris giving Sterling a bath. Preston looked a bit strange, but I couldn't figure out why. Then I saw the damage.

"In the doorway of my bedroom was a huge round spot, approximately two feet wide. The spot was a strange mix of beige and red.

"Preston had pulled my zipped make-up bag off the dresser, unzipped it, and opened everything he could open. Preston had covered himself and the floor in my brand-new bottle of foundation. He had smeared his face, body and of course the floor with my lipsticks.

"All I could do was laugh. Chris was still pretty mad, but I think he then saw the humor in it all. I had to ask, 'Did you take any pictures?' I think I have trained him well, because he said yes, he had taken three. I miss my make-up, but these pictures are priceless because they show how truly mischievous my little Preston is!" ❤

Photo Tips: Capturing Action

by Anita Matejka

PHOTOS BY ANITA MATEJKA

Snapping photos during a sporting event isn't always an easy feat. Getting as close as possible and using the right speed of film are important steps in getting the photo you want. Here are a few more suggestions to help you capture active moments on film:

◆ Get closer! Because most sports are played on a field or in a large gym, getting close to the action isn't always easy. Do whatever you can to get closer. Get out of your seat and move as close as you can to the floor, sidelines, etc. Also, use your zoom lens—the longer the better!

◆ Use high-speed film. If you're outside on a sunny day, you can get by with a medium-speed film, but if you're in a gym with poor lighting, you'll get better results with a higher speed, which lets more light in. And unless you have a mammoth flash attached to your camera, your flash isn't going to benefit you in a gym if you're sitting more than 12 feet away from the action. Check your camera's manual for the exact distance your flash will light.

◆ Anticipate the play. If you can, keep your camera targeted on your subject, keeping your shutter button depressed half way. When you're ready to take the photo, hold the shutter button down so your camera will take several shots quickly. This way you're sure to catch the photo you want as you see it happening.

◆ Don't forget the "benched" moments. Take pictures of your athlete during time-outs, strategizing with a fellow teammate or coach, or catch her reactions to the game while she's on the bench.

boys will be boys

Scrapbook their tough tender and silly sides

AS I PULLED into the driveway one day, I noticed my seven-year-old son, Benji, and his four-year-old brother, Peter, vigorously hammering away at the concrete wall that divides our driveway from our front yard. I was shocked.

I fully expected my sons to see me, stop what they were doing, and at least look a little worried at being caught. Instead, they continued hammering. "What in the world are you doing?" I asked pointedly. Without missing a beat, Benji exclaimed, "Mom, if you look close, you can see shiny sparkles in there. It's gold, and we've just got to keep digging until we find it!"

As the mother of five boys, that was not the first—nor will it be the last—time my boys will surprise me. Let's see, there was the day I arrived at Benji's basketball game only to find him pressing down the court in his snow boots. (What's a star player to do when he can't find his shoes?) Or the day I walked down the hallway and was met by a large snake. ("But Mom! I found him in the front yard! His name is Gizmoluke!") I was in for a big surprise the day Peter came in after playing on the trampoline with his arm dangling limply and two bones protruding. (I suppose I shouldn't have been too surprised, since he'd done the same thing the previous summer.)

At times, I don't know how many more surprises I can take. But every once in a while, one of my boys will do something amazing. Like when Benji left a group of friends and ran to give me a big hug. Or like the day Nick sat in a hospital room softly playing the guitar for a dear friend who was dying of cancer. As I listened to Nick's gentle music, I realized something I hadn't before. Maybe a boy who can tenderly care for a lost snake can also have compassion on a friend who is suffering. Perhaps a boy who can play an entire basketball game in his snow boots can make his own choices in life, regardless of what others may say.

IF YOU HAVE A BOY IN YOUR LIFE, no doubt you've been surprised like me at his energy, creativity and tender heart. The challenge at times is capturing that creativity on a scrapbook page. Well, if you've run out of boy page ideas, you're in for a big surprise! Here's a sampling of terrific readers' pages that celebrate boys and being their mom.

> BY DEANNA LAMBSON

"A Boy Is a Treasure"

by Toni Holoubek
Rockford, IL

Supplies *Patterned paper:* Paper Adventures; *Title:* Mary Engelbreit, Creative Imaginations; *Computer font:* CAC Pinafore, downloaded from the Internet; *Eyelets:* The Stamp Doctor; *Gems and beads:* Westrim Crafts; *Embroidery floss:* DMC; *Charms:* S. Axelrod Co.; *Mesh:* Magic Mesh, Avant Card; *Die cuts:* The Beary Patch, Creative Imaginations, Deluxe Cuts, Scrap-Ease, Stamping Station; *Chalk:* Craf-T Products; *Buttons:* Hillcreek Designs; *Craft wire:* Artistic Wire Ltd; *Poem:* Downloaded from *www.twopeasinabucket.com.*

Capture a boy's sense of adventure with a layout that highlights his love of "treasure." Count him among the prizes! Toni included the following poem on her treasure-themed layout:

Little boys' pockets hold magical things
Earthworms, apple cores, a mess of string.
But this *treasure* is nothing to the wealth one finds
In little boys' hearts and little boys' minds.

"Play It!"

by Helen Williams
Wodonga, Australia

Supplies *Computer fonts:* Garamond ("Soccer" and "Live It, Breathe It"), Microsoft Word; Annifont ("Play it!"), downloaded from the Internet.

Record a boy's energy on a layout that matches his zest for life. Show him actively engaged in a sport. Energize your page title with an exclamation point!

"I Will Remember You"

by Polly Lund
Providence, UT

Supplies *Letter stickers:* Stickopotamus; *Heart punch:* EK Success; *Computer font:* CK Italic, "The Best of Creative Lettering" CD Combo, *Creating* Keepsakes; *Other:* Spritzer and hemp.

All too soon, little boys grow up. Take a moment to record the big and little things that you'll remember about your little boy. Polly created a lift-up flap to record more priceless memories of Hunter. Her journaling:

"Hunter: Soon you will grow up, and you won't remember what you were like when you were young—your words, your discoveries, your face—but I will always remember you as a small boy. You are more wonderful, fun and fulfilling than I ever imagined. . . . You are my first child, and you taught me how much I could love."

Excerpts from inside lift-up portion:

"I will remember how you love to stay in the bathtub, sometimes until your fingers and toes have turned to prunes."
"I will remember how you jump off anything you can find, no matter how high."
"I will remember how you cover your ears with my hands and bury your head in my arms when you are frightened or uncomfortable."
"I will remember your sweet kisses. I love those."
"I will always remember how you whisper 'mama.' "

"A Two-Year-Old Son"

by Hope Store
Sioux Falls, SD

Supplies *Patterned cardstock:* Source unknown; *Star punch:* Marvy Uchida; *Square punch:* McGill; *Computer font:* Black Boys on Mopeds, downloaded from the Internet; *Poem (adapted from original):* Source unknown.

Depending on what time of day you snap a photo of your little guy, he could be laughing, sleeping, teasing or hiding! Hope combined eight photos on one page to share the big picture of raising a two-year-old.

"Day Dream"

by Patti Tschaen
Holmdel, NJ

Supplies *Computer fonts:* 2Peas Distressed (journaling) and 2Peas Stonewashed ("Day Dreams"), downloaded from *www.twopeasinabucket.com*; *Chalks:* Decorating Chalks; *Rubber stamps:* Shadow Stamps, Hero Arts; *Stamping ink:* Tsukineko; *Button:* Making Memories.

Patti couldn't help but notice the dreamy look on her son's face as he waited for his events at a swim meet. Says Patti, "I thought it might be fun to have him express his dreams so he could look back on them 10 years from now and see what he's accomplished or how his dreams have changed."

Patti's printer doesn't handle 12" x 12" pages. To get around this, she tears smaller pieces of paper, adheres them to a sheet of 8½" x 11" paper with repositionable adhesive, then prints.

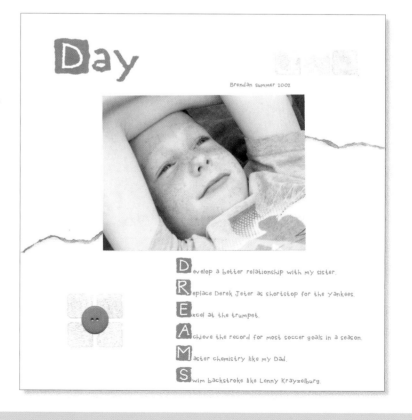

Your first word was "car" but it quickly changed to " kruck". Santa brought you a Tonka **Mighty** Dump Truck for Christmas. You load up the back and dump it right back out and pretend to rev up the engine, brrrrmmm, brmmmmm, brmmmmm. There is now a distinguishable difference between trucks: **BIG** trucks and trucks. You have your little yellow Dodge Ram **Monster** truck and your **BIG** dump **truck**. It is fun to see how you make the comparison. When driving down the road in our car you point out all the trucks you like. The ones with **BIG** tires are your favorite. We have watched the Monster truck shows on television and you ooohhh and ahhh it is so cute. You are such a **BOY**.

"Big Truck"

by Ashley Gull
Salt Lake City, UT

Supplies *Lettering template:* Blocky, Provo Craft; *Computer font:* Tahoma, Microsoft Word; *Chalk:* Stampin' Up!; *Pop dots:* Therm O Web.

What is it with boys and trucks? Ashley made tracks—yes, tire tracks—on her pages by ripping the shapes from black paper and cutting diagonal treads with a craft knife. She then chalked around the treads with black and adhered them as a border with pop dots. Hang on to this idea because a boy never grows out of his fascination with trucks!

A Fun "Boy" Border

Boys may come in all shapes and sizes, but some things stay the same. Spotlight them in a clever border! Here, Ginger Johnson of American Fork, Utah, created a custom look with a torn-paper dump truck (complete with button wheels), a Band-Aid and a tree punch. Her poem? "Little trucks and mounds of dirt . . . Band-Aids on those things that hurt . . . Climbing trees and running for miles . . . My little boy just makes me smile!"

Supplies *Patterned paper:* Provo Craft; *Vellum:* Memory Lane Paper Co.; *Dump truck:* Ginger's own design; *Tree punch:* Family Treasures; *Computer font:* CK Girls, "The Best of Creative Lettering" CD Vol. 4, *Creating Keepsakes; Buttons:* Dress It Up, Jesse James & Co.; *Other:* Brads.

Little trucks and

mounds of dirt...

Band-aids on those

things that hurt...

Climbing trees and running for miles...

My little boy just makes me smile!

The moment that one gives close attention to anything, even a blade of grass, it becomes a mysterious and awesome, indescribably magnificent world in itself.

Tristan May 2002

"Even a Blade of Grass"

by Tracy Kyle
Coquitlam, BC, Canada

Supplies *Vellum:* Paper Adventures; *Computer font:* Tall Paul, downloaded from the Internet; *Quote:* Downloaded from *www.twopeasinabucket.com.*

Think Tracy had to make several enlargements of her favorite photos on these pages? She didn't! Here's her secret: The bottom photos on both pages are 4" x 6" photos directly from the developer. The extra strips of grass along the sides are cut from duplicate photos. The photo under the vellum was a panoramic print made from a regular negative. (You don't even need a panoramic camera!) When making a panoramic from a regular negative, remember that you'll lose a little bit of the image on the top and the bottom. In Tracy's case, it was well worth it!

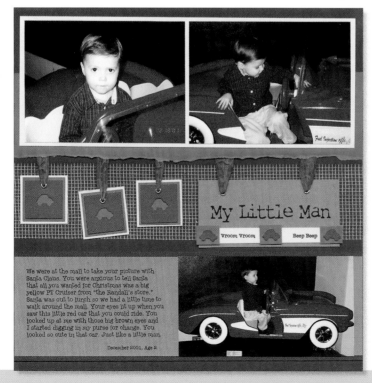

My Little Man

Vroom Vroom   Beep Beep

We were at the mall to take your picture with Santa Claus. You were anxious to tell Santa that all you wanted for Christmas was a big yellow PT Cruiser from "the Randall's store." Santa was out to lunch so we had a little time to walk around the mall. Your eyes lit up when you saw this little red car that you could ride. You looked up at me with those big brown eyes and I started digging in my purse for change. You looked so cute in that car. Just like a little man.

December 2001, Age 2

"My Little Man"

by Amber Crosby
Houston, TX

Supplies *Mesh:* Magic Mesh, Avant Card; *Punches:* EK Success (car) and Family Treasures (square); *Eyelets:* The Stamp Doctor; *Paper yarn:* Twistel, Making Memories; *Computer fonts:* CK Gutenberg (title) and CK Stenography (journaling), "Fresh Fonts" CD, *Creating Keepsakes.*

Whether your boy is big or small, a red convertible is sure to rev his interest. Amber played up her car theme with vibrant touches of red and prominent car punches.

"Welcome the Task"

by Kerri Bradford
Orem, UT

Supplies *Football photo:* Shotz, Creative Imaginations; *Snaps and eyelets:* Making Memories; *Computer fonts:* PaletteD and NicholasCocT Reg, URW Software; CK Constitution, "Fresh Fonts" CD, *Creating Keepsakes.*

Do you ever take so many photos at a big game that you have no room left for journaling the post-game highlights? Kerri solved this problem by creating a "lift-up flap" that reveals the journaling underneath. She attached the flap to the background with a shoelace tied through eyelets.

"Hershey Kissy Eyes"

by Pam Easley
Bentonia, MS

Supplies *Patterned paper:* Creative Imaginations; *Silver paper:* Solum World Paper; *Vellum:* Pixie Press; *Square eyelet, vellum tag and metal tag:* Making Memories; *Computer font:* Riverside, downloaded from the Internet.

When Pam looks into Jake's deep, dark eyes, she sees rich chocolate kisses. Fortunately, Pam found decorative paper and stickers that were just the right flavor. She accentuated Jake's beautiful eyes by ripping two strips of vellum to soften the photo and let her son's "Hershey kissy eyes" shine through.

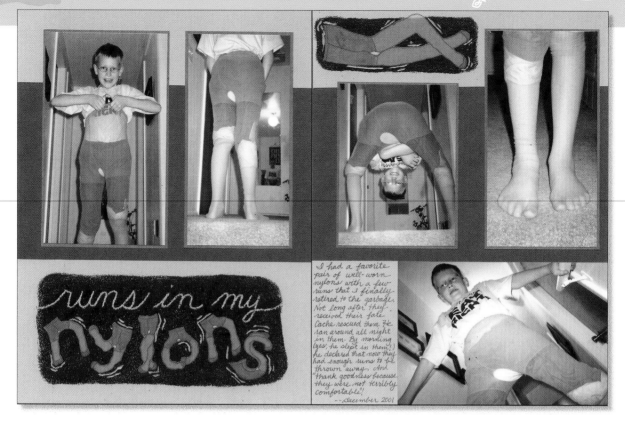

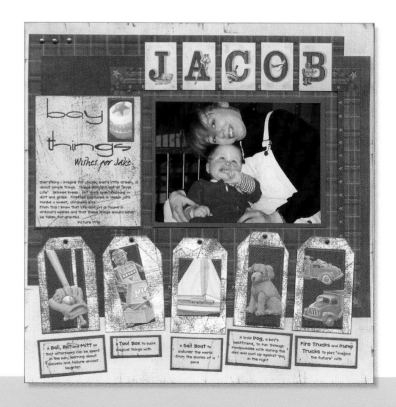

"Runs in My Nylons"

by Darcee Thompson
Preston, ID

Supplies *Vellum:* Paper Adventures; *Pen:* Tombow; *Colored pencils:* Prismacolor, Sanford; *Chalk:* Craf-T Products; *Embossing powder:* Stampendous!.

When Darcee finally discarded a well-worn pair of nylons, she had no idea they'd be rescued and worn by her son Cache. He pulled and tugged and even slept in them! Darcee created a unique title by covering the lower part of her page with embossing powder. Before heating it, she etched out the lettering with a stylus.

"Boy Things"

by Nicole Gartland
Portland, OR

Supplies *Papers:* K & Company; *Stamping ink:* Ranger Industries; *Computer fonts:* Speed Bowling (title) and Sulatko (subtitle), downloaded from the Internet; CK Handprint (journaling), "The Best of Creative Lettering" CD Combo, *Creating Keepsakes.*

What wishes do you have for your boy? Nicole realized that every dream she had for Jacob was simple—hot days spent running in the grass, a loyal dog and more. She created five tags, each representing a wish for Jake.

Nicole inked each tag with a brayer and ink, then cut images from embossed paper for each of her wishes. This page is a reminder that life and joy are found in the ordinary things.

"Where Are You Going?"

by Christine Brown
Hanover, MN

Supplies *Patterned paper:* Colors By Design; *Computer fonts:* Idealist (titles), downloaded from the Internet; Arial (journaling), Microsoft Word; *Chalk:* Craf-T Products; *Punches:* Emagination Crafts (heart), Family Treasures (large leaf), Marvy Uchida (large flower) and McGill (large swirl); *Craft wire:* Artistic Wire Ltd.; *Paints:* Delta Technical Coatings; *Foam squares:* Therm O Web; *Foam tape:* 3M; *Transparency sheets:* F & M Enterprises. *Idea to note:* Christine created an aged look for her "window frame" by painting streaks of black, brown and white paints on gray cardstock.

What mom doesn't watch her little guy out the window and think how fast he's growing up? Christine does, and created a "window" setting for a treasured photo of her favorite little guy.

To create her window look, Christine positioned the whole window area on a double layer of foam tape and covered the area with transparency. She left the photo flat. The flowers are positioned behind the transparency, with the hearts in front of the transparency.

"Balance"

by Marie Hazzard
Springfield, PA

Supplies *Velveteen paper:* Wintech; *Vellum:* DMD Industries and The Paper Company; *Fiber:* DMC; *Computer fonts:* Brush Script MT (title), Microsoft Word; Art Brush (journaling), downloaded from the Internet.

Marie created her original title background by printing her own skateboard photo on a 4" x 12" piece of vellum. She hopes the stitches in the photo corners are the only kind she sees! Her touching journaling:

He thinks only of ollies.
I think about broken bones.
He thinks about grinding the rails.
I think about trips to the hospital.
He thinks about skateboarding glory.
I think there must be something less dangerous.
He sees an overprotective mom.
I see a little boy who is not so little anymore.

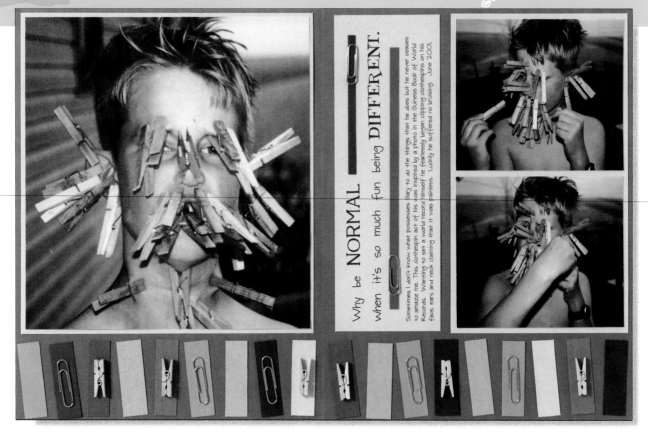

"Why Be Normal?"

by Angie Cramer
Redcliff, AB, Canada

Supplies *Computer fonts:* 39 Smooth ("Normal") and Fontdinerdotcom ("Different"), both downloaded from the Internet; CK Journaling (journaling), "The Best of Creative Lettering" CD Combo, *Creating Keepsakes; Other:* Mini clothespins, paper clips and thread.

Being a boy means coming up with bizarre ideas that no one's ever dreamed of before.

Ouch—perhaps someone should have hidden that *Guinness Book of World Records*! Angie found a much less painful way to use clothespins by attaching the mini variety to her pages with clear thread.

10 Macho Techniques for Boy Pages

What can you do to make your boy pages look more macho? Consider the following:

- Rub sandpaper or steel wool over your crinkled background or accent to give it a rough, worn feel.
- Place a metal washer under eyelets or fasteners, or hang them with a tag.
- Use ordinary office staples or a prong fastener (from an office supply store).
- Trace letters on quick-rust, medium-weight steel and cut out to create a title. (See www.quickruststeel.com for details.)
- Use window screen material (Magic Mesh is self-adhesive) for an accent or title.
- Add wire, string, chain or hemp for a "rough and tough" enhancement.
- Use an entire page of baseball card sheet protectors for an easy page. Fill each pocket with trimmed photos or enhancements.
- Write title words on aluminum foil blocks and adhere with fasteners.
- Dry emboss on heavyweight foil, copper, aluminum or brass paper.
- Use corkboard as a background. (Check acidity for one-of-a-kind photos.)

"Tough and Tender"

by Amy Brenton
Tucson, AZ

Supplies *Patterned paper:* SEI, Inc.;
Vellum: Close To My Heart; *Computer
font:* Helena's Hand, downloaded from
the Internet; *Tags and charm letters:*
Making Memories; *Eyelets:* Impress
Rubber Stamps; *Ribbon:* C.M. Offray
& Son.

Sure he growls. He throws his
action figures into death-defy-
ing spirals, yet there's still that
sweet boy underneath who thinks
you make the best Campbell's
chicken noodle soup in the world!
Amy captured the dual personality
of little Philip at age five. Take a
minute to jot down the things
that make your little guy "tough
and tender."

*Philip at five years old...
You're always talking about beating
the bad guys or throwing your
action figures into death defying
leaps, and even growling when
you're upset. But under all that
boyishness, I know there is a
sweet guy who will want a hug
from his mom, tell her she smells
good, and then mention that she
makes the best Campbell's Chicken
Noodle Soup in the world!*

July 2002

"Dino-mite Boy"

by Michelle Tardie
Richmond, VA

Supplies *Patterned papers:* Crackle (picture
matting) and Tan Check Essentials (journaling
block), Debbie Mumm for Creative
Imaginations; *Computer fonts:* P22
Garamouche Regular, www.impressrubber-
stamps.com; 39 Smooth (larger print in journal-
ing), downloaded from the Internet; *Dinosaur,
topper (chalked brown) and leaf cutouts:* The
Beary Patch; *Lettering template:* Spunky, Déjà
Views, The C-Thru Ruler Co.; *Chalk:* Craf-T
Products; *Eyelets:* The Stamp Doctor; *Mesh:*
Magic Mesh, Avant Card; *Stamping ink:*
Tsukineko.

What better way to highlight a
T-Rex sized smile than on a
dinosaur page? Michelle gave her
preprinted page title a prehistoric,
Jurassic look by chalking it with
brown chalk. She created an even
darker edge by daubing a bit of ink
on her letters and photo mat before
chalking. Now that's a mammoth idea!

*One of the things I love
most about you is your
T-Rex sized smile.
You just have one of
those smiles that makes
everyone else around
you want to smile too.
You crack me up
every single day with
something you say or
sometimes just a look
you give me. I'm so
thankful to have you as
my son, and I'll love
you through all of the
ages.*

"You're My Best Friend"

by Lee Anne Russell
Brownsville, TN

Supplies *Chain:* Impress Rubber Stamps; *Chalk:* Craf-T Products; *Computer fonts:* BaabookHmk ("Best Friend"), Hallmark Scrapbook Studio, Sierra Home; Poppycock ("You're My"), downloaded from the Internet; *Pop dots:* All Night Media; *Title:* From a line in a Tim McGraw song. *Idea to note:* Lee Anne wrinkled the paper for her photo mat, then ironed it.

Every boy needs a best buddy, and Lee Anne was pleased to capture this picture in front of a dark, weathered fence. She later re-created the weathered fence on her pages by cutting strips of paper and chalking them to match.

Even though the photo mat colors are very different, they're brought together with a stitch of a ball chain and two dangling hearts. Just like these two friends who just belong together!

"Camp"

by Leslie Herbert
Queen Creek, AZ

Supplies *Computer fonts:* 2Peas Distressed ("camp"), downloaded from www.twopeasinabucket.com; Marydale (journaling), downloaded from the Internet; *Eyelets and paper yarn:* Making Memories; *Pen:* Zig Writer, EK Success; *Tag:* Leslie's own design. *Idea to note:* Leslie cut out the block letters for her "camp" title.

Lots of tears were shed the day Zach went to camp—not by him, but by his mom! Leslie wanted to record the worry and emptiness she felt that week, so she extended the margins on her computer and started typing. After printing out her journaling, Leslie drew a thin black line around the edge of the tag, the journaling and specific words. Highlighting the words "let you go," "hug," "I love you," "gone," "cry," "wings" and "home" seemed to say it all.

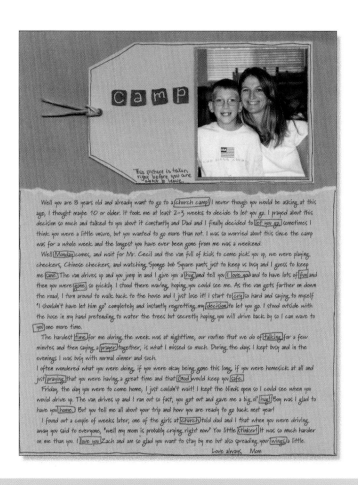

"Cool Kid"

by Stacy McFadden
Victoria, Australia

Supplies *Colored tags:* Making Memories; *Embroidery floss:* DMC; *Beads:* Bizarre Beads; *Eyelets:* Doodlebug Design; *Chain:* Impress Rubber Stamps; *Computer fonts:* Zapfino (title), downloaded from the Internet; Times New Roman (journaling), Microsoft Word; *Gel pens:* Marvy Uchida.

Let a favorite boy know through a striking, "cool kid" layout what you love about him. Here, Stacy used a dramatic black background, colorful metal-rimmed tags, a ball chain and more to let Nicholas know he is adored.

"Goofball"

by Tara Whitney
Valencia, CA

Supplies *Computer font:* P22 Garamouche, downloaded from the Internet; *Vellum:* Paper Adventures; *Eyelets:* Doodlebug Design.

Yep, little boys know how to get Mom's attention, as shown in Tara's journaling: "Okay . . . why? I just don't get this whole new silly thing you have going on. You are constantly trying to say and do the weirdest things to get attention. I am assured by all that it is just a phase, but sheesh . . . WHAT are you thinking, my little man? I can just see your future as the class clown. You are lucky we love you, you little goofball."

the **goofball** that is my son

Okay...why? I just don't get this whole new silly thing you have going on. You are constantly trying to say and do the weirdest things to get attention. I am assured by all that it is just a phase...a four year old thing. But, sheesh...WHAT are you thinking my little man? You like to make goofy faces at the camera, tell jokes that make no sense, copy things we say and then laugh hysterically at yourself, and just babble incoherently to no one in particular. This is a whole new world for me. I can just see your future as the class clown. You are lucky we love you, you little goofball.
January 2002

GIRL power

17 layouts on girls' endearing qualities

Sure, they're sugar and spice and everything nice, but they're also much more—darling and daring, intelligent and innovative, moving and moody, caring and complex. Girls. They can disarm you with their charm and quickly capture your heart. Why not capture a few of the qualities that make girls so endearing?

Celebrate the special girl in your life with a tribute page that highlights her crowning achievements, unforgettable favorites or most memorable personality traits (especially since they've been known to change with mercurial speed).

Whether you're creating a page about your daughter, sister, cousin or friend, you're sure to find inspiration in the following layouts. From going wild with the accessories to going against the grain, from fun hairstyles to funny faces, these pages all have something in common—they all show why it's great to be a girl!

BY DENISE PAULEY

"YES, GIRLS CAN"
by Nancy Rogers > Baton Rouge, LA

*

Through your pictures and journaling, reinforce that girls can do anything they set their minds to.

*

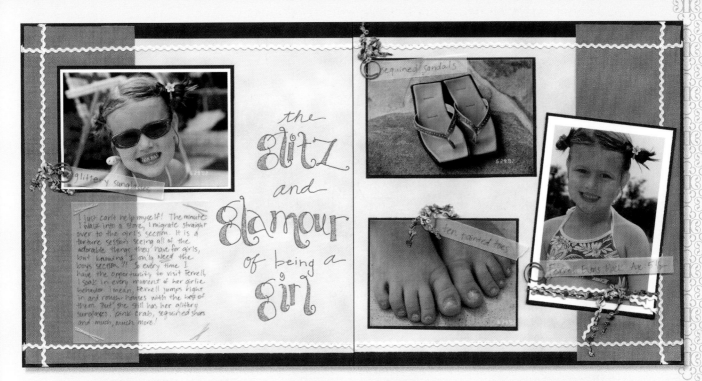

"GLITZ AND GLAMOUR"
by Tracie Smith > Smithtown, NY

✳

Add glitz and glamour
to a girl layout with glitter
and crystal lacquer.

✳

SUPPLIES
Bookbinding paper: Books by Hand
Patterned paper: Making Memories
Vellum: The Paper Company
Pen: Zig Millennium, EK Success
Crystal lacquer: Crystal Effects, Stampin' Up!

Fibers: From www.fibersbytheyard.com
Circular paper clips: Clipiola
Embroidery floss: DMC
Glitter: Magic Scraps
Rickrack: Michaels

"BLOSSOMING"
by Kristi Barnes > Kaysville, UT

SUPPLIES
Letter stickers: David Walker, Colorbök
Silver eyelet: Making Memories
Pen: Zig Writer, EK Success
Flower accents: Colorbök
Other: Glass bead

✳

Add feminine touches to
a girl layout with a "blossom"
theme, flower accents
and a glass bead.

✳

"THAT GIRL THING"

by Nicole Gartland > Portland, OR

SUPPLIES
Tag words: Dolphin
Tags: Making Memories
Embossing powder: Ranger Industries
Pigment powder: Radiant Pearls,
Angelwing Enterprises
Computer fonts: Dragonwick (large title),
Festival Flourish (small title), New
Romantics ("I used to do") and Teen Light
(journaling), downloaded from the
Internet

Contrast the girl you
were in the past with the
girl you are today.

Journaling to note:
"I used to be SUCH a girl. There wasn't
anything I'd do without make-up on. I
spent hours thinking about clothes and
shopping for something new, something
cool to wear. I actually used my round
brush and blow dryer. I applied nail
strengthener daily and always knew where
my file was. I didn't always look great, but
I tried.

"Now, I do little most days. My hair is
usually left loose, undone and barely
brushed, or in a ponytail. Make-up does
get applied, but I have to be GOING SOME-
WHERE before I take the time. . . .

"I sometimes miss being the girl I used
to be. Really, I do. I liked that confidence
that comes from knowing there's no dirt
smeared on the back of my shirt (mysteri-
ously shaped like a toddler hand) and that
my hair, if not looking wonderful, isn't
making people wonder if I even OWN a
hairbrush. I miss the cool clothes. I miss
finding a new shade of eye shadow. . . .

"But, mostly, I just like that I'm now,
finally, comfortable with being plain old
me. That girl thing was a lot of fun, but
without it, I've found that I don't mind my
face without blush, pale though I am. That
I can still feel pretty without spending
hours styling my difficult hair. And most,
interestingly, that no one around me seems
to really notice, let alone mind.

"But the greatest thing about being
plain old me is that it frees me up to do
the things I love—take walks, be Mama,
scrap, visit with pals—without having to
stop by a mirror first."

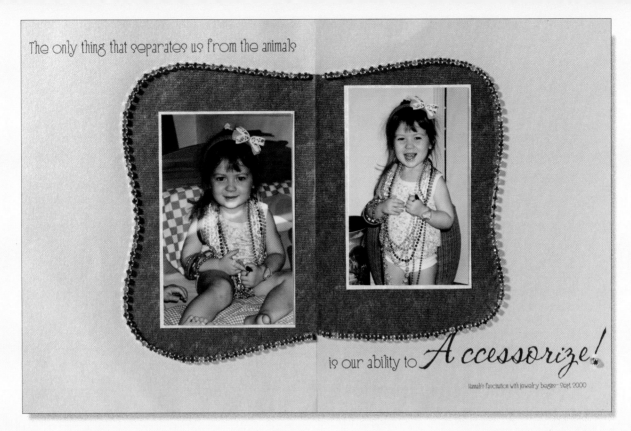

The only thing that separates us from the animals

is our ability to Accessorize!

Hannah's fascination with jewelry begins~ Sept. 2000

"ACCESSORIZE!"
by Shannon Watt > Van Nuys, CA

A rhinestone border is a "gem" at adding color and sparkle to a layout with a jewelry theme.

SUPPLIES
Silver metallic cardstock: Bazzill Basics
Purple paper: Bravissimo
Computer fonts: CAC Shishoni Brush (title) and Rumbascript (journaling), downloaded from the Internet

Rhinestone strands: Decorative Details
Deacidification spray for purple paper: Archival Mist, Preservation Technologies

"LAUREN"
by Polly McMillan > Bullhead City, AZ

SUPPLIES
Paper: MPR Paperbilities (corrugated white), Pages in a Snap (rust) and Provence (blue swirl)
Vellum: Paper Adventures
Fabric butterfly: Creative Co-op, Inc.
Computer font: Scrap Cursive, "Lettering Delights" CD, Inspire Graphics
Blue ribbon: Jo-Ann Crafts
Gold brads: Premier Group
Heart fastener and brad: American Pin & Fastener
Pen: Zig Millennium, EK Success
Chalk: Craf-T Products
Pop dots: All Night Media
Fabric trim: Wrights
Ideas to note: Polly cut three rectangles from her green vellum, then positioned pop dots beneath paper strips to elevate the words "Live," "Love" and "Laugh." She also used pop dots to mount the matted photo.

Add a feminine touch to a photo by framing it with delicate ribbon.

"THIS ABOVE ALL"
by Cindi Peterson > Issaquah, WA

❊

Use photographs to show
the many sides of a girl, from serene
to spunky.

❊

SUPPLIES
Patterned paper: Scrappin' Dreams
Vellum: Pebbles in my Pocket
Computer font: CK Bella, "The Best of
Creative Lettering" CD Vol. 3, *Creating Keepsakes*
Ribbon: Stampin' Up!
Other: Eyelets

"A KALEIDOSCOPE OF EMOTIONS"
by Renee Camacho > Nashville, TN

SUPPLIES
Patterned paper: Karen Foster Design
Computer fonts: 2Peas Flip Flops (title) and
2Peas Fairy Princess (journaling), downloaded
from *www.twopeasinabucket.com*
Dotlets: Doodlebug Design
Vellum: Paper Adventures

❊

Use brightly colored paper with a wavy
pattern to emulate a girl's shifting
emotions.

❊

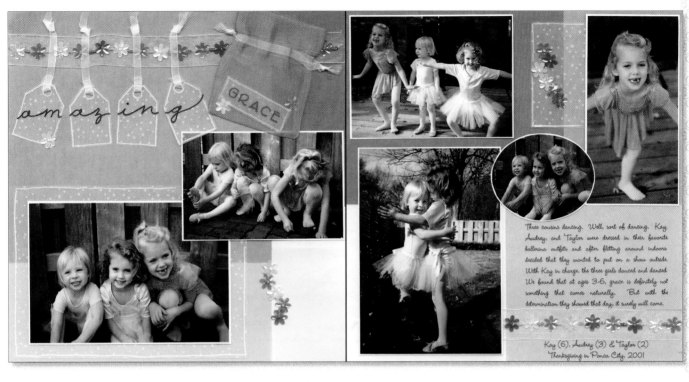

"AMAZING GRACE"
by Jennifer Ditz > Cincinnati, OH

✻

Add sheer beauty to girl pages with
vellum tags and photo mats.

✻

SUPPLIES
Colored vellum: Pixie Press
Computer fonts: Wendy Medium
("Amazing" and journaling) and Cricket
("Grace"), downloaded from the Internet
White pen: Galaxy Marker, American Crafts
Ribbon/beaded trim: Hirschberg Schutz & Co.

Sheer drawstring bag: Bag-Its
Ribbon: C.M. Offray & Son
Chalk: Craf-T Products
Tags: Jennifer's own designs
Idea to note: Jennifer created her multi-
colored background with blocks of vellum.

"THE GIRLS"
by Jennifer Wohlenberg > Stevenson Ranch, CA

SUPPLIES
Textured white cardstock: Memory Lane
Computer font: Minya Nouvelle, downloaded
from the Internet
Mulberry spring roll: Pulsar Paper Products
Nailheads: Scrapworks
Heart: Cut by hand
Idea to note: Jennifer adhered her spring roll
frame with wonder tape.

✻

Frame a girl photo
with pink paper tied
playfully at the corners.

✻

"TWO BRAIDS"
by Dawn Brookey > La Crescenta, CA

✽

Unwrap paper yarn, then braid it to
create a playful border.

✽

SUPPLIES
Vellum: Paper Adventures
Paper yarn: Twistel, Making Memories
Eyelets: Impress Rubber Stamps (round)
and Stamp Doctor (scallop)
Computer font: Babelfish, downloaded
from the Internet
Letter stickers: David Walker, Colorbök

"KARISSA"
by April Cullett > Roseburg, OR

✽

Hold a photo shoot featuring your
favorite girl!

✽

SUPPLIES
Patterned papers: Hot Off The Press
(cement) and Rocky Mountain Paper Co.
(mottled)
Lettering template for title: Fat Caps,
Frances Meyer
Computer font: Arial Black, Microsoft Word
Portraits: April Cullett Photography

Craft wire: Artistic Wire Ltd.
Chalk: Craf-T Products
Vellum: Strathmore
Eyelets: Scrap Arts

Shy   Shocked   HYSTERICAL   Leery   Suspicious

Thoughtful   Focused   Scared   Distracted   Annoyed

GOOFY   Giggly   ANNOYED   Vain   Silly

She's All That

Elizabeth on her 17th Birthday

"SHE'S ALL THAT"
by Erin Lincoln > Frederick, MD

❋

Pull out your camera and capture a friend's playful expressions.

❋

SUPPLIES
Patterned paper: Scrapbook Sally
Computer fonts: 2Peas Jilted Bride and adapted 2Peas Wide Load, downloaded from *www.twopeasinabucket.com*; CK Journaling, "The Best of Creative Lettering" CD Combo, *Creating Keepsakes*
Eyelets: Doodlebug Design and Impress

Rubber Stamps
Rubber stamps: PSX Design
Stamping ink: Stampin' Up!
Brads: Making Memories
Chalk: Craf-T Products
Fiber: On the Surface
Other: Staples, alphabet beads and craft wire

"ALL GIRL"
by Angelia Wigginton > Belmont, MS

SUPPLIES
Circle punch: EK Success
Computer fonts: Boyz Are Gross (title), downloaded from the Internet; CK Diva (journaling), "The Best of Creative Lettering" Vol. 4, *Creating Keepsakes*

❋

Combine brightly colored paper squares for borders and photo mats that are as cheerful as the subject of the page.

❋

ALL GIRL

"I HOPE YOU DANCE"
by Shannon Jones > Mesa, AZ

✳

Apply pink ink to photo corners for
an extra-feminine touch.

✳

SUPPLIES
Patterned paper and letter stickers:
K & Company
Butterscotch flat tops: Stamp Doctor
Alphabet stamps: PSX Design

Pen: Zig Writer, EK Success
Stamping ink: Tsukineko
Ribbon: Jo-Ann Crafts
Photo corners: Kolo
Beads: Beads Elite

"CURLS"
by Nikki Krueger > Liberty, MO

SUPPLIES
Patterned paper: Paper Adventures
Vellum: Chartham
Circle punches: McGill
Computer fonts: Planet Benson (title),
downloaded from the Internet; 2Peas
Commercial Break (journaling), down-
loaded from the website
www.twopeasinabucket.com

✳

Focus on a favorite
feature (in this case,
curls) of a favorite girl.

✳

Try This Technique: Printing on Tags

by Lynn Montgomery

Is there such a thing as a tag-aholic? I can barely make a page these days without attaching some cute little tag to it. Although I love using tags, I hate trying to write on them—especially the teeny, tiny ones. I can never write small enough to fit everything I want to say. To solve this problem, I started running the tags right through my computer printer (nothing has gotten jammed so far … knock on wood!). I can adjust the size of the text to fit on the tag, and I can even adjust the color to match my layout. Here's how:

❶ Type the journaling for your tag using any word-processing program. Estimate the correct size for the tag and print it out. Using a light source, such as a window or lamp, hold your tag behind the journaling on your printout to see if it's the correct size. If your journaling is too big or too small, make adjustments on your computer and print another copy. Repeat this step until your journaling is the right size for your tag.

❷ Once the journaling will fit onto the tag, use a small adhesive square to adhere the tag right over the top of the journaling on your printout. Make sure the tag is centered properly (using the light source). Run the paper with the tag attached to it through the printer again. This time your printing should come out directly on the tag. Gently remove the adhesive from the tag, and it's ready to use!

Hate writing on small, store-bought tags? Run them through your printer! *Page by Lynne Montgomery.* **Supplies** *Computer font:* CK Script, "The Best of Creative Lettering" CD Vol. 1, *Creating Keepsakes; Flower punch:* All Night Media; *Glass marble:* Panacea; *Window screen:* Home Depot; *Other:* Fibers and eyelets.

kids or not, *7* good reasons to scrapbook

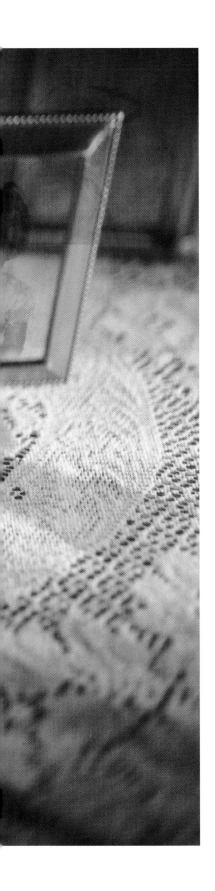

for my

EYES

only?

When I was five, my mother took me shopping at the most fascinating place in the world, Mott's Five and Ten Cent Store in Fort Worth, Texas. For 25 cents, we got a yellow scrapbook with scissor artwork on the front and a price penciled in on the back.

"Mama, dime stores smell funny," I announced, to her dismay. We walked home and excitedly began to paste my "artwork" into the scrapbook. I was surprised she'd saved so much—these were crayon creations only a mom could love!

Years went flying by. I had my career but no children, and I began to dread the holidays. After a particularly difficult season, I needed a vacation, so my husband and I headed to Scottsdale, Arizona. Intrigued by what I saw in two scrapbook magazines there,

I rushed out and purchased a huge stash of paper, scissors, how-to books, stickers and other products.

Then it hit me. "I don't have any children," I thought, feeling panicked. "The scrapbooks I've seen are full of children's pictures. What can I put in mine? There's nobody to inherit them, and the only people who may ever see them are me and my husband."

I decided to move ahead anyway, and as I created my scrapbooks, I found they're perfect for so much more than just showcasing children's pictures. Here are seven good reasons to scrapbook:

1 Celebrate lives. Honor your own life and those who gave you life. Your scrapbook validates your existence and helps you remember the contributions you've made.

According to Dara Biegert and

by Judy Rutledge

Figure 1. Scrapbook your work adventures and the fun you've had. *Page by Kristin Mill.*
Supplies *Patterned paper:* Paperbilities; *Title letters:* Kristin's design, patterned after an advertisement; *Punches:* EK Success (small swirl), McGill (large swirl); *Computer font:* Market, Print Shop, Broderbund.

Sue Brown, co-owners of Memory Catchers in Flower Mound, Texas, "Whether you have kids or not, you have a life to celebrate. You've experienced life moments that you need to record. Scrapbooking's a craft that lets you express your creativity."

Scrapbooking lets you list the good things you've done and the good times you've had. In Figure 1, Kristin Lennox Mill of Indianapolis, Indiana, highlights her time as the "perky" spokeswoman for Dayton Mall in Ohio. In Figure 2, Jennifer Kofford of Layton, Utah, lists what she loved most during her job as a copywriter. What memories come to mind of the places you've worked?

Write down the funny things that happened as you were growing up. Record items such as:
• What was your father's favorite joke?
• What made your mother laugh?
• What makes you smile?
• Was your father in the armed services?

It's important to document and record everything you know about your parents. While I'm not sure my mother would approve, I make sample pages for many scrapbook stores using my favorite picture of her. I love seeing her smiling face when I walk into a store, and this is one of the ways I choose to honor her memory.

2 Enjoy yourself. These scrapbooks are about you, your ancestors (see Mary Larson's page in Figure 3), your life and your accomplishments. Whether anyone else feels the same satisfaction or not, create them because *you* enjoy them. Feeling a little stressed or unmotivated? Create a scrapbook page about your discomfort, paste a funny cartoon on it, and explain how you're feeling. It's *your* book.

Gather any certificate or award you ever received and put it in your scrapbook. Did you write a great paper in high school or college? Put it in your book and read it occasionally. Have you taken a class recently? If you received a certificate of completion, put it in your scrapbook.

Did you do volunteer work? Write the details on a page and add appropriate illustrations, whether you have photographs or not. Did you plant a beautiful garden, mentor someone, learn a new skill, buy your first home, or start your own business? Did you travel anywhere or do a great presentation? Write about it, adding a postcard or magazine cutout.

3 Break the rules. You are the boss of your scrapbooks. You are in control. Remember, there's no rule that every scrapbook needs photos of children. Travel, pets, best friends and gardening are great page themes as well. In Figure 4, Laura Hudson of Boise, Idaho, shares how her Golden Retriever, Bear, has an affinity for peanut butter. She snapped a picture of him after he'd cleaned out an entire jar!

Both my aunt and I made an entire scrapbook of our cats. Another album, my "Y2K Scrapbook," contains photographs of Scottsdale, the garden my husband and I've cultivated, and our beautiful amaryllis plants in bloom. Yet another scrapbook contains pictures and descriptions of classic cars we've purchased and restored.

What do you collect? Take photos of your collections and scrapbook why you like certain pieces. Says Zuma Knight, owner of The Scrapbook Store in Arlington, Texas, "Many of my customers don't have children. They love scrapbooking about their lives, their husbands, their vacations and their new homes. I always take my scrapbooks to family reunions, and at least one or two people look through the albums the entire time we're there." →

things i LOVE about DSW

After nearly four years at Euro RSCG/DSW Partners, I decided it was time to move on. I started there in the media department in March 1996, just after returning from my mission. I left as a copywriter in February 2000 to go work as a Senior Copywriter at pointClick, an Internet start up. Even though it was a relief to leave the stress, politics and pace of the ad agency business behind, I was still sad to leave. I made some great friends, had plenty of laughs and went to some excellent company parties. I also learned a ton and gained experience that will help me the rest of my professional career.

monday bagels and o.j.

my office

funky decor

games in the Lounge

Figure 2. Share what you've loved about certain jobs and the things you've learned. *Pages by Jennifer Kofford.* **Supplies** *Colored pencils:* Prismacolor, Sanford; *Pen:* Zig Writer, EK Success. *Ideas to note:* To keep her layout from looking "blocky," Jennifer tilted a few of her pictures slightly and introduced subtle diagonal lines through angled pieces of cardstock.

SISTERS

Figure 3. You're a descendant of noteworthy people before you. Help scrapbook their lives. *Page by Mary Larson.* **Supplies** *Patterned paper:* Scrap-Ease; *Lettering template:* Kiki, ScrapPagerz.com; *Photo corners:* Canson; *Circle punch:* Family Treasures; *Wheels:* Mary's own designs, created with the help of a Coluzzle template from Provo Craft; *Computer font:* CK Journaling, "The Best of Creative Lettering" CD Combo, *Creating Keepsakes.*

Figure 4. Pets and their peculiarities and sweetness make perfect subjects for page layouts. *Page by Laura Hudson.* **Supplies** *Patterned paper:* Bo-Bunny Press; *Paw print die cut:* Accu-Cut Systems; *Computer fonts:* CK Fill In (title) and CK Journaling (journaling), "The Best of Creative Lettering" CD Combo, *Creating Keepsakes.*

Figure 5. You may not have kids at home, but you can still scrapbook grandkids, cousins, nieces, nephews and more. *Page by Mary Lavery.* **Supplies** *Patterned paper:* Hallmark; *Vellum:* The Paper Company; *Clear photo corners:* Pioneer Photo Albums; *Pens:* Zig Scroll & Brush and Zig Writer, EK Success; *Lettering:* CK Delight, "The Art of Creative Lettering" CD, *Creating Keepsakes; Flower accent:* Actual flower from one of the girls' dresses.

4 Create a diary with pictures.
Express personal feelings. Maybe you're "fifty-something" and thinking about retirement. Go get some "glamour shots" done and create a few pages showing how you looked at different times in your life. Add historical facts and how events have affected you. You can find helpful resources at *www.historychannel.com* and *www.dmarie.com/timecap.*

Laura Gregory and Vickie McCullough, co-owners of The Scrapbook Page in Fort Worth, Texas, were impressed by a customer who said, "I want people to remember the way I was when I was living. *Life* is a scrapbook. Friends and family like looking at my scrapbooks because the pages include pictures of them, too."

5 Get closure. Journaling can be cathartic and is a good way to get closure on painful issues. The hardest pages to create are those about the death of loved ones. Do them as soon as you're able, even if it takes you two or three years to get started.

Design the pages with colors, papers and embellishments your loved one would enjoy if he or she saw them. Keep the pages upbeat and positive. Write a letter saying how much you miss someone and include the letter on the scrapbook page.

6 Share the joy. Scrapbookers with children at home can encourage non-parents and "empty nesters" to craft scrapbooks for nieces, nephews, cousins and friends. Bonnie Turpin, who teaches heritage scrapbooking at The Scrapbook Store located in Arlington, is a non-parent who's crafted scrapbooks for her nieces and nephews. Says Bonnie, "I do it to preserve our family history. I want these children's children to know where they came from. I love delving into the history of the great-grandparents."

your albums will be treasured.

If you're a grandparent, take pictures of your grandchildren and help scrapbook their experiences. In Figure 5, Mary Lavery of Quincy, Illinois, designed a sweet page about her granddaughters' participation as flower girls at a wedding. I'm sure the girls' parents—not to mention the girls—were delighted.

7 Get your mind off the pain.
Journaling in a scrapbook is therapeutic for both mind and body. It's hard to be depressed when you're creating layouts. You forget your aches and pains each time you look through them, if only for a few moments.

While my aunt endured poor health the past 15 years and rarely added journaling to her albums, I can't help but think she lived to the age of 94 by staying involved with her albums. I still remember her organizing the photos, sorting them into big envelopes, and finally placing her photos in the albums. Both Bonnie and I understand this and have occasionally thought, "Oh, Lord, please don't take me before I finish these scrapbooks!"

My late cousin's children were close to tears when they finally got to see my aunt's pictures of their father as a young man. It helped fill a gaping hole about their heritage, and they can now learn about their late father, grandfather and great-grandfather.

Whether you have children or not, your albums will be treasured sometime, somewhere, by someone. Other people will be thrilled to help pass your memories along. The most important thing is to care and to share. ♥

You Never Know

When I first started scrapbooking, I studied magazines and began practicing with scores of cat photos. Surprisingly, when my aunt and uncle died and I was helping sort through their belongings, I was amazed to find 15 scrapbooks and photo albums. I'd never known it, but my aunt was a scrapbook addict, too!

Although my aunt had never married, she'd carefully organized each album for her nieces and nephews. There, in a box in the back of a musty closet where I'd played hide-and-seek as a child, was a goldmine of memories.

We discovered albums with photos of my aunt's many friends, one with photos of her cats (complete with all their tags and papers), one with postcards of all the places she'd visited, and one with wonderful photos of Granny and Pa. The box also contained precious pictures of her and her siblings as children. "Excited" doesn't come close to how I felt when we discovered this box! You never know how or when your scrapbooks will touch another person's life.

12 Fresh Layouts That Celebrate

Relationships

Express your feelings for loved ones

Love—it may be the most powerful word in the world. It's also a strong emotion that connects us, that motivates us to live each day. What would life be like without our treasured relationships with family and friends? Late at night after my children are asleep, I often sneak into their rooms and watch them sleep. I sometimes contemplate what life would be like without them. I'd miss Kade's impeccable integrity, Collin's unselfish ways, Brecken's thoughtful notes and Sage's slobbery kisses.

I'm sure you've scrapbooked about school, birthdays and summer vacations. But have you scrapbooked your relationships with loved ones? We've made it easy for you. Just create one layout each month, and by the end of the year you'll have 12 amazing layouts that celebrate your relationships with favorite people (and pets).

BY LISA BEARNSON

thers Teachers Cousins Parents Children Neighbors Mentors Gran
aches Pets Deity Friends Aunts Co-workers You Significant Other Sisters Brothers Teacher Cousins Parents Children
Deity Friends Aunts Co-workers You Significant Other Sisters Brot
nds Aunts Co-workers You Significant Other Sisters Brothers Teacher Cousins Parents Children Neighbors Mentors
Neighbors Mentors Grandparents Uncles Supervisors Coaches Pe
es Co-workers You Significant Other Sisters Brothers Coaches Pets Deity Friends Aunts Co-workers You Significant O
gnificant Other Sisters Brothers Teachers Cousins You Sisters Brot
es Supervisors Coaches Pets Deity Friends Aunts Co-workers You Significant Other Sisters Brothers Coaches Pets De

JANUARY

Page by Maya Opavska

You! One of the most important relationships you can have is with yourself.

That's right—create a page about yourself. Where are you spiritually? Emotionally? Physically? Intellectually? How do you celebrate your life and all the goodness you represent? Do you like who you are? Maya Opavska created this layout to celebrate the journey of her relationship with herself.

Supplies *Decorative paper:* Pebbles in my Pocket; *Textured cardstock:* Provo Craft; *Letter stamps:* PXS Design; *Stamping ink:* Stampin' Up!; StazOn and Brilliance, Tsukineko; ColorBox, Clearsnap; *Computer font:* CK Sketch, "The Art of Creative Lettering" CD, *Creating Keepsakes; Metal letters, corners, snaps and circles:* Making Memories; *Fibers:* 7 Gypsies; *Other:* Staples. *Idea to note:* Maya concealed very personal and heartfelt journaling under her photo, which lifts up.

FEBRUARY

Page by Michelle Tardie

Significant Other

Create a page about the special relationship you have with the man in your life.

Create a layout commemorating that special someone in your life. Why did he capture your heart? Why is he your type? What qualities do you love about him? What does he do that makes you feel special and loved?

Supplies *Patterned paper:* Karen Foster Design; *Computer font:* 2Peas Chestnuts, downloaded from *www.twopeasinabucket.com*; *Screw snaps:* Making Memories; *Stickers and letter stickers:* Nostalgiques, EK Success; *Metallic rub-ons:* Craf-T Products.

Idea to note: Michelle distressed the patterned paper with sandpaper.

MARCH

Pets Writing your journaling in a poetic format is a fun way to remember a pet.

Have you ever had a special friendship with a pet, past or present? Maybe it's a furry cat that curls up on your lap every time you watch TV. Maybe it's a ferret that never grows tired of playing. Maybe it's the fish in a serene aquarium you enjoy watching after a long day at work.

Even if you're not an animal lover, dig deep inside to remember a special pet. If it's hard for you to be serious in your journaling, try writing a silly poem like I did on the page here.

Page by Lisa Bearnson

Supplies *Patterned paper:* Perfect Match, American Crafts; *Stickers:* Sue Dreamer, Colorbök; *Eyelets:* Making Memories; *Computer font:* CK Extra, "Fresh Fonts" CD, *Creating Keepsakes*.

APRIL

Pages by Loni Stevens

Parents Gather memorabilia about your parents. Include a letter from your parents, plus photos from the day you were born.

Supplies *Oval metal frame, "Memories" bubble phrase and "Treasure" plaque:* Li'l Davis Designs; *Metal frame:* Making Memories; *Conchos:* Scrapworks; *Acrylic paint:* Delta Technical Coatings; *Computer fonts:* 1942 Report and Linenstroke, downloaded from the Internet; Cezanne, P22 Type Foundry; *Postage stamp:* Nostalgiques, EK Success; *Other:* Ribbon, foam core, transparencies, beads and mini brads.

Ideas to note: Loni created a mini shadow box from foam core, then dropped the beads and bubble phrase in and covered them with a transparency. To draw attention to the pictures of her dad the day she was born, Loni created a frame by sewing around it without thread. You end up only seeing the needle holes.

We all have a mom and a dad. Have you scrapbooked your feelings about these two amazing people? Remember, you don't have to focus on just a traditional parent. Maybe you have a special bond with a stepmother, a foster dad or even a best friend's parent.

Notice the nice touches on Loni Stevens' layout above. She included a letter her dad wrote to her on her eighteenth birthday, along with photos taken the day she was born. Loni also tugs at your heart with the thoughtful words she wrote about her dad (they're printed on two pieces of cardstock and attached with brads at the top).

Mentors Grandparents Uncles Supervisors Coaches Pets Deity Friends Aunts Co-workers You Significant Other Sisters Brothers Teachers Cousins Parents Children Ne
Coaches Pets Deity Friends Aunts Co-workers You Significant Other Sisters Brothers Teachers
her Sisters Brothers Parents Children Neighbors Mentors Grandparents Uncles Supervisor Coaches Pets Deity Friends Aunts Co-workers You Significant Other Sisters Br

MAY

Page by Teri Anderson

Grandparents

Even if you never knew your grandparents, you can still capture the bond you share with them.

I recently walked into a friend's musty basement and had to close my eyes—the smell brought back vivid memories of my grandma's cellar. I sat and reminisced about my wonderful grandmother and my relationship with her.

Even if your grandparents are no longer around, capture what made your relationship unique. Teri Anderson barely knew her great-grandparents, yet did a beautiful job capturing their kinship.

Supplies *Patterned paper:* Chatterbox; *Computer font:* Problem Secretary, downloaded from *www.scrapvillage.com*; *Letter stamps:* Hero Arts; *Metal stamps:* FoofaLa; *Stamping ink:* Close To My Heart; *Metal:* Once Upon a Scribble; *Circle punch:* Marvy Uchida; *Heart and circle clips:* Making Memories; *Other:* Fibers and string.

JUNE

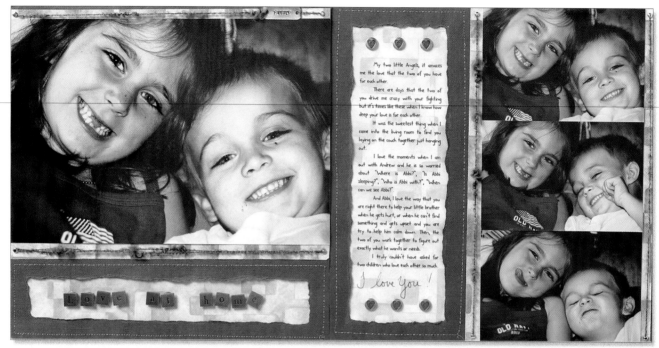

Pages by Melissa Reynolds

Children

Scrapbook your perspective of your children's relationship.

Even if you're not a parent, you probably have a relationship with a child—perhaps a niece, a cousin or the next-door neighbor.

Highlight the fun memories you've had with your favorite child. Or, follow Melissa Reynolds' lovely example here of journaling about your perspective of your children's relationship.

Supplies *Patterned paper:* Paper Adventures; *Vellum:* Close To My Heart; *Tag:* QVC; *Mesh eyelets and letters:* Making Memories; *Computer font:* CK Handprint, "The Best of Creative Lettering" CD Combo, *Creating Keepsakes; Other:* Fibers and thread.

JULY

Pages by Erin Lincoln

Brothers and Sisters

A page layout is the perfect place to express feelings about a sibling.

I have four sisters, and their companionship means the world to me. They know when to listen and not give advice. They know when to show up on my doorstep with a hot meal. They know when to invite my children to their houses so I can have a quiet afternoon to myself.

If I died tomorrow, would my sisters really know how I feel about them? A scrapbook page is the perfect place to express your feelings. In the pages above, Erin Lincoln shares her "big and little sister" story.

Supplies *Patterned paper and stickers:* Chatterbox; *Computer font:* CK Regal, Becky Higgins' "Creative Clips & Fonts for Special Occasions" CD, *Creating Keepsakes; Snaps, plaque and metal word:* Making Memories; *Slide holders:* Two Peas in a Bucket; *Rub-ons:* Chart-pak; *Eyelets:* Magic Scraps.

Idea to note: Erin painted the slide holders to match the paper.

AUGUST

Pages by Caroline Davis

Mrs. Weldon, my 12th grade biology teacher, was one of the most important cheerleaders during some of my toughest years. She took the time to find out what made me tick and what ticked me off! She had faith and confidence in my abilities despite my insecurities.

What type of teacher, mentor or coach made a difference in your life? For Caroline Davis, it's her boss, who has been an incredible mentor. She created a pocket on her layout that contains three smaller pages detailing different attributes that her mentor, Kerig, possesses. Detailed journaling is tucked behind each page.

Teachers, Mentors and Coaches

Showcase a close relationship with a boss who's a mentor and friend.

Supplies *Poemstones:* Sharon Soneff, Creative Imaginations; *Metal letters, eyelets and rub-ons:* Making Memories; *Letter die cuts:* Roxy, QuicKutz; *Embossing powder and page protectors:* Close To My Heart; *Brads:* Impress Rubber Stamps; *Computer font:* Sweet Pea, downloaded from the Internet; *Foam tape:* 3M; *Hole punch:* Fiskars.

Ideas to note: For her "Boss" title, Caroline ran a cardstock strip through her Xyron machine, adhered her die-cut letters, then sprinkled the strip with embossing powder and heated it. She used a sharp knife to remove molten powder from the letters. Caroline repeated the process several times.

Mentors Grandparents Uncles Supervisors Coaches Pets Deity Friends Aunts Co-workers You Significant Other Sisters Brothers Teachers Cousins Parents Children Net
Coaches Pets Deity Friends Aunts Co-workers You Significant Other Sisters Brothers Teachers
her Sisters Brothers Parents Children Neighbors Mentors Grandparents Uncles Supervisor Coaches Pets Deity Friends Aunts Co-workers You Significant Other Sisters Br

SEPTEMBER

Page by Kerri Bradford

Supervisors and Co-workers How do you feel about your "professional pals"?

In many companies, we're not supposed to be friends with co-workers and supervisors, yet some of my most treasured relationships are with my "professional pals." Have you captured this unique friendship on a page? Why do you like working with your supervisor? Have you bonded with a co-worker?

Supplies *Textured and patterned paper:* Provo Craft; *Mesh:* Maruyama, Magenta; *Quote:* Tiny Tales, My Mind's Eye; *Typewriter stickers and tape measure:* Nostalgiques, EK Success; *Quote eyelet and metal accent:* Making Memories; *Silver charms:* Once Upon a Charm; *Computer font:* Typewriter, downloaded from the Internet; *Fabric:* Hancock Fabric; *Walnut ink:* Anima Designs; *Other:* Brad.

OCTOBER

Neighbors Neighbors often make the best friends. Celebrate your friendship on a layout.

Have you ever moved next door to someone and thought, "She's not my type—we'll never be friends"? Often you discover you have a lot more in common than you thought. Perhaps your differences are what attract you to each other. Or, maybe you find a kindred spirit in your neighbor or acquaintance. On the layout at right, Angela Ash lovingly captures her relationship with Bill and Eloise Petty, her neighbors in Conyers, Georgia.

Page by Angela Ash

Supplies *Stitched paper, heart accents, sticker pins and letters:* Stitches, SEI; *Computer font:* CK Typewriter, "Fresh Fonts" CD, *Creating Keepsakes.*

NOVEMBER

Deity Don't be afraid to write how you feel about a higher being.

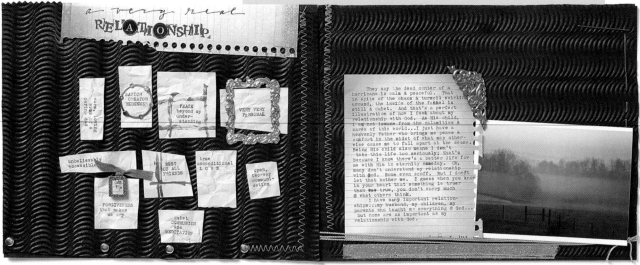

Pages by Rebecca Sower

Your relationship with God or a higher being is very personal. It's something to hold sacred and dear to your heart but also to share with those you love, says Rebecca Sower. Don't be afraid to write what you feel inside. Your posterity will thank you someday.

Supplies *Textured paper:* Artistic Scrapper for Creative Imaginations; *Frames:* Anima Designs; *Brads:* Office Depot; *Embossing powder:* PSX Design; *Twill tape:* Manto Fev; *Metallic pen:* Krylon; *Pen:* Zig Writer, EK Success; *Letter stickers:* Nostalgiques, EK Success; *Letter stamps:* PSX Design; *Stamping ink:* All Night Media; *Metallic rub-ons:* Craf-T Products; *Other:* Photo corner, cording, notebook paper, thread and a Corona typewriter.

DECEMBER

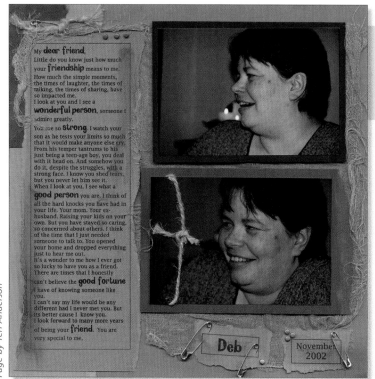

Page by Teri Anderson

Friends A tribute to a special friend is an important addition to your scrapbook.

Can you imagine the holidays without friends? December is the perfect time to reflect on these relationships. These are the people who brighten your life on cloudy days—the pals who accept you for who you are and love you despite your imperfections. In the page at left, Teri Anderson tells about her friendship with Deb. ♥

Supplies *Computer fonts:* PC Keyhole, Provo Craft; Times New Roman, Microsoft Word; *Brads:* American Pin & Fastener; *Metallic rub-ons:* Craf-T Products; *Other:* Jute, safety pins and netting.

through the year

Have you ever stopped for a moment to reflect on how the seasons influence your daily life? Capture how the seasons affect what you see, do, think, hear, smell and feel by taking pictures of scenes that change with each season, such as your home or yard. At the end of the year, you'll have four photographs of each scene—one taken each season—to show exactly what you see throughout the year. Here are some fun ideas to get you started:

- You and your family as you're heading out the door (What are you wearing? What are you carrying?)
- Your flowerbeds, yard and garden
- How you've decorated the main living areas of your home

- The dinner table as you sit down to eat (What are you eating? What does the table look like? Are you inside or outside?)
- Your closet (Is it full of sweaters or tank tops?)

- What you buy at the grocery store
- Where and how you exercise
- Your backyard (Is your summer furniture arranged on the patio? Is there a huge snow fort in the middle of the yard?)

ARTICLE BY CATHERINE SCOTT

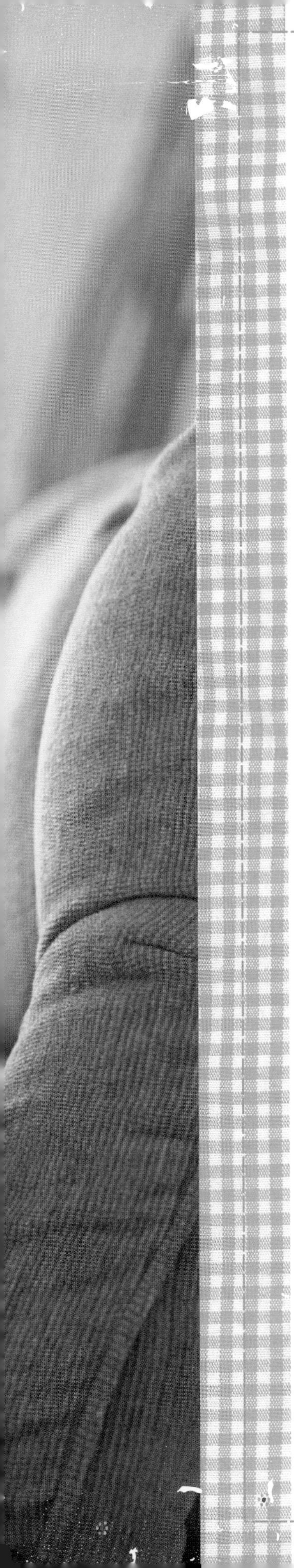

UP CLOSE
&
personal

BY HEIDI SWAPP

CREATE A COOL SELF-PORTRAIT

As a freshman in college, I signed up for a required humanities class. Not only did it seem like a huge waste of time, it was held at 7:30 a.m. (what was I thinking?). During the class, the professor flashed masterpiece after masterpiece past us. The paintings really didn't mean anything to me until we got to the artists' self-portraits.

I soon found myself fascinated, especially after the professor described what was going on in each artist's life as he or she created the work of art. The professor used excerpts from the artist's journals and letters to provide insight into what the artist was thinking. Little did I know how much these self-portraits would influence me later.

PHOTO © SKYLAR NIELSEN

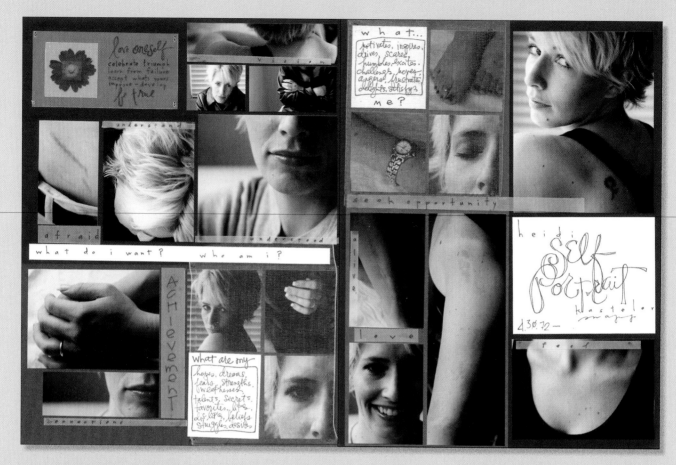

Figure 1. Share what you like or dislike about yourself. *Pages by Heidi Swapp.* **Supplies** *Vellum:* Making Memories; *Other:* Organza and flower.

⁜ I SCRAPBOOK MYSELF

A little over two years ago, I was asked to create a "goals and challenges" layout for a *Creating Keepsakes* class. At that time, I was going through a transition. I had just given birth to my third child, and I was trying to figure out how to balance multiple demands and the desires of my heart. I was questioning who exactly I was and wanted to be.

I asked my cousin Nanci to take pictures of my favorite and not-so-favorite body parts (including physical imperfections like scars and birthmarks). The request was a bit awkward, but she was totally game. I explained exactly what I wanted, and she took just the pictures I was looking for.

When my layout came together (Figure 1), all of my journaling was in the form of questions. This really reflected how I felt at the time. I wondered if *Creating Keepsakes* would find the layout too "real" and raw, but I sent it off anyway. The layout was used and eventually returned. Recently, while preparing for a CKU class, I came

Live a balanced life. Learn some and think some, draw and paint. And sing and dance. And play and work everyday some. — robert fulghum

Figure 2. Scrapbook goals such as creating better balance in your life. *Pages by Heidi Swapp.* **Supplies** *Vellum, rub-ons, snap, stick pin, beads and jump ring:* Making Memories; *Craft paint:* Delta Technical Coatings; *Mini tag:* Avery; *Stamps:* Postmodern Design; *Other:* Photo corners, ribbon and silk flower.

Ideas to note: With the help of a friend, Heidi applied Simply Stated rub-ons to her hands and back. After a quick photo shoot, she printed the photo on regular computer paper. Heidi roughed up the image with sandpaper.

across the layout and felt a strong rush of emotion. It was like I was being transported back in time—I could remember perfectly how I'd felt while creating it. Even more amazing was that I could compare my feelings then with my feelings now, and I marveled at the growth I've experienced, growth only I can really understand.

❖ WHY YOU SHOULD SCRAPBOOK YOU

Sure, I could have written my feelings in a journal, but creating scrapbook pages was so much revealing and memorable. The photos, colors, images and design all combined to send a powerful message, and the creative process was another "aha" in my personal evolution.

Creating a self-portrait layout is a way to capture *you* at that moment. It's a way to capture your joys, hopes, fears, struggles and emotions. What better way to see your personal growth, understanding and development?

Although others will treasure it, a self-portrait layout is for *you*; it's to capture *your* perceptions. It's an artistic combination of explicit (clearly stated or shown) and implicit (suggested) expressions. It's a powerful way for you and others to learn who you are.

❖ WHAT TO SCRAPBOOK

Think you might give a self-portrait a try? Consider one or more of the following approaches:

• **Your Roles.** Roles and responsibilities change all the time, as do

our feelings about them. Scrapbook how your roles and responsibilities define you, give you purpose, and dictate how you choose to live your life.

• **Your Life.** Scrapbook your surroundings, your job, your schedule and the people around you. These details change often, but still reflect you.

• **Your Appearance.** Record how you look right now. Share what you like or dislike. (See Figure 1.)

• **Your Aspirations.** What goals are you working toward? Scrapbook them! (See Figure 2.) It's a well-known fact that writing down goals makes it more likely that you'll achieve them. Imagine the extra incentive you'll have with a scrapbook page as well!

FULFILL
LOVE
Life
OPPORTUNITY
SPIRIT
DREAMS
EXPERIENCE
LEARN
family
HKS
ENJOY
Passionate
love
INSPIRE
it's so amazing to me how no matter how you think you can plan or how you think you have control of your life... and then you realize that you don't! sometimes i totally just feel along for the ride. there's some strange balance of making things happen and being in the right place at the right time. i look at my life, and i could never have predicted any of it.
live
2003
my work feels like play. i love the challenge and the accomplishment. i can't imagine not having this. but the balance eludes me. i can't stop and relax. it moves too fast. too much of a thrill.

Figure 3. Tell what drives and inspires you. *Pages by Heidi Swapp.* **Supplies** *Alphabet charms and jump rings:* Making Memories; *Ribbon:* May Arts, Bucilla; *Craft paint:* Delta Technical Coatings; *Rubber stamps:* Inkadinkado, Missing Like Stamp Co., Postmodern Design, PSX Design, Stampa Rosa; *Other:* Canvas.

Idea to note: Heidi brushed craft paint on letter stamps and stamped onto a piece of canvas. She started in the middle and worked her way out.

- **Your Family.** The people closest to you help shape who you are as a woman, mother, wife, daughter or friend. Scrapbook these people's impact on your life.
- **Your Beliefs.** Scrapbook what you believe and where you're at in your spiritual life. It will serve as a benchmark as you experience new things and gain more understanding.
- **Your Abilities.** What are you good at? What do you like to do? Scrapbook what makes you unique and special. Focusing on your best attributes will help you grow toward the good in yourself.
- **Your Inspiration.** Scrapbook what drives you (Figure 3), what you find truly motivating and inspiring. This will reflect where you're at in life and what you want.

GETTING READY

Determine your approach, then find, take or schedule *current* photos of yourself. They can be casual or elaborate—it's up to you. If you choose to do a photo shoot, consider beforehand what you want to reflect. Wear your favorite clothes. Include the colors and styles you like best. The idea is to be as "timely" as possible—to show how you look *now*. For quick ideas on setting up your own photo shoot, see "Photographing You" on page 81.

It's not always easy to take an "up close and personal" look at ourselves. Be brave—take the leap. Even with all our imperfections, we have so much to celebrate and embrace. A self-portrait scrapbook page can help you document your personal growth and discovery.

A SAMPLING OF SELF-PORTRAIT PAGES

We loved Heidi's concept so much that we asked nine scrapbookers to create self-portrait pages as well. Following are their inspiring examples.

⁙ 27 YEARS

by Tara Whitney
Mission Viejo, CA

Tara wanted to create a self-portrait layout but "stalled" when it came to lots of in-depth journaling. Instead, she simply took several of the thoughts she'd written down and turned them into a list. The number of words was so close to her age that Tara added a few more and used the number in her title.

- Use photo-editing software to create a funky border effect for your focal-point photo.
- To create her contact strips, Tara resized three photos of herself to approximately 1" x 1" each. After opening a new, 1" x 11" image in Paint Shop Pro, Tara copied and pasted each photo as a new layer into that image, creating a long strip that she output on her photo printer.
- Tara started with her favorite color (celery green) and added

other colors she liked. "I think this combination really comes across as *me*," says Tara. "I'm funky, unconventional, and maybe just a little bit cool."

Journaling Excerpt
"Tall, mommy, woman in love, photographer, kind, lazy but busy, insane, casual, creative, realistic, mellow, giving, insecure, open-minded, unorganized, growing and trying, introverted extrovert, family, dieting, beach lover, friend"

Supplies *Computer font:* Plastique, downloaded from the Internet; *Pen:* Zig Writer, EK Success; *Photo-editing software:* Auto FX.

If the unexamined life is not worth living,
then I figured it was time to sit down and write
a little bit about mine - parts that make me
whole, pieces in the puzzle of me. 26 years and a
lot of growing has made me comfortable in the
skin that I am in. Mother, wife, creator, friend,
daughter - each "window" of my life has left me
with different experiences, the joy of
motherhood, the delight of being in love, the
passion I have for creating, the friends that I
have made along the way.
These windows have not always been free of
cracks, for I have had my share of struggles in
life - dealing with my parents' divorce,
surviving in NYC on my own, heartbreak, loss of
loved ones, but looking back through these
windows, I would not change one thing, for these
experiences have made me who I am, and you know
what. . .
I really like what I see.

Supplies *Transparencies:* Apollo (sheets) and Magic Scraps (designs); *Computer fonts:* Mom's Typewriter (journaling), Harting Plain (title and "Who Am I" in window boxes) and Dirty Ego (remainder of title), downloaded from the Internet; *Camera and face stamps:* Leavenworth; *Clock stamp:* Postmodern Design; *Poetry dog tags:* Chronicle Books; *Label tape:* Dymo; *Metal tag:* Making Memories; *Ribbon:* C.M. Offray & Son; *Square punch:* Marvy Uchida; *Acrylic letter "r":* Coffee House Designs.

A LIFE UNEXAMINED
by Nia Reddy
Brooklyn, NY

To showcase some of her traits, Nia created mini "windows." She based her journaling around how these traits have changed her as a person and shaped who she is.

• Print "Who Am I?" on transparency sheets and use them for "windows." Attach words that describe who you are.

• Overlay your picture with multiple transparency sheets to signify your many layers.

Journaling Excerpt
"If the unexamined life is not worth living, then I figured it was time to sit down and write a little bit about mine—parts that make me whole, pieces in the puzzle of me. 26 years and a lot of growing have made me comfortable in the skin that I am in. Mother, wife, creator, friend, daughter—each "window" of my life has left me with different experiences, the joy of motherhood, the delight of being in love, the passion I have for creating, the friends that I have made along the way.

"These windows have not always been free of cracks, for I have had my share of struggles in life … but I would not change one thing, for these experiences have made me who I am, and you know what … I really like what I see."

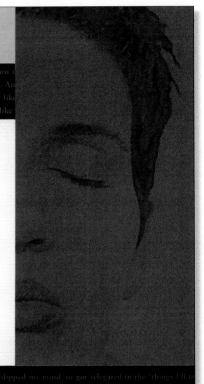

[this just in:]

An urgent message for Aidan and Coleman Zielske: Hi guys, it's me, Mom, and I had to share something important with you, before it slipped my mind, or got relegated to the "things I'll tell them one of these days" file. I hope this won't come as a huge surprise to you both, but here it is: **I'M NOT PERFECT**. Okay, whew! Now that it's out there, let me explain…

There are days when we have reached our limits. You know the ones. Cole invades your personal space. Aidan won't let you touch anything in her room. And me, well, I'm busy trying to explain why hormones make Mom yell so loudly. I've been thinking alot lately about what it means to be a parent, and to tell you the truth, half the time, I act like I don't have a clue.

Your Dad, on the other hand, doesn't need any clues. For him, it's like a fish to water, with no instruction needed on how to navigate the currents. Me, sometimes it's like a fish out of water, flopping around on the dock, trying to figure out what happened to the water, and why I'm having

so much trouble breathing. A little dramatic, I know…but that's your mother talking, and that's also why we thank God everyday for Daddy.

I don't always know the right thing to do. I've heard it said, "Wow, it'd be great if there was a manual for parenting with all the answers." Well, we have that already. You call him "Daddy." But I don't always find that reservoir of patience, that endless ability to selflessly step outside of myself and rise above to meet any occasion. It's part of who I am, and something I'm working on, too.

But here's another thing, that's not "just in." I love the two of you in a way that defies all rational behavior. From the minute each of you wonderful, beautiful, amazing creatures came into my world, I have been blessed. Wholly and unconditionally blessed. I would, without a doubt, trade my life for yours without a second thought.

Although far from perfect, which we have thusly established, here's **WHAT I AM**: the one who will be at your bedside in the middle of the night

without question; the one who will sing duets with you from the "Grease" soundtrack; the one who will play hockey in the dining room, laugh at your jokes, marvel at your artwork, hold you when you're sad, bring you Cheetos upon request, make you endless supplies of chocolate milk, help you learn lyrics to countless songs from the '80s, make you special meals so you don't have to eat what Daddy and I are eating, kiss your cheeks until they're chapped, eat Fla-Vor-Ice with you every day, make you feel as safe as humaly possible in this uncertain world, pray with you at night, and then get down on my knees and be more thankful than any other imperfect soul could ever be, for the two of you.

So, that's it, in a nutshell. And aptly spoken, from your nutty Mom. I'm not perfect, but my love for you is. It's honest, pure and from the absolute gut of my being. I will work on the yelling part, and remember to be more fun and patient. Does it sound like a deal to you? Okay, good…I'm starting now. **8.03**

[imperfect]

Supplies *Computer fonts:* Old Typewriter (title), downloaded from the Internet; Adobe Garamond and Gill Sans (journaling), Adobe Systems; *Ribbon charms:* Making Memories; *Photo paper:* Premium Luster, Epson; *Photo-editing software:* Photoshop, Adobe Systems.

⁜ THIS JUST IN
by Cathy Zielske
St. Paul, MN

At the end of a long, trying day, Cathy sat down and typed a letter for her kids to read when they're older. "I wanted them to know that I'm not perfect—that I don't always know the right things to say or do," says Cathy. "At the same time, I wanted to tell them that the one thing I am absolutely positive of is my love for them."

- Cathy opted for a single photo because she felt a series would be too "obvious" and she needed more space for her journaling.
- To create an abstract effect on her photo, Cathy applied a charcoal drawing filter in her photo-editing software. "This layout was about words, not images," notes Cathy. "That's exactly what I wanted to achieve."

Journaling Excerpt

"I don't always know the right thing to do. I've heard it said, 'Wow, it'd be great if there was a manual for parenting with all the answers.' Well, we have that already. You call him 'Daddy.' But I don't always find that reservoir of patience, that endless ability to selflessly step outside of myself and rise above to meet any occasion. It's part of who I am, and something I'm working on, too."

Supplies *Computer fonts:* 2Peas Spread Sunshine ("Look Through"), downloaded from *www.twopeasinabucket.com*; 1942 Report, downloaded from the Internet; *Computer software:* Photoshop 6.0, Adobe Systems.

LOOK THROUGH MY EYES, LOOK THROUGH MY HEART

by Rhonda Stark
Plymouth, MN

Rhonda had recently read *How to Photograph Your Life* by Nick Kelsh, and she knew just what approach she wanted to take. "He wrote about taking pictures of things that identify a person, a portrait without the person being in it," says Rhonda.

"I thought about what my kids might think identifies me. I didn't want them thinking I was just about cooking and cleaning and laundry and all those things I do each day. I wanted to create something that showed them that, yes, I do those things, but that those are not what I am all about. That there is a reason I do those things, and that there is more to me than they see."

• To create photo squares that are the same size, Rhonda used Photoshop's Rectangle Tool to create individual white borders over the layers of pictures. She merged all the layers of the white border, creating one layer, then placed a drop shadow on the merged layer. Instead of setting the angle of the light source from above, she created it from below (at -60 degrees). "This gives the illusion that the pictures and papers were placed on top of the white, as if they were cropped using a square punch," says Rhonda. "I like my layouts to look as realistic as possible."

• To give her "My Heart" and "My Eyes" titles a sense of depth, Rhonda applied the Emboss effect in Photoshop.

Supplies *Clay:* Creative Paperclay ("a wife" word tile) and Sculpey, Prēmo (dark page accents); *Square brads, metal letters and page pebble:* Making Memories; *"A" and "N" letter tiles:* Westrim Crafts; *Gold letter tags:* DieCuts with a View; *Arrow:* Caroline Moon; *Label tape:* Dymo; *Leather:* Silver Creek Leather Co.; *Clear gloss:* Diamond Glaze; *Letter stamps:* Barnes & Noble (large) and PSX Design (small); *Photo-editing software:* Photoshop Elements, Adobe Systems. *Other:* Embossing powder, walnut ink, domino tile, muslin, twill tape and metal tags. *Idea to note:* Sara created the brown paper by dribbling walnut ink back and forth on art paper.

I AM

by Sara Tumpane
Grayslake, IL

After dealing with both positive and painful issues in her personal and business life, Sara has found herself reflecting on who she is. At Heidi's invitation, she created a self-portrait page.

"I usually journal about events or photos, not feelings," says Sara. "This was a big stretch for me, but a good one. I learned a lot about myself and how I'm changing and growing."

• Sara displayed positive, strengthening words on the right-hand side of her layout. She included other reflective thoughts in a small muslin pocket that's more private.

• The photo, taken under low lighting conditions, shows Sara in a reflective state. To improve its quality, Sara tweaked the photo in Photoshop Elements. She selected the "Enhanced" feature to give the photo a more ethereal effect.

• Note how the clay sections reinforce Sara's desire to "mold" herself for the future.

Supplies *Patterned paper and vellum:* Chatterbox; *Textured cardstock:* Bazzill Basics; *Transparency overlay:* Artistic Expressions; *Ball chain:* Making Memories; *Typewriter key letters:* FoofaLa; *Computer font:* Facelift, downloaded from the Internet; *Photo-editing software:* Photoshop Elements, Adobe Systems.

⚛ PORTRAIT OF ME
by Stacy McFadden
Victoria, Australia

Stacy couldn't wait to create a cover page for her self-portrait album—she realizes the importance of documenting her memories along with her family's. When she couldn't find a high-quality picture of herself, Stacy used a photo-editing program to turn one of her best photo options into a hand-sketched look.

• Stacy used photo-editing software to give her digital picture a "colored pencil drawing" look. She output the picture on textured cardstock for a "canvas" feel.

• Stacy didn't want the "factual" part of her history to be prominent, so she hid it behind the photo as a pull-out with a small tab. Along the side are strips with descriptive words about Stacy that she will elaborate on in her album.

On the layout:

S We grow neither better M

I Or worse as we get older L

But more like ourselves E

september 2003

It is so hard to believe, but my 40th birthday is just around the corner. Where did the time go? It seems like just yesterday that I could snuggle in my parents' laps... just yesterday that I was a little girl playing with my Barbie dolls... just yesterday that I was a teenager experiencing my first 'crush'... just yesterday that I graduated from high school...and from college. It seems like it was just yesterday that my Daddy walked me down the aisle...and just yesterday that I became a Mommy.

So how is it, then, that just today I realized that I am turning the corner from summer to winter? And that the fine lines around my eyes aren't so fine anymore? And that my once athletic figure can now officially be called middle-aged? And my wardrobe is decidedly not so hip anymore?

I don't know the answers to these questions, but the other thing I realized just today is that I am right where I should be. And through the wisdom of my years I am now comfortable following the beat of my own drum. I no longer have to think twice about what others think. I no longer need to put on an act to impress people – I am comfortable and confident just being *me*.

And just knowing that I have finally arrived at *me* makes me SMILE

S M I L e

Supplies *Textured cardstock:* Bazzill Basics; *Patterned paper:* Pamela Martin, Creative Imaginations; Karen Foster Design; *Computer font:* 2Peas Chestnuts, downloaded from *www.twopeasinabucket.com*; *Alphabet stamps:* PSX Design; *Stamping ink:* Paintbox (rainbow pad), Clearsnap; Brilliance (black), Tsukineko; *Embossing powder:* Cloisonne, Tsukineko; *Metal alphabet charms and eyelet:* Making Memories; *Slide holders:* Two Peas in a Bucket. *Idea to note:* Christine inked the slide holders with rainbow pigment ink, then embossed it.

SMILE

by Christine Brown
Hanover, MN

As she approaches her 40th birthday, Christine has been thinking a lot about where the time has gone. "I realize I'm entering the 'fall' of my life," says Christine, "but I also realize that I'm right where I should be. I'm more comfortable and confident in showing my true self than I've ever been before. That's a great reason to smile."

• Scrapbook a photo of what you look like today. The close-up here plays up Christine's broad smile and light-yellow eyes, but documents that she is aging a little as well. "I don't mind this," says Christine. "I and others can see that I'm still myself, beaming underneath it all."

• Christine dressed" the layout just how she would dress herself—soft and feminine with simple jewelry, while still maintaining an air of professionalism and polish.

Journaling Excerpt

. . . "So how is it, then, that just today I realized I am turning the corner from summer to fall? And that the fine lines around my eyes aren't so fine anymore? And that my once athletic figure can now officially be called middle-aged? And my wardrobe is decidedly not so hip anymore?

"I don't know the answers, but the other thing I just realized today is that I am right where I should be. . . . I no longer have to think twice about what others think. I no longer need to put on an act to impress people—I am comfortable and confident just being me. And just knowing that I have finally arrived at *me* makes me SMILE."

Supplies *Patterned papers:* Chatterbox, Karen Foster Design and Making Memories; *Computer fonts:* CK Newsprint, "Fresh Fonts" CD, *Creating Keepsakes*; CAC Shishoni, downloaded from the Internet; *Oval label holder, ribbon and ribbon charm:* Making Memories; *Circle charm and jump rings:* Westrim Crafts; *Index tabs:* Z-International, Inc.; *Alphabet blocks:* FoofaLa; *Chalk:* Craf-T Products; *Stamping ink:* Ancient Page, Clearsnap. *Idea to note:* Mellette's husband, Joe, took the photographs in their garage.

COMPLETELY ME
by Mellette Berezoski
Crosby, TX

Mellette has always felt that physical, emotional and spiritual aspects make up who she is. When creating her self-portrait layout, Mellette included these areas in a notebook-style setting. "I've kept journals since I was a young girl," says Mellette, "and writing has always been a very natural and wonderful outlet for me to express my thoughts. I created a small notebook to house my journaling and additional photos."

• To create the journal, Mellette made a template the same size as the pages and pierced evenly spaced holes down the left-hand side. She placed the template on top of each page for perfect placement of the holes. Next, Mellette attached the four pages with jump rings. They hold the notebook together nicely without being too bulky.

• To symbolize her old-fashioned views and values, Mellette aged her plaid paper by rubbing chalk over the front, then inking the edges with an ink pad.

Journaling Excerpt
"I am an emotional person. I cry at movies, can be completely moved by a song on the radio, and take other people's words to heart. I can be easily heartbroken, and have been told that I am too sensitive many times in my life. But I love deeply, and am not afraid to put my entire heart into something or someone I truly care for.

"I am 35 and know all too well that being this way sometimes hurts. To love deeply means to hurt deeply as well. I know that because I have felt that. But I would cry a million tears just to know and feel the fullest capacity of my heart. And every morning, when I wake up to my husband and children, I feel that too."

PHOTOGRAPHING *you*

PHOTOS BY NANCI JARMAN AND ALVARO REDDY

TAKE A SENSATIONAL SELF-PORTRAIT

BY ALLISON TYLER JONES

While capturing yourself on film may not be tops on your to-do list, it's a worthwhile exercise. Here's a little technical know-how to help you produce revealing results.

TOOLS

Two tools that can help ensure your success are the right camera and a tripod. Look for the following:

- A delayed-action timer (typically gives you 10–20 seconds to get in the picture)
- A wireless remote that lets you trigger the shutter
- A cable release if you have a single lens reflex (SLR) camera.

With the cable-release accessory, you can release the shutter on a tripod-mounted camera. A tripod will keep your camera in a fixed position while you pose for your portrait.

- A digital camera. It's a real plus since you can see the results immediately and make adjustments as you go.

TECHNIQUES

Once you've got the right tools handy, try these simple ideas for sensational self-portraits:

- **Stand in front of the bathroom mirror.** Turn your camera's flash feature off, then pose in front of a mirror and photograph your reflection (Figure 1). Hold your camera at waist level—you'll be cropping out

that portion of the photo anyway. You'll need to play with the camera angle a little, so take several shots. Use a film speed of 800 or faster for the best results.

• **Photographing your body parts.** Considering holding your camera at arm's length and taking pictures? This isn't recommended, especially with point-and-shoot cameras. The minimum "focusing distance" is typically longer than arm's length, and attempting this type of shot will usually result in a blurry mess.

Instead, move in closer with a zoom lens and pick up the body parts that are unique to you. Maybe it's those piano fingers that are so admired; perhaps you consider your eyes your best asset. Focus on what's unique about you, even if it's not pretty.

• **Take a still shot by a window.** Find a window with nice light, set up a chair, place your camera on a tripod and you're ready to shoot (Figure 2). You can hang up a background (such as a sheet) or, better yet, zoom in enough and you won't have to worry about the background at all (Figure 3). When shooting with window light, use film speeds of 400 or 800 for best results.

Try these exercises and see what you learn about yourself. You could be surprised! Once you get over being self-conscious, shooting a self-portrait can be fun. Just remember: Don't give up too soon. Keep shooting until you get a photo that captures the real you.

Allison Tyler Jones is the co-author of Designing with Photos *and co-owner of Memory Lane Photo and Paper Arts in Gilbert, Arizona.*

Figure 1. Holding your camera at waist level, photograph your reflection in a mirror.

Figure 2. Set up a tripod near a window with nice light.

Figure 3. Zoom in for a sensational photo with a trouble-free background.

the rest of the story

Create an album that's a welcome switch

Figure 1. Capture thoughts that seem to float around in your head and pin them down on a page layout. *Page by Rebecca Sower.* **Supplies** *Patterned paper:* The Paperie; *Rubber stamp:* Inky After Dark; *Date stamp:* OfficeMax; *Stamp ink:* Creative Beginnings; *Computer font:* Teletype, Print Shop Premier, Broderbund; *Other:* Brass hardware, button, wire and running-shoe picture from *Sports Illustrated.*

At bottom left, Rebecca scrunched up a running-shoe picture, rubbed over it with steel wool, then sponge-stamped it with stamping ink.

On turning 40

It's less than two years away...if I could choose what I'd like to do when I turn 40...

...I would *not* like to be at my surprise party where everyone is laughing and the room is full of black balloons;
...I would love to be at a sidewalk cafe in Paris with my husband;
...I would like to reflect back on my first 40 years with the satisfaction of a job well done;
...I would like to make big plans for my next 40 years;
...I would like to have a stylish haircut, and still look acceptable in jeans;
...I'd like to be running at least a mile every day;
...I hope to feel younger than that poor, tired mom that I was when I was 30 with a toddler and infant in the house;
...I want to garden like my grandmother and play ball with my kids;
...as always, I want to be the best wife and mom that I can be.

EVER DONE SOMETHING that was perfectly permissible, yet for some reason you felt you needed to justify it? That's how I used to feel about my morning walks. No one in my family gave me any flack over taking the time for myself, but I still found myself wanting to explain how important this time was for me.

I created a layout about the walks (page 84), but it didn't really "fit" into the other albums I'd completed to date, so I set the layout aside. One day, not much later, I

ARTICLE BY REBECCA SOWER

watched a spider build her web outside my window. I learned an important lesson from watching that spider, so guess what? I created a scrapbook layout telling all about it (page 85). But this layout didn't flow well with my other albums either.

Then there was the time (somewhere around Thanksgiving) that I jotted down 10 small reasons I had to be happy *that day*. I didn't worry about "family," "faith" and the other *big* blessings. Instead, I just focused on *that-particular-day* reasons, like "not running out of gas before I got to the gas station," "hearing a favorite song from high school on the radio" and more. The exercise was so fun that—yep—I wanted to create a layout for my list of that day's blessings.

Figure 2. Share the personal reasons you chose an activity. *Page by Rebecca Sower.* **Supplies** *Computer font:* StarBabe, Card Studio 2, Hallmark; *Rubber stamps:* Close To My Heart (sun) and Hot Potatoes (leaf); *Embossing powder:* Mark Enterprises; *Fibers:* Rubba Dub Dub Products.

Next I found myself creating a layout about all the orders I dish out to my children day after day (page 86). Soon I was working on a scrapbook page about all the photographs I *wish* I'd taken. Before long I was creating another page about why I'm not going to purchase any more decorator magazines until my children are older (page 86).

Before I knew it, I had the makings of a completely separate album. I call it my "Rest of the Story" scrapbook. You should try it.

What! Does this mean I'm supposed to start yet another scrapbook?

Of course not. Still, it could prove to be a refreshing diversion from some of your other scrapbook projects. Here are some great reasons to start your own "Rest of the Story" album (or at least start a file for one):

♦ **It's fun.** This album is so unlike the traditional approach to albums. It isn't deep. It isn't soul-searching or life-changing. It's not about hopes, dreams, aspirations and heart's desires. To call it therapeutic would be a stretch. It's just *real facts* in a lighthearted and creative format. It's personal, but not so personal

possible topics

Coming up with topics for your "Rest of the Story" album can be tricky. Just think of all the topics that aren't good fits for your traditional albums. A few examples could include:

♦ A list of the books you'd like to read when you find time

♦ How you always seem to pick the slow line at the grocery store

♦ What section of the newspaper you like to read first and why

♦ How you wish Sunday mornings weren't quite so hectic

♦ Why you like to visit a particular section of the bookstore

♦ Your mission to perfect a particular recipe

♦ Your plans for organizing your household

♦ Why you don't like to shop at the mall (me either!)

♦ What makes you tick and what ticks you off

♦ Any "Why am I doing this?" situation

♦ A description of your dream house

♦ How a certain movie or book affected you

♦ Your housework routine (this could come in handy for your offspring someday)

♦ What you'd do if you had a day all to yourself

Machine-stitch around your page and journaling blocks to create a spider-web feel.

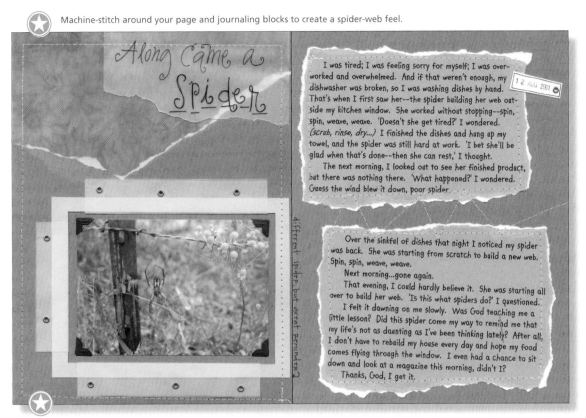

For a novel photo frame, fold vellum rectangles in half, slip the folded vellum over a cut-out frame, then secure it with eyelets.

Figure 3. Share a story or experience that doesn't seem to fit well into your traditional scrapbooks. *Pages by Rebecca Sower.* **Supplies** *Patterned vellum:* Autumn Leaves; *Eyelets:* Impress Rubber Stamps; *Journaling font:* Chris, Card Studio 2, Hallmark; *Pen:* Zig Writer, EK Success; *Date stamp:* OfficeMax.

that others can't look at it.

◆ **It's fulfilling.** No, it's probably not going to be coffee-table material; but it will help you pin down all those experiences and thoughts that you find floating around your head on a regular basis. For instance, I've been watching "40" loom over me since I turned 35. Now it's less than two years away. I'm by no means dreading it, but I have had some *ideas* about turn-

ing 40 that have passed through my mind now and then. My "Rest of the Story" album has proved the perfect place to tack down those ideas (Figure 1).

◆ **It's insightful.** You and those who live with you will both benefit from this album. You'd probably feel strange creating a layout about how you wish all customer-service departments were like the one at American Girl (yes, they literally *saved* my daughter's Christmas last year). But in your "Rest of the Story" album, it fits perfectly. And now my daughter has an even bigger appreciation for the gift that had a small crisis behind its arrival.

◆ **It's (dare I say it?) selfish.** Perhaps "personal" would be a better word. What I mean is that the album is *yours* and you can present and say anything *you* want

in it. Your "Rest of the Story" scrapbook is not something you're creating for others.

For instance, as I create the pages for my child's album, I focus on that child. I create any projects with her in mind, and I stay within certain "boundaries." By that I simply mean I wouldn't include a layout about why I prefer to shop for groceries early on Thursday morning or why I'd like to start a Bible study group in my home. But your "Rest of the Story" album gives you freedom— to include anything you want.

◆ **It's your chance to be daring.** You have my permission to push the limits. Try something a little out of creative character for you. Sometimes in our traditional albums, we (understandably) attempt to present layouts and journaling in a more organized

Interested in other ideas for theme albums? Check out our sister publication, *Simple Scrapbooks*, which has a strong theme-album focus. Visit *www.simplescrapbooksmag.com*

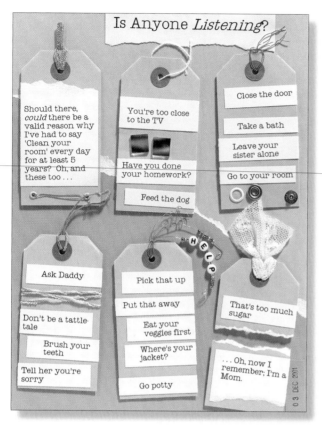

Is Anyone *Listening?*

Should there, *could* there be a valid reason why I've had to say 'Clean your room' every day for at least 5 years? Oh, and these too . . .

You're too close to the TV

Have you done your homework?

Feed the dog

Close the door

Take a bath

Leave your sister alone

Go to your room

Ask Daddy

Don't be a tattle-tale

Brush your teeth

Tell her you're sorry

Pick that up

Put that away

Eat your veggies first

Where's your jacket?

Go potty

H·E·L·P

That's too much sugar

. . . Oh, now I remember: I'm a Mom.

0 3 DEC 2001

Figure 4. Ever had one of those "Why am I even bothering?" moments? This album is the perfect place to document it. *Page by Rebecca Sower.* **Supplies** *Cardstock, tags and alphabet beads:* Impress Rubber Stamps; *Computer font:* Teletype, Print Shop Premier, Broderbund; *Mirror tiles:* Darice; *Fibers:* On the Surface; *Date stamp:* OfficeMax; *Other:* Beads, wire, snaps, lace, hemp cord, ribbon and string.

and refined manner. With your "Rest of the Story" scrapbook, there are no creative rules!

Use leftover photos or no photos. Tear quotes out of magazines and stick them on the page. Try your hand at painting, then include the results in your album. Tear or punch your photos. Present your journaling with a different twist. Think of all those times you thought a technique or object looked really cool but were afraid the scrapbook police might arrest you. Now's your chance!

Not that you couldn't before, but your "Rest of the Story" album lets you scrapbook *anything.* Go ahead—have a good time with it. Let this be your one album where you don't feel any pressure or restrictions. Laugh at yourself, talk to yourself, sing if you like as you create this scrapbook. Try a little scrapbooking *freedom!* ♥

I think I'm going to stop buying those home decorator magazines. Every now and then, when I'm in line at the grocery, I'll pick up one and put it in the cart.

Usually it's a few days before I have the chance to flip through it. Page after page of meticulously decorated, furnished and *clean* rooms.

Then I feel that same little wave of despair that I've felt before. I keep my eyes locked on the magazine...that way I don't have to face the wooden train tracks and puzzle pieces scattered all over the living room floor, and the furniture that should've been dusted a week ago...is that a piece of popcorn under the sofa?...

'Mom, have you seen my clarinet?!'

snaps me back to real life.

Oh yeah, that's what the magazine pictures lack--reality, *my* reality. Wait a minute, I *love* my reality.

'Did you leave it in the van again?'...

1 1 DEC 2001

LIFE

not just yet

Create wrinkled-paper pockets by spraying cardstock with water, scrunching and unscrunching the paper several times, then letting it dry.

Figure 5. Create reminders to "hang in there" and keep a proper perspective. *Pages by Rebecca Sower.* **Supplies** *Computer font:* StarBabe, Card Studio 2, Hallmark; *Date stamp:* OfficeMax; *Tag:* Avery; *Laminating machine:* Xyron; *Eyelets:* Impress Rubber Stamps; *Fibers:* On the Surface; *Other:* Game piece, puzzle piece, candy wrapper, magazine page section.

Journaling Ideas:
Remembering Small Details

by Denise Pauley

Record the small details and events that make your relationship special. Each year, include the notes on an anniversary layout. *Page by Denise Pauley.* **Supplies** *Vellum:* Paper Adventures; *Red and silver textured paper:* Books by Hand; *Computer font:* Bickley Script, Microsoft Word; *Pen:* Zig Millennium, EK Success; *Muslin bags:* Impress Rubber Stamps; *Aluminum tags:* Anima Designs; *Other:* Brads.

As each year of marriage passes (and as I get older ... and older), I tend to forget some of the small details and events that have made our relationship special—the inside jokes, the day trips, the favorites, the arguments. To preserve them, I've decided to adapt my practice of writing "love notes" to my family into a new "anniversary anecdote" tradition. Each year, I plan to create a layout that features several tidbits that my husband and I can recall from the previous year ... anything interesting, funny or noteworthy that made it meaningful.

For "privacy," I like to enclose the notes in pockets, such as little muslin bags. You can also tuck them into small envelopes, conceal them under flaps, or be bold and include your notes right on the page. (However, I fully expect that these snippets will be enlightening to our children someday—just when they're convinced that old Mom and Dad never had a life other than being their mom and dad!)

If you'd like to make up for lost time, simply complete a layout that covers the elements you remember from the early years of your marriage—the bad and the good. Just make sure you're specific! The entire concept will be pointless if you pull out a strip of paper years from now, read the inscription and ask, "Now what does *that* mean? I don't remember that at all!" The notes should be brief but include enough information to trigger a recollection of a memorable time.

ILLUSTRATION BY CAROL NORBY

What's in Your Closet?

Closet?

SEE WHAT IT SAYS ABOUT YOU

Bedroom closets, hall closets, walk-in closets, cedar closets. For some of us they're a place to hide things. For others, they're a spot where everything has a place. No matter what you use them for or what you find in them, closets conceal glimpses of our pasts, presents and futures.

As a child, the house I grew up in had lots of small, dark closets. Almost every one of those closets had, and still has, items that tell a story or fetch a memory.

For example, besides the typical spring jackets and winter coats, the hall closet upstairs holds such treasures as my parents' wedding album, antique coats and hats, an old poker chip set we loved to play with, and—best of all— a fake-fur jacket.

by Mary Larson

Figure 1. A closet can contain much more than clothes. This one held Bobby Sherman pictures, a doll collection, handkerchiefs and Raggedy Ann books. *Pages by Mary Larson.* **Supplies** *Background paper and vellum:* Making Memories; *Reverse computer font for lettering:* Asia, downloaded from the Internet; *Computer font for journaling:* Greetings Monotone, downloaded from the Internet; *Other:* Dowel rods and Italian paper clips (Clipiola). *Ideas to note:* To make interesting frames for two of her photos, Mary scanned the pictures, reduced, tiled and printed them, then overlaid them with vellum.

As a young girl, I loved to snuggle in the jacket's soft fur and smooth satin while I watched TV in the den. I don't know where the jacket came from and I never remember my mom wearing it, but I remember the coat's feel and how warm it was.

To this day, the cedar closet in my parents' basement holds my childhood dance-recital costumes, my father's "marryin' and buryin' suit," and his uniform from the Navy. Keep looking and you'll also find old prom and formal dresses from the '60s, plus Jackie Kennedy-style hats.

A Personal Journey

When I go back home to visit, I often find myself searching my parents' closets for items that bring back personal memories. The fact that I find so many things gives me a hint of the era in which my parents grew up—the Great Depression. It was a time when certain items were scarce and everything was saved, not thrown away. Items were repaired, not replaced.

Growing up with my parents as an example, I find myself in the same predicament. I have a hard time getting rid of anything that

> I keep anything that holds a special memory for me or a loved one, and I attach sentiment to almost every object I own.

once belonged to someone I love, or that I think I might use or wear again. I keep anything that holds a special memory for me or a loved one, and I attach sentiment to almost every object I own. Okay, I'll admit it—I hoard.

A much nicer way of putting it is that I'm a "collector." It's no wonder my closets are overflowing with baby items, toys, clothes or shoes. From old record albums to ski clothes (hey, I used them 15 years ago), my closets are full!

A Packed Closet

Recently, I decided to alleviate some of the clutter in the walk-in closet in our master bedroom. When you have to move three boxes and squeeze sideways past the laundry baskets to get to your clothes, it's time to organize! Besides the normal clothes and

Figure 2. Whether we're talking designer handbags or canvas totes, the purses in your closet communicate loads about your lifestyle. *Page by Denise Pauley.* **Supplies** *Wood veneer and velveteen paper:* Paper Adventures; *Computer fonts:* Arial Narrow (journaling), Microsoft Word; Sixty-Seven (title), downloaded from the Internet; *Letter stickers:* Making Memories; *Teddy-bear template:* Pebbles in my Pocket; *Pen:* Zig Writer, EK Success; *Other:* Leather and brads; *Bags:* Denise's own designs.

shoes, my closet contains other items. Craft supplies for "future" projects take up one corner, while "collections" take up another.

While organizing my closet, I found a set of Raggedy Ann and Andy books that I'd read as a young girl. I also found a folder full of Bobby Sherman pictures. When I was about 10 years old, I had a huge crush on this pop star and kept pictures of him from teen magazines. It was so fun to reminisce about those "giggly" girl times.

Done with Dolls

At the back of the closet was a box of dolls. Before scrapbooking, I used to collect and customize dolls. This box was just one of many I still have around the house, and it reminded me of a hobby I used to enjoy.

Unfortunately, with four sons, I have little use for the box of dolls anymore!

How about Hankies?

I began a handkerchief collection a couple of years ago. My mother had many handkerchiefs, and I remember ironing them. Not so long ago, an older cousin of mine gave me more antique handkerchiefs. My grandmother and my great-aunt, as well as other ancestors, had owned them. One of these days, some of those handkerchiefs will be framed and hung above my bed.

Scrapbooking the Contents

While I had everything out of the closet, I documented the objects by snapping pictures of them. My sons were hovering around, wanting to know what the items were and why I still had them. My kids weren't interested in the dolls, but they did think it was funny that I had so many pictures of a pop star they'd never seen! Making a layout of this venture (see Figure 1) was a great way to record my past through writing and photographs.

Your Turn

So, what's in your closet that tells something about you? Is your closet tidy and organized—or messy and cluttered? I once knew a woman who insisted on burgundy plastic hangers for her closets. Knowing that about her, I could tell she was precise, particular, and very, very neat. I decided right then that she could never see the

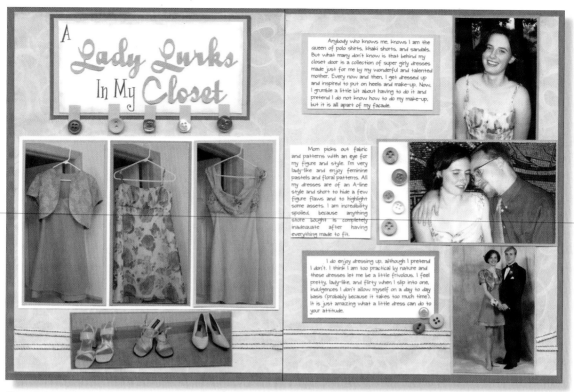

Figure 3. Lovely dresses convey a sense of beauty and class. **Pages by Erin Lincoln. Supplies** *Patterned paper:* David Walker, Colorbök; *Vellum:* Paper Adventures; *Chalk:* Craf-T Products; *Buttons:* Singer; *Ribbon:* Ribbon Textiles; *Computer fonts:* Quiggly-Wiggly and Girls Are Weird (title), downloaded from the Internet; CK Journaling, "The Best of Creative Lettering" CD, *Creating Keepsakes. Idea to note:* Erin printed her title in reverse, then cut it out with an X-Acto knife.

inside of my closets—it would be too embarrassing!

What's in your bedroom closet? Do you keep only necessities like clothes and shoes, or is it filled with items from your past or items for your future? Does it contain a favorite outfit from five years ago? How about 20 pairs of black pumps so you'll have the perfect match? A friend of mine keeps embroidered pictures from her grandmother in her closet.

What's Your Bag?

When Denise Pauley of La Palma, California, looked in her closet, she was bombarded with bags. She has all sorts! From the brief-cases she carried as a career woman to the huge tote bag she now carries as a mother, the bags are a reflection of what she was doing at the time she carried

them. The layout in Figure 2 shows Denise's pile of bags, plus the stories behind them.

Favorite Outfits

Erin Lincoln of Frederick, Maryland, usually finds herself in shorts and sandals. Peek in her closet, however, and you'll see a different side to her. Erin's mother makes beautiful dresses so Erin will look just right on special occasions. For the layout in Figure 3, Erin highlighted a few of her dresses as they appear on her and when they're hung up.

Our closets contain our pasts, our lives. They're an indication of the way we live and what's impor-tant to us. So, the next time you're cleaning out that closet, pay attention to what you find. You might just have the makings

of a great layout that'll help future generations get to know you better! ♥

Note: This article is designed to help you uncover and scrapbook who you and loved ones are. What did you find in your closet?

inside your JEWELRY BOX

SCRAPBOOK THE
MEMORIES WITHIN

by Denise Pauley

My jewelry box can best be described in one word: hodgepodge. Truth be told, most of its contents aren't even jewelry! Nestled among the bracelets, watches and rings is everything from notes to newspaper clippings, pins to postcards. They're just odds and ends, really, but they mean more to me than all the jewels they're stored beside.

I often wonder what my great-great-granddaughter would do if she inherited my jewelry box as it stands today. Would she immediately sift through the compartments to locate the most valuable jewels? Would she be intrigued by any of the items I've saved? Would she wonder why I kept the delicate gold chain with the broken clasp, the blue poker chip and a handful of little rocks?

Sure, it's easy for anyone to find the "valuables" in your collection. A gold watch, an emerald bracelet or diamond earrings are obviously significant, at least monetarily. But if you're like me, some of the items that have the most "worth" aren't the ones that cost the most. They're the pieces that have a history, a meaning, a story . . . and that story deserves to be told.

What treasures are hidden in your jewelry box? Will future generations know their significance? Since we're so interested in leaving a legacy through our scrapbooks, it seems a shame to let the importance of these future heirlooms go unrecorded.

What do you or those you love keep in your jewelry boxes? We were curious, so we asked some of the scrapbookers we know. While some didn't feel their jewelry boxes were scrapworthy, others felt the items within should be mentioned. Here's how Alannah Jurgensmeyer, Vivian Smith and Katherine Brooks chose to scrapbook those items.

Figure 1. If you've got one item that outshines the rest, devote an entire, beautiful layout to it. *Page by Alannah Jurgensmeyer*. **Supplies** *Patterned paper:* Karen Foster Design; *Beads:* Magic Scraps; *Gold threads:* On the Surface; *Mini-eyelets:* Creative Impressions; *Metal corners:* Boutique Trims; *Colored pencils:* Prismacolor, Sanford; *Computer fonts:* Bickley Script (italicized text), Corel Draw 10, Corel; CK Classic ("Beautiful Bangle"), "The Art of Creative Lettering" CD, *Creating Keepsakes*.

A Precious Object

When you look through your jewelry box, does a particular item immediately grab your attention? If you have something that's particularly beautiful, meaningful or important, create a special layout to spotlight it.

Alannah Jurgensmeyer of Rogers, Arkansas, designed "My Beautiful Bangle" to do just that (Figure 1). In addition to photos of the gorgeous piece, she journaled about it and even adorned her layout with ornamental photo corners to further the theme. The result is a beautiful page that will explain to her children's children why the bracelet is part of their family history.

Alannah chose to scrapbook the bracelet because "each slide represents something: my college alma mater, my firstborn, my second born, my 30th birthday, an apology, and several other holidays such as Christmas and less significant birthdays. I love it that each day when I choose my jewelry I'm also reminded of some of the most special times in my life."

The Highlights

Maybe you'd rather discuss several objects that have a special meaning instead. Vivian Smith of Calgary, Alberta, Canada, took this approach and did a lot of reminiscing in the process (Figure

2). Along with small photos of each item, Vivian included the reasons they're special. Beyond discussing the jewelry, she shares fond memories of her travels and friendships as well.

Among Vivian's treasures? An intricate fish pendant with a tail that flips back and forth, a cross pendant with gold recovered from a sunken galleon, a pinky ring that matches a good friend's, a globe ring that reminds her of a gypsy's crystal ball and more.

Katherine Brooks of Mesa, Arizona, used a similar method for her "My Jewelry Box" layout (Figure 3). In addition to a border photo encompassing a lot of her jewelry, the layout also singles out

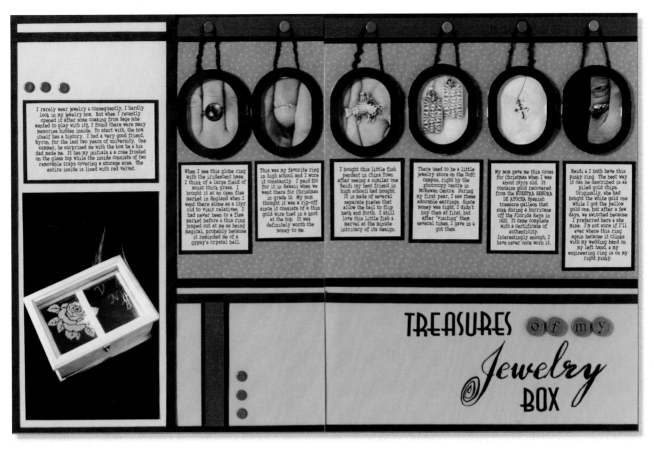

Figure 2. Little history-rich details can turn your trinkets into treasures. *Pages by Vivian Smith*. **Supplies** *Patterned paper:* O'Scrap!, Imaginations!; *Letter stickers:* Flavia, Colorbök ("Jewelry"); Asia ("Treasures" and "Box"), Shotz letters by Danelle Johnson, Creative Imaginations; *Flat-top eyelets and eyelet words:* Making Memories; *Fiber:* Rubba Dub Dub, Art Sanctum; *Circle template:* Coluzzle, Provo Craft; *Pop dots:* Stampin' Up!; *Computer font:* CK Corral, "Fresh Fonts" CD, *Creating Keepsakes. Idea to note:* Vivian used a circle template to create her photo frames. She then pop-dotted them and hung them with fiber from flat-top eyelets.

her favorite objects, collections and the stories behind them. By reading the journaling on Katherine's layout, it's easy to sense her love for her family and her fascination with opals, her mother's rings and her grandmother's roadrunner pendant.

Are many of your keepsake items not even jewelry? Create a layout to explain and capture the memories behind them. Who knows? Someday you could be looking through your jewelry box and wonder why you saved that video game token or broken seashell! If you have a lot of bits and pieces, simply do a quick inventory list to touch upon the reasons you're holding onto them. Or, include an explanation in your journaling as Alannah did.

The Icing

Though its contents may be beautiful, some people might consider the actual jewelry box the icing on the cake—an heirloom as valuable as everything within. Perhaps you own a gorgeous keepsake box you received for a special occasion, one inherited from your grandmother, or a cool satchel you found in an antique shop. Whatever its past, give the future a reason to cherish it as much as you do. Record its importance and the memories it invokes.

The Questions

If you're still having trouble getting started or finding focus for your layout, try asking yourself the

following questions. Your answers might even inspire you to create an entire theme album devoted to the topic!

- Find your most cherished piece of jewelry. Who gave it to you and why? Is it a priceless inherited brooch, a handmade friendship bracelet or a pretty promise ring? What are the reasons it's still so important to you today?

- When you open your jewelry box, what's the first object that catches your eye? Are you drawn to it simply because it's gorgeous or because of a sentimental attachment?

- Is there a piece of jewelry you'll never wear again but can't bear to give up? If so, is there a

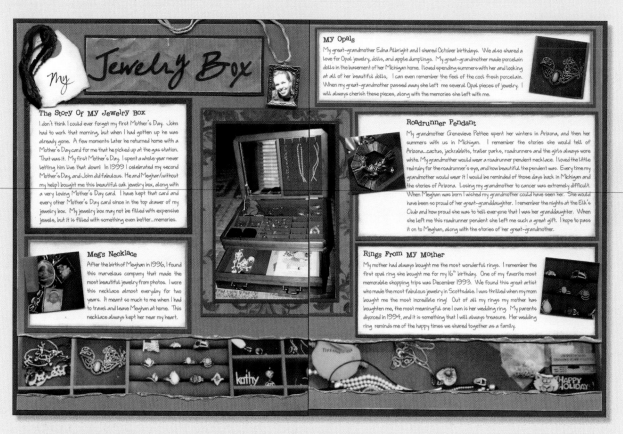

My Jewelry Box

My Opals

My great-grandmother Edna Albright and I shared October birthdays. We also shared a love for Opal jewelry, dolls, and apple dumplings. My great-grandmother made porcelain dolls in the basement of her Michigan home. I loved spending summers with her and looking at all of her beautiful dolls. I can even remember the feel of the cool, fresh porcelain. When my great-grandmother passed away she left me several Opal pieces of jewelry. I will always cherish these pieces, along with the memories she left with me.

The Story Of My Jewelry Box

I don't think I could ever forget my first Mother's Day. John had to work that morning, but when I had gotten up he was already gone. A few moments later he returned home with a Mother's Day card for me that he picked up at the gas station. That was it. My first Mother's Day. I spent a whole year never letting him live that down. In 1999 I celebrated my second Mother's Day, and John did fabulous. He and Meghan (without my help) bought me this beautiful oak jewelry box, along with a very loving Mother's Day card. I have kept that card and every other Mother's Day card since in the top drawer of my jewelry box. My jewelry box may not be filled with expensive jewels, but it is filled with something even better...memories.

Roadrunner Pendant

My grandmother Genevieve Pettee spent her winters in Arizona, and then her summers with us in Michigan. I remember the stories she would tell of Arizona...cactus, jackrabbits, trailer parks, roadrunners and the girls always wore white. My grandmother would wear a roadrunner pendent necklace. I loved the little red ruby for the roadrunner's eye, and how beautiful the pendent was. Every time my grandmother would wear it I would be reminded of those days back in Michigan and the stories of Arizona. Losing my grandmother to cancer was extremely difficult. When Meghan was born I wished my grandmother could have seen her. She would have been so proud of her great-granddaughter. I remember the nights at the Elk's Club and how proud she was to tell everyone that I was her granddaughter. When she left me this roadrunner pendent she left me such a great gift. I hope to pass it on to Meghan, along with the stories of her great-grandmother.

Meg's Necklace

After the birth of Meghan in 1996, I found this marvelous company that made the most beautiful jewelry from photos. I wore this necklace almost everyday for two years. It meant so much to me when I had to travel and leave Meghan at home. This necklace always kept her near my heart.

Rings From My Mother

My mother had always bought me the most wonderful rings. I remember the first opal ring she bought me for my 16th birthday. One of my favorite most memorable shopping trips was December 1993. We found this great artist who made the most fabulous jewelry in Scottsdale. I was thrilled when my mom bought me the most incredible ring! Out of all my rings my mother has bought/given me, the most meaningful one I own is her wedding ring. My parents divorced in 1994, and it is something that I will always treasure. Her wedding ring reminds me of the happy times we shared together as a family.

Figure 3. A wonderful selection of stories can help highlight your beautiful collection. *Pages by Katherine Brooks.* **Supplies** *Patterned paper:* K & Company; *Computer fonts:* Problem Secretary (subtitles), downloaded from the Internet; CK Bella (title), "The Art of Creative Lettering" CD; CK Journaling (journaling), "The Best of Creative Lettering" CD Combo, *Creating Keepsakes; Circle and square punches:* Family Treasures; *Chalk:* Craf-T Products; *Frame:* Memory Lane; *Fibers:* Rubba Dub Dub, Art Sanctum; *Tag:* Katherine's own design; *Other:* Ribbon.

noteworthy reason that deserves further explanation?

• What is your most unusual object? Why and where did you get it?

• What was the first piece of jewelry you ever received? Who was it from, and does it still hold meaning for you today?

• Do you collect anything that you keep in your jewelry box? Your collection doesn't have to be jewelry. Maybe you keep certain types of memorabilia (like coins, shells or baubles) and have a special reason for doing so.

Are you enamored with one type of precious stone or metal? Some people prefer gold to silver or platinum to gold. Others prefer sapphires to pearls. What are your favorites?

• Are there any pieces you regret buying?

• Have you ever received any jewelry that you didn't like?

• Are there any items you want to see passed down from generation to generation? If so, that's a good enough reason to create a layout about your jewelry box. You'll want to make sure others know the history of and hopes for the items. ♥

I own a gold watch that once belonged to my grandmother. Although I love it for that reason alone, I have no idea where she got it, how often she wore it, or if it held a special place in her heart. Knowing the details would help me treasure the watch even more.

So, although you may think it's unimportant or that you don't have the time, try to set aside one scrap session to browse through your jewelry box. Look for any memories that should be recorded. You can even make a color copy of your scrapbook layout to tuck among the keepsakes. Future generations will be glad you did.

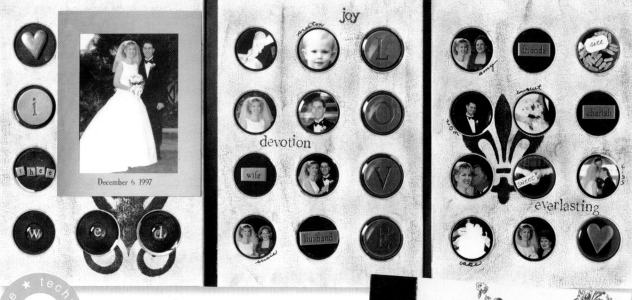

Altered Coin Book

This tri-fold book started out as a coin collection folder (Figure 1). The format is great for vacation or wedding scrapbooks because you can use so-so photos.

Use a circle punch to trim your photos, then emphasize your favorite images with watch crystals. You can also encapsulate rice, sand, shells and more. Here's how to alter a coin book:

❶ Cut the folder into three separate boards. Paint the punched sides with acrylic paint. Set them aside to dry.

❷ Select three coordinating papers. Apply adhesive to the board covers, then smooth your papers over them. Trim away the excess paper with a craft knife.

❸ Using an inkpad and a stippling brush, "pounce" the painted side of each board to create an aged look. For added visual texture, rub the entire surface with metallic rub-ons or stamp it with a crackle-textured rubber stamp.

❹ Reassemble the book with book binding tape, book repair tape or masking tape. (I found black masking tape at a teachers' supply store.) Make sure you leave enough space between each board to allow the book to close properly. You'll need to apply another thin strip of tape or cardstock in the creases so the tape doesn't stick together.

❺ Punch and set two large eyelets in the center coin circle on the left board. Thread ribbon through the holes with the ribbon ends on the outside. (You'll wrap the ribbons around the book to keep it closed.)

❻ Punch your photo elements with a circle punch. Arrange your photos and embellishments so that bulkier openings (circles with watch crystals in them) will be "received" by flat openings on the opposing page when you close the book.

❼ Stamp words and images on the inside of the book with solvent ink.

Variation: Use this technique as an accent block on a scrapbook page.

—*Ann Pelke, Peoria, AZ*

Figure 1. Showcase small photos in pages created from a coin folder. *Pages by Ann Pelke.* **Supplies** *Patterned paper:* Anna Griffin; *Textured cardstock:* Bazzill Basics; *Circle punch:* EK Success; *Rubber stamps:* Inkadinkadoo ("Words of Wisdom") and unknown (foam stamps); *Stamping ink:* Ancient Page, Clearsnap; StazOn, Tsukineko; *Pen:* Slick Writer, American Crafts; *Watch crystals:* Deluxe Plastic Arts; *Clear 3-D stickers, letter charms, metal frame and eyelet words, quote and hearts:* Making Memories; *Acrylic paint:* Ceramcoat, Delta Technical Coatings; *Metallic rub-ons:* Craf-T Products; *Ribbon:* Berwick; *Book tape:* Highsmith.

YOUR DREAM JOB

If my nose isn't buried in a Patricia Cornwall novel, I'm watching "C.S.I." or "Crossing Jordan." Yep—Emily Magleby, mild-mannered scrapper, stay-at-home mother of a two year old, would love to solve crimes from the trace materials left behind.

What does it say
about you?

by Emily Magleby

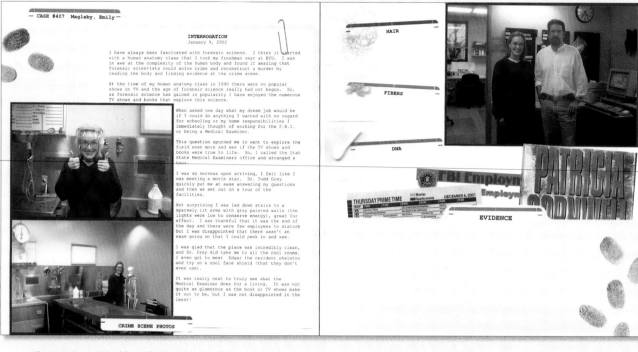

Figure 1. Forensic junkie Emily Magleby visited the state medical examiner's office—on assignment, of course! *Pages by Emily Magleby.* **Supplies** *Ink pad:* VersaColor, Tsukineko; *Computer font:* Courier New, Microsoft Word; *Memorabilia pockets:* 3L Corp.; *Other:* Avery labels and paper clips.

Use fingerprints and a Courier computer font to lend a scientific, "official" touch.

The forensic bug bit first while I was a freshman in college. While taking Zoology 260 ("Human Anatomy"), I studied cadavers and spent hours in the lab examining everything from nerve paths to tendons. Even though I reeked of formaldehyde, I was hooked! Unfortunately, my path into medicine ended the next summer with my Organic Chemistry class. After that, my schooling took a different turn.

Even though I've never held a medical job, the human body still fascinates me. I get my "fix" with forensic-themed TV shows such as "C.S.I." or "Crossing Jordan." When they're on, my husband, Matt, knows I'm not to be dis-turbed. I get totally absorbed in the puzzles that are so conveniently solved in a 60-minute time slot.

I'm such an inquisitive person, I called the state medical examiner's office in Utah and asked if I could come for a tour. Dr. Todd Grey, Chief Medical Examiner, said yes! We made an appointment, then I visited the office. I was both anxious and excited, but Dr. Grey put me at ease as he answered questions and led me downstairs for a tour.

The low-level lighting and gray paint on the walls were just what I'd expected. I watched, fascinat-ed, as Dr. Grey showed me every-thing from an exam room (with autopsy tables all in a row) to a small, closet-sized room that housed "containers" of autopsy findings. Even though I didn't get to see an autopsy in progress, I loved getting a firsthand look at where the evaluations take place.

At the end of the tour, Dr. Grey was kind enough to snap a picture of me wearing a face shield (these are worn during an examination). I thanked him for his time and left, thrilled with the opportunity I'd been given. Am I ready to pur-sue years of medical school and training, long hours and less-than-pleasing surroundings? No—but I'll live the forensic life vicariously through the actors who help keep it so intriguing!

I scrapbooked my experience at

(continued on page 102)

Figure 2. Bench-press champ and scrapbooker Lana Rickabaugh would love to dedicate her time to bodybuilding. *Pages by Lana Rickabaugh.* **Supplies** *Sparkly paper:* Diamond Dust, Paper Adventures; *Metallic paper:* Accu-Cut Systems; *White gel pen:* Marvy Uchida; *Lettering template:* Spunky, Déjà Views, The C-Thru Ruler Company; *Computer font:* Boys on Mopeds, downloaded from the Internet; *Embossing tool:* Li'l Boss, Paper Adventures; *Paper crimper:* Fiskars; *Other:* Eyelets, brads and a prong fastener.

Lana printed the words "True Stories of a Wannabe," then embossed them with silver embossing powder to create a metallic effect. She used an embossing tool and paper crimper to add patterns to her metallic paper.

Figure 3. Scrapbooker Rhonda Solomon is crazy about color! Ever since she was a child, Rhonda's been captivated by the color names for crayons, cosmetics, haircolor and more. She'd love to come up with her own. *Pages by Rhonda Solomon.* **Supplies** *Lettering template:* Pebbles in my Pocket; *Linen thread:* Normandy, Hillcreek Designs; *Computer font:* Courier New, Microsoft Word; *Hole punch:* Family Treasures; *Chalk:* Craf-T Products; *Pop-up glue dots:* Glue Dots International; *Shelves, frames, crayons, tags and lipsticks:* Rhonda's own creations; *Pen:* Zig Writer, EK Success; *Other:* Badge clip and paint color samples.

Rhonda created a "dream" business card, complete with photo, company name, lamination and clip. Elsewhere on her layout, she layered and chalked cardstock to create a feeling of depth for her accent bases and photo frame.

SILVER SCREEN DREAMS

I'M NOT SURE EXACTLY HOW IT BEGAN
BUT WHEN I WAS IN JUNIOR HIGH
I STARTED WATCHING OLD MOVIES.
INSTANTLY I WAS HOOKED AND EVER
SINCE I HAVE THOUGHT THAT BEING
A FILM HISTORIAN WOULD BE
A DREAM JOB. OVER THE YEARS I'VE
AMASSED QUITE A LIBRARY OF
VIDEOS AS WELL AS BOOKS ABOUT
OLD MOVIES. EVERYTHING ABOUT
CLASSIC HOLLYWOOD FASCINATES
ME FROM HOW THE MOVIES WERE
MADE TO THE STARS THAT WERE
IN THEM. IT MAY NOT BE MY CAREER
BUT IT HAS BECOME A FUN HOBBY.

- RUDY VALEE, WHO WAS IN
  55 FILMS, HAS THE SAME
  BIRTHDAY AS ME - JULY 28
- ACADEMY AWARD WINNER
  WALTER HOUSTON BEGAN
  HIS CAREER AS AN
  ENGINEER - MY PROFESSION
- THE MOVIE, THE PROGRAM
  HAD SCENES FILMED AT MY
  COLLEGE - DUKE UNIVERSITY
- PAUL NEWMAN WHO WON
  A BEST ACTOR OSCAR
  WAS BORN IN THE SAME
  TOWN AS ME - CLEVELAND, OH

Figure 4. Love old movies? Scrapbooker Lisa Brown does, and would love to be a film historian. She's interested in everything from movie stars to how the movies were made. *Pages by Lisa Brown.* **Supplies** *Vellum:* DMD Industries; *Circle punch:* Paper Shapers, EK Success.

Lisa made copies of black-and-white pictures of classic film stars, then overlaid them with colored vellum for artistic effect.

Career Choices When CK editors were asked what their dream jobs would be, their answers ranged from chef to archeologist to detective. Following is a sampling of dream career choices:

the state medical examiner's office (Figure 1), and in talking with other scrapbookers, I've discovered others' dream jobs as well. From Lana Rickabaugh's vision of body-building greatness (Figure 2) to Lisa Brown's love of old movies (Figure 4), ideas for great scrapbook pages abound. Look at Figure 3, and you'll learn all about Rhonda Solomon's secret inkling to create and name colors.

What's your dream career? Scrapbook it and what it says about you! The "Career Choices" sidebar at right will help get you started. ♥

- Artist
- Architect
- Engineer
- Educator
- Explorer
- Professional athlete
- Interior decorator
- Food taster
- Inventor
- Film star
- Veterinarian
- News reporter
- Doctor or nurse
- Movie critic
- Fashion model
- Novelist
- Trainer

What appeals to *you*?

uniquely you

Share who you and others are

Figure 1. Let your child know what you feel makes her stand out the most. *Page by Rebecca Sower.* **Supplies** *Date stamp and sticker:* Making Memories; *Stamping ink:* All Night Media; *Textured paper:* Provo Craft; *Paint:* Golden Artist Acrylics; *Pen:* Zig Writer, EK Success; *Other:* Vintage button and gauze ribbon.

"No one is more you-er than you!"
— Dr. Seuss

I LOVE the children's book *You Are Special* by Max Lucado. It's the story of a make-believe guy who lives in a make-believe town where people go around sticking yellow stars and gray dots on each other based on the way they view the recipients and their actions. The poor little subject of the story is covered with gray dots—so many that he convinces himself he's not a good person. He feels that way until he meets his maker, then everything changes (ha, now you have to buy the book).

Although the target audience for the book is obviously a child, how many of us adults go through life viewing ourselves through others' eyes? What is it about human nature that makes the negative shout loud and clear, while the positive sits quietly to the side?

ARTICLE BY REBECCA SOWER

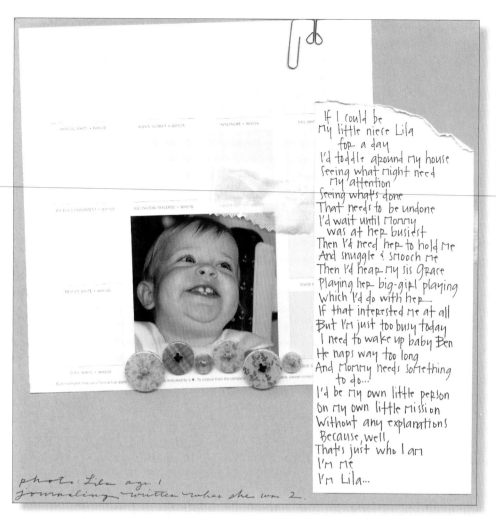

Figure 2. Poor little middle child (I was one, too). Help the child feel special by attributing what's unique and nice about him or her. *Page by Rebecca Sower.* **Supplies** *Paint swatch card:* Glidden; *Buttons:* Laura Ashley, EK Success; *Pen:* Zig Writer, EK Success; *Other:* Vintage fabric and paper clips.

What We Are

This article is not intended to be a personal therapy session for you. However, as they say, "if the shoe fits." You and I are incredibly unique individuals. Our mannerisms, traits, personalities, preferences and whims are ours and ours alone. Have you zeroed in on what is unique to you? And what about the characteristics you've noticed as being unique to the ones you love? If you haven't focused on these things, now is the time.

Although I want to encourage you to create some "uniquely you" layouts for the non-you people in your life (also known as *others*), I hope to motivate you to create some pages about a very important person in your life—*you!*

These won't be the layouts you might first envision. No, not the one about your role as mother, wife or friend. Not a "my favorite things" page that lists all the things you love (but which many people know about already).

I want you to take a deep breath, followed closely by a long,

hard look at you and *who you are.* Because who you are is a gift. A gift to your family. A gift to your friends, and a gift to this great, big planet earth. The questions in the "Questions to Ask Yourself" sidebar (see facing page) can help you get started.

Tell Them About It

If you have children, it's probably easy for you to create a "uniquely you" layout about each child. (See Figures 1 and 2.) Many of us have already done that. Have you created

Create some pages about a very important person in your life—you!

Figure 3. Tell someone how much you love and appreciate his unique qualities. *Page by Rebecca Sower.* **Supplies** *Paints and acrylic gel medium:* Golden Artist Acrylics; *Stickers:* Nostalgiques, EK Success; *Mini fasteners:* Impress Rubber Stamps; *Alphabet stamps:* PSX Design; *Stamping ink:* All Night Media; *Pen:* Zig Writer, EK Success; *Watercolor paper:* Molly Hawkins.

a "uniquely you" layout about your mom, your husband, your good friend? If not, let me show you how to *force* some feelings. No, I don't mean it like that—not false feelings or superficial praise. What I'm referring to is heartfelt feelings that are definitely there, just not easily accessible.

Here's an exercise: Think of someone who could use a little boost right now. Let's say it's your husband. Number a piece of paper from one to ten. Look at a favorite picture of your husband,

Questions to Ask Yourself

The answers to the following questions are unique to each person.

Why not use a few as starting points for a "uniquely you" page layout?

- What is a compliment you receive on a regular basis?
- What is something you have made by hand?
- What talent do you consider your favorite or best?
- What are your beauty secrets?
- What have you done in life that you're most proud of?
- What inanimate object or objects do you treasure?
- What can usually make you smile?
- What do you most enjoy doing when you're alone?
- What are at least five things your hands do during the course of a day?
- What are the pet names others have for you?

- What are your housekeeping secrets?
- What is your favorite dish to cook?
- How do you feel about nature?
- What do you do when something breaks?
- What would you do if you won $1,000,000?
- What do you consider life's necessities?
- How do you instantly react when faced with a crisis?
- What word best describes your "style"?
- What makes you cry?
- Do you daydream?
- In three words, describe your heart.

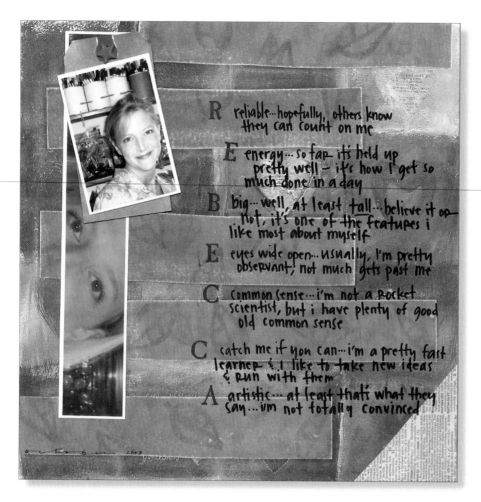

R reliable...hopefully, others know they can count on me

E energy...so far it's held up pretty well - it's how I get so much done in a day

B big...well, at least tall...believe it or not, it's one of the features i like most about myself

E eyes wide open...usually, I'm pretty observant; not much gets past me

C common sense... i'm not a Rocket scientist, but i have plenty of good old common sense

C catch me if you can...i'm a pretty fast learner & i like to take new ideas & run with them

A artistic... at least that's what they say...i'm not totally convinced

Figure 4. As uncomfortable as it may seem, creating a page that lists your unique characteristics will mean a lot to those you love. *Page by Rebecca Sower.* **Supplies** *Patterned papers:* Sarah Lugg (background), unknown (green) and Design Originals (dictionary); *Alphabet stamps:* The Missing Link; *Stamping ink:* All Night Media; *Pen:* Galaxy Marker, American Crafts; *Paints:* Golden Acrylic Glazes; *Fastener:* Making Memories; *Other:* Thread and manila tag.

draw a deep breath, and let those things you appreciate most about him float to the surface.

Now, maybe you're mad at your guy because he didn't take out the trash this morning. Get over it. Take the trash out yourself and notice how the world doesn't end. Didn't he do about a thousand nice things for you just last week? (See how the negative always demands the most attention?) Where was I? OK, so start jotting down what surfaces. Not lengthy paragraphs, just telegraph-style notes. For me, it was easy. (See Figure 3.)

If you think that was difficult, wait until you see what I'm going to ask you to do next. The *same* type of list about (ta-da) *you*! And yes, you need to hold a photo of yourself so you'll remember what you look like. What are the things you appreciate (even adore) about yourself? No, not the things someone else appreciates about you. What do *you* truly view as likable about you? What are the unique characteristics that set you apart? They're there, just buried deep. (See Figure 4.)

It's All About You

Remember, it's not so much what other people see you as (although we have to be honest and acknowledge that it plays a part). But what unique traits and qualities do you see in yourself? How about in those you love? Take a little time to start digging up what those characteristics are. They're there—you just have to discover them. And remember, *you be you!* ♥

For additional ideas on creating a page about who you are, see "Up Close and Personal" on page 68.

What unique traits and qualities do you see in yourself? How about in those you love?

dear diary . . .

If you don't tell your story, who will?

Figure 1. Describe your path in life. *Page by Tracy White.* **Supplies** *Stickers:* Mrs. Grossman's; *Letter rub-ons:* Chatterbox; *Computer font:* Baskerville, Adobe Systems.

my path

HONEST, I had a happy childhood, but if you read my teenage diary, you'd think I led the most miserable life. My entries went something like this: "May 14—My life's over. I didn't get asked to the prom." Or, my next entry (months later): "November 6—I'm so depressed. I got a ticket while driving to school and . . ."

On days that got a little rough I turned to my diary and poured my heart out, sobbing all the while. Invariably, life would return to normal and I'd abandon my diary for another dreary day.

I'm glad my diary served as a confidant while I processed my teenage angst, but it doesn't show a complete picture of me. Instead it paints a lopsided picture of a teen who continually suffered from growing pains.

I recently looked through my scrapbook and realized that it, like my teenage diary,

ARTICLE BY TRACY WHITE

WHEN I'M 64

When I close my eyes, I can see the future I want.

I imagine myself wearing an oversized straw sun hat as I putter around my garden. One cat rubs against my leg as I stoop to pull a weed, while the other lays around, soaking in the morning sun. I imagine bees flitting from the tall hollyhocks to the stalks of lavender, which gently bend in the breeze.

Birds chirp. Bees buzz. Cats purr. And I am content to wander.

I imagine that I'm an artist. Of which medium, I've yet to discover. Perhaps it's paint, film, ceramics, pastels or words, but I'm an artist nonetheless. My studio is a small one-room building with loads of windows that allow the light to flood in and warm me as I work.

My life is simple and so are my needs. But my simplicity is contrasted with a rich inner peace. I imagine that I'm comfortable with my eclectic life and people can see that peace residing in me.

TODAY'S DREAMS BECOME
TOMORROW'S REALITIES

Figure 2. Share what you envision for your future. *Page by Tracy White.* **Supplies** *Patterned paper:* Daisy D's; *Computer font:* High Tower Text, downloaded from the Internet; *Flowers:* Making Memories; *Brads:* Lasting Impressions for Paper; *Chalk:* Craf-T Products. *Idea to note:* Tracy darkened the flower color with chalk.

doesn't offer a complete snapshot of me. Sure, it showcases photos of my recent trip to NYC, details my travels through my master's program and highlights my career, but it doesn't get to the heart of me. If someone picked up my album, he or she wouldn't know much more about me than the basic milestones of my life.

So I decided to create a scrapbook about me—a photo journal, so to speak. I know—another album? Most of us feel so far behind on our scrapbooks that we can't fathom the thought of starting another project. But why not?

This album tells *your* story, and if you don't tell your story, who will?

I divided my photo journal into three sections: perspective (where I've been), personality (who I am) and hopes (where I want to go). Once I decided on a structure, I gave myself permission to treat this album as a "perpetual scrapbook"—a place filled with ongoing reflection. This means that:
♦ I'll never finish this album because I'm always growing and changing.
♦ I want to be able to go back and respond to earlier entries. Again, I'm growing and I want my photo

journal to reflect my changes.

Deciding on my album's structure was the easy part. Figuring out what I wanted to say was harder. So I came up with some journaling prompts that made writing my story a little easier.

Perspective

Have you ever noticed that as time passes you view past events differently? All of a sudden the sharp details of the day soften and you're able to revaluate the events, your feelings and other people's actions. At times this reflection can help you realize that a seemingly

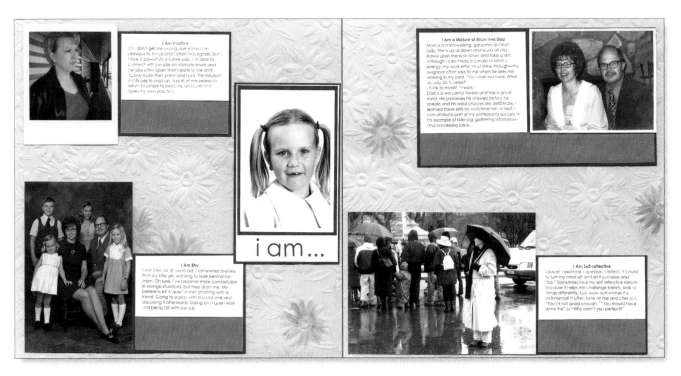

Figure 3. Journal the personality traits that influence your actions and thoughts. *Pages by Tracy White.* **Supplies** *Letter stickers:* SEI; *Embossed paper:* K & Company; *Computer font:* Century Gothic, Microsoft Word; *Vellum:* Mrs. Grossman's; *Chalk:* Craf-T Products.

insignificant moment has influenced you greatly. It's important to scrapbook your path (Figure 1).

Remember, my goal with my photo journal is to create a fleshed-out picture of me. So when working on my perspective pages, I plan on reviewing past *events* (retrospective) and past *feelings* and *thoughts* (introspective).

The following list of Perspective Prompts is designed to help you examine moments in your life and identify what they mean to you. This list is not comprehensive, but it may be helpful in thinking of additional questions that will help you with your journaling.

Perspective Prompts
◆ What are the defining moments in your life? Why are they defining? How did your life change because of those moments?

◆ Describe your feelings on a certain day (such as a wedding or the birth of child). Why do you think you felt that way? Do you still feel that way? Why or why not?

◆ Which political, economic or world events have influenced you? Why? How did you react, feel and think? How did these events change your life?

◆ What decisions of yours have positively or negatively impacted your life? In hindsight, why did you make those decisions? If you wish you made a different decision, why? What have you learned from the experience?

Personality

In creating my photo journal I decided that an important component was my personality traits—my likes and dislikes, what I value and believe in, as well as those quirky idiosyncrasies that make

me, me (Figure 3).

One rule of thumb: Delve deeper with your answers. Here's what I mean: Rather than saying "I love rainy days," tell *why* you love them. This will help flesh out your personality pages.

The following list of Personality Prompts may help trigger parts of your personality you've yet to uncover in your scrapbooks. Again, the list isn't comprehensive, so use it as a springboard. (Who knows, with this journaling your great-grandchildren may finally figure out where their dry sense of humor comes from!)

Personality Prompts
◆ What do you value? Honesty? Thrift? Education? Something else? How do you embody these values? Who do you know that embodies these values? Examine your past experiences. What events

or people influenced you to value these items?

◆ What are your political, religious, philosophical and sociological beliefs? Who or what influenced you to hold these beliefs? How have your beliefs changed through the years? How have people treated you differently as your beliefs have changed?

◆ What activities rejuvenate you? What makes you feel at peace? What activities frustrate you? How do you behave when you engage in these activities?

◆ How do you express love for people? Through actions, words, gifts or something else? How do you want a loved one to express his or her feelings for you? Why? How do you feel if someone shows you that he or she loves you in a different way?

◆ What sets you apart from your siblings, parents or friends? What role do you play—leader, peacemaker, comic relief or something else—when you're around them? Are you comfortable in the role? How does it change when you're around different people?

◆ How do you react in stressful situations? Social situations? Embarrassing moments? What does your reaction say about you?

Hopes

When I was 18 my best friend and I had crushes on two guys who happened to be best friends. Linda and I figured out a way we could stay friends forever: we dreamed of marrying the two guys, buying homes next to each other, having kids at the same time and living happily ever after. It would be perfect! Today, I smile when I think of that youthful outlook.

At 35, I have plenty of dreams I've yet to accomplish—I just hope they're a little more grounded in reality than my high-school fantasies! My hopes say a lot about me and shed light on my values. What do you hope for? The following Hope Prompts may help you identify your fondest wishes:

Hope Prompts

◆ Complete the following sentence and supply details and reasons for your statements: "When I am 83, I will . . ."

◆ What do you hope to achieve physically, emotionally, mentally, financially, artistically and spiritually? Why? What are you doing to achieve these aspirations? (See Figure 2.)

◆ What do you hope to teach people around you? What are you doing to implement it?

◆ What do you hope for your children, loved ones and friends? What can you do to help these hopes come true?

◆ If you won the lottery, what would you spend the money on? Why? What does that say about you?

◆ What kind of world do you hope to live in? How are you making the world a closer representation of your ideal? Are you active in politics? Are you a volunteer?

I'm still working on my photo journal and plan to work on it for years to come. I want this book to be a representation of *me*—of my successes and strengths along with my foibles and insecurities. It's a place where I can track my maturation; I can't wait to see how I turn out!

Give yourself permission to do something for you. Whether you hide your photo journal under your bed and lock it with a key, place it on your nightstand, or proudly share it with your family, this special book will help ground you on those harried days and give you courage on the tough ones. ❤

More Journaling Tips from Tracy

Do you skip journaling on your scrapbook pages or get stumped when you'd like to express your thoughts? Ever wish someone would whisper a great journaling idea in your ear? *The Journaler's Handbook: Everyone Has a Story* is a book/CD combo by CK editor-in-chief and journaling guru Tracy White. In the combo, Tracy offers advice and activities to help you get past your fear of journaling. This easy-to-use reference includes sections for your most important scrapbook pages (birthdays, vacations, childhood and more). Available October 2004. $29.95. To order, visit *www.creatingkeepsakes.com/shop* online.

ILLUSTRATION BY DEBBIE DRECHSLER

life's to-do lists
SCRAPBOOK YOUR DREAMS AND YOUR GOALS

How many of us write lists every day? We jot down which groceries to pick up, bills to pay, people to call and chores to eliminate. Many of us have imaginary to-do lists in our heads and hearts as well. They may not come to mind often, but they're there nonetheless. Let me explain.

Life is a series of events, big and small. We tend to mentally "check" off milestones (such as getting married, having a child or buying a house) as we reach them. These can include birthdays, plans for retirement, job promotions and more. The milestones are the things we hold on to, work for, and celebrate when we achieve them.

BY JENNIFER WOHLENBERG

A Girl

and

her

Goals

Go to Italy like Grandma and Grandpa

Go to Sacramento (that might be cool)

Learn how to be a professional artist in college

Learn how to scrapbook like Mommy

Go to Colorado where it's snowy

Learn how to swim

Maybe I'll be a lawyer when I grow up like Daddy

Go to Legoland and ride roller coasters

Have a dog

Move to a place near Legoland so I don't have to drive

Brenna's list of goals, in her own words 2002

Figure 1. Scrapbooking a child's goals can offer a revealing peek into his or her hopes and dreams. *Page by Jennifer Wohlenberg.* **Supplies** *Rubber stamp:* Magenta; *Letter stamps:* All Night Media; *Stamping ink:* Archival Brilliance, Tsukineko; *Computer font:* SandraOh, downloaded from the Internet.

 MORE ABOUT GOALS

While some of our goals may be big steps like marriage, others are hobby oriented. Perhaps you'd like to make a quilt, climb Mount Everest or learn to scuba dive. Still others are travel related. You might want to go on a cruise, visit the countries your ancestors came from, or have lunch in a café in Paris. Other goals could include volunteering your skills or conquering a fear.

Life goals can range from the tiniest of hopes to the most monumental of dreams, but writing them down tells powerful things about us. By doing so, we not only give others an inside look at our aspirations, we give ourselves concrete goals to achieve. We see how far we've come.

Goals Change

Our goals change as we grow. A five year old's dream of becoming a doctor may turn into a teenager's dream of starting his or her own rock band. A mother's dream of someday traveling on her own may become a grandmother's dream of learning to dance. Plotting the changes shows powerful insight into our emotional growth as we age.

What a man wants

I asked Brad if he could name ten goals to achieve for the rest of his life. He looked at me somewhat incredulously. "I survived law school, got married, had kids, and bought a house! What more could I want from life?" First, I laughed, but I needed to know seriously, was there anything else he dreamed of? He told me to give him a few minutes, he had to think. After ten minutes of silence, I got a short email with five goals listed. At first, I thought he was joking. When I told him these were silly, he shot me a hurt look – he had really given this some thought, and these were his true goals. So I asked for more clarification. Once he'd elaborated, I had a much better understanding of the ideas he had for the future. I can't say I agree with all of them (I like Winter!) but I can say that I'm privileged to have a peek into his dreams.

Maintain cutting-edge PC (translation – enjoy his free time)
This one is pretty self-explanatory. The computer is Brad's primary hobby, toy, and relaxation. He does not play or watch sports, so this is the one way that he winds down after a long day of work. Ensuring that it is always running at top speed is very important to him.

Eliminate Winter (translation – make all his days sunny)
Brad hates winter, so his ultimate goal is to have a home in both the United States and in Australia, so that he'll never have to experience another cold day.

Pay for kids' college (translation – provide for his family)
One thing that worries him deeply is how to pay for three college educations at once. While I take a "Cross that bridge..." approach, I know that it's something that he ponders often.

Definitive right-of-way reform (translation – do something instrumental during his career)
Brad's career involves a lot of wrangling with right-of-way issues, so a dream of his is to be a force in the enactment of legislation that would clear up a lot of the confusion, and help make his job a lot easier!

Have a big funeral (translation – live a good life)
When a longtime family friend died, Brad said one of the things that impressed him the most was the sheer number of people who attended the funeral services. All of them said that this man had deeply affected them in some way, and that they would miss him dearly. Brad said it inspired him to want to live in a way where he could touch many lives and show kindness to as many people as possible.

2002

Figure 2. Persuade the man in your life to share his goals, no matter how reluctant he may be. It's worth the effort! *Page by Jennifer Wohlenberg.* **Supplies** *Letter stickers:* Sonnets Flea Market Alphabet, Creative Imaginations; *Computer font:* CK Man's Print, "The Best of Creative Lettering" Super Combo, *Creating Keepsakes; Number stamps:* PSX Design; *Stamping ink:* Stampin' Up!.

✓ *A Child's Goals.* I asked my seven year old to tell me about her to-do list. At first, she looked at me quizzically, but I didn't want to sway her opinions, so I gave her as little prompting as possible. After a few moments of thought, she easily listed 10 things she wanted to do (Figure 1).

I had to hide my delight as I wrote down my daughter's to-do list word for word. I really liked the juxtaposition of her wanting to travel to an exotic place like Italy, while her next thought was of Sacramento! I could see my daughter's brain wrestling with the idea of being her own person, where art is her true love, or wanting to be more like Mommy and Daddy, pursuing interests in scrapbooking and law.

I loved the Legoland references most and consider this page a treasure, not just for her, but for us as well. I gained some great insights, and I plan to ask her the same questions at each birthday to see how her plans evolve.

✓ *A Husband's Goals.* If you can persuade your husband to do it, recording his goals can be eye-opening (Figure 2). When I asked my husband to share his goals, at first he said he had

Looking at this picture, taken on graduation day in June of 1990, it's so easy for me to see how naïve this girl was, how unaware of what life had in store for her. She had many plans, all written down to the last detail, and her headstrong ways didn't allow for any deviation in those plans. First, to UNLV for a Business Degree with an English Minor, and then off to California to pursue a writing career, hopefully in the entertainment field, but any kind of writing career would do. There would be a husband and some kids, but those would come later, once this girl had fulfilled her own goals, because first she had to make something of herself. Little did this girl know, within a year she would drop out of college to follow a boy (a boy!) to California. Little did she know, within two years, that relationship would collapse and she'd be on her own in Los Angeles. Little did she know, in just over three years, she'd be married to the man she'd always hoped to find. There would be no college degree, no big career, no book contract. Not yet, anyway. Instead, there was only the hardest job in existence — mothering three feisty little girls. Though the girl in the picture may have scoffed at such a future, the woman I am now says that's okay. Our life may not have turned out quite the way we planned, but it turned out to be more than that girl could ever have imagined. I look back with few regrets because I have found so much to celebrate in the path taken.

Figure 3. A teenager's dreams can look much different from the reality ahead. Journal your expectations as a teen. *Page by Jennifer Wohlenberg.* **Supplies** *Patterned papers:* Emagination Crafts and Magenta; *Computer font:* Rage Italic, downloaded from the Internet; *Fiber:* Rubba Dub Dub, Art Sanctum.

none. Later, after some urging, he wrote down five objectives. It still took a bit of elaboration before I got the full meaning of his ambitions (and he wasn't exactly comfortable with the exercise), but I think the resulting page will give our family insight into what drives the man we share our lives with.

✓ *A Teenager's Goals.* I was fortunate to find a journal that I kept during my senior year of high school. In it, I had written down some goals that I hoped to achieve before my 10-year class reunion (Figure 3). I'm struck now by how many of my goals involved "having" something rather than "doing" something. As a teen, I was very preoccupied with the idea of a mansion on the beach, a closet full of designer clothes, and a convertible in my garage.

I'm nearly 13 years out of high school now, and I ask myself, did I meet the goals on my list? Well, not all, but the really important ones. I don't regret not having met a few of them, like owning a house on the beach. The mom in me says it would be a nightmare keeping sand out of the carpet!

✓ *Your Goals.* As I celebrate my 30th birthday this year, I'm also emerging from seven years of diaper duty and some of the most intense years of motherhood I could have imagined. I find

As I approach my 30th birthday, I realize that there are many dreams that I've accomplished, but also many more left to fulfill. As the girls grow older and become more independent, I hope that I can step back a little from the sacrifice of mommy-hood and re-focus on my own future and achieve these things for myself. I have so many goals, but so little time.

August 2002

- Write a book
- Move out of California
- Travel to Ireland
- Learn how to quilt
- Help other women with PPD
- Finish my degree
- Host a dinner party
- Spend a Christmas in the snow

Figure 4. Devote a page to your current aspirations. *Page by Jennifer Wohlenberg.* **Supplies** *Specialty paper:* Tiziano Papers; *Computer font:* Scrap Sweetness, downloaded from *www.letteringdelights.com*; Times New Roman, Microsoft Word; *Stamping ink:* Shadow Inks, Hero Arts; *Clock pieces:* From *www.skybluepink.com*.

myself with two kids in school and more breathing room than I've had in years. I've had time to contemplate and scrapbook my own goals for coming years (Figure 4). While doing a page like this might seem daunting (who wants to add another item to the to-do list), I found it energizing after years of thinking "children first."

While we may have many aspirations ahead of us, it's also good to look back at what we've accomplished. Many times, amidst the busy-ness of our lives, we take what we have for granted. Journaling a page about these triumphs (Figure 5) can help us reflect on our good fortune and our achievements. It also provides something

WHERE TO FIND GOAL QUOTES

Want to find great quotes that deal with setting and reaching goals? Check out these sites:

✓ *www.quotegarden.com/goals.html*

✓ *www.sparkpeople.com/start/quotes_goalsetting.html*

✓ *www.randomterrain.com/quotes/goals.html*

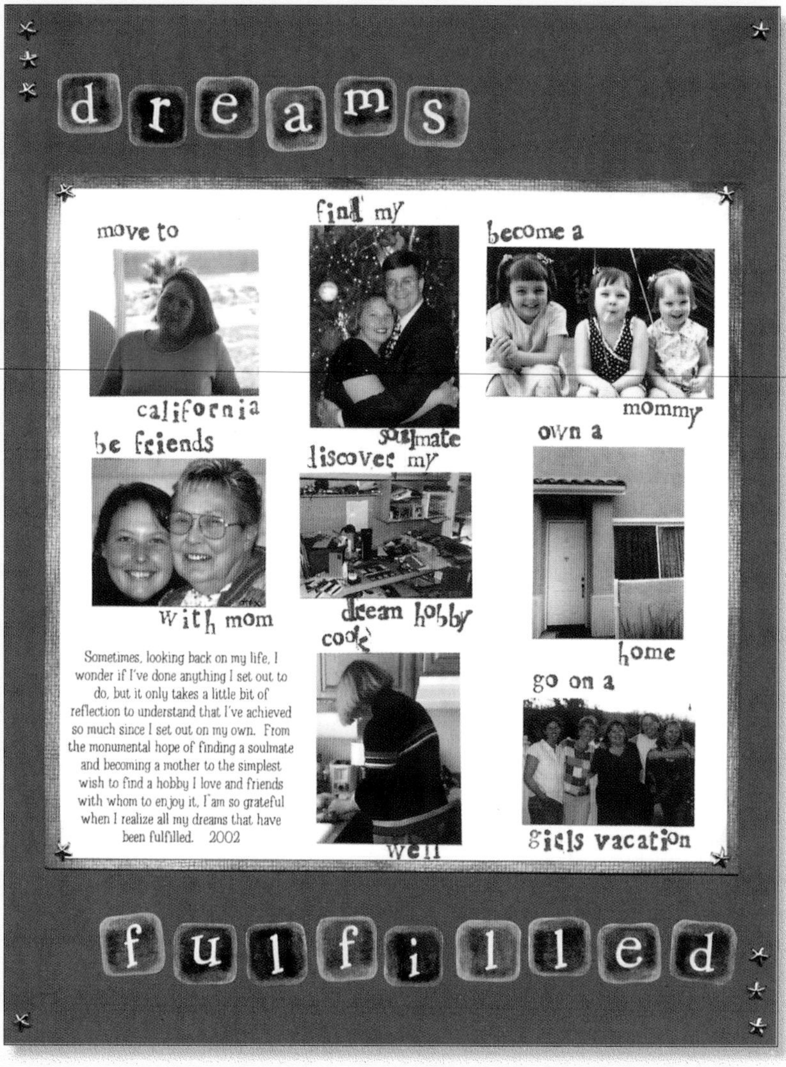
dreams
move to
california
find my
soulmate
become a
mommy
be friends
with mom
discover my
dream hobby
own a
home
cook
well
go on a
girls vacation
Sometimes, looking back on my life, I wonder if I've done anything I set out to do, but it only takes a little bit of reflection to understand that I've achieved so much since I set out on my own. From the monumental hope of finding a soulmate and becoming a mother to the simplest wish to find a hobby I love and friends with whom to enjoy it, I'm so grateful when I realize all my dreams that have been fulfilled. 2002
fulfilled

Figure 5. Look back at your life and pay tribute to your achievements. *Page by Jennifer Wohlenberg.* **Supplies** *Computer font:* CAC One Seventy, downloaded from the Internet; *Letter stickers:* Sonnets Flea Market Block Alphabet, Creative Imaginations; *Letter stamps:* PSX Design; *Stamping ink:* Stampin' Up!; *Star nailheads:* JewelCraft.

tangible so future generations can understand more about us and what we valued most.

Looking back at my high school list and considering my past achievements, I wonder how my current list will appear when I'm 40, 60 and 80. Will I think my goals as a 30 year old are trivial, or will I think I've finally figured out what's important? Will I meet all my goals? What will my next ones be? I'm also eager to learn about my daughter's goals and what she feels they'll be five years from now.

The act of recording these objectives—my daughter's, my husband's and my own—has been illuminating. Not only does it help solidify what's most important to us, it gives others insight into our deepest desires. So, the next time you're writing yourself a list of chores to conquer, grab another piece of paper, a cup of tea, and a quiet moment. Jot down those things you hope for the most—the silly, the imperative, the frivolous, the significant, the sublime.

Whatever your heart wishes for, whether it's one thing or twenty, record them. Revel in your achievements, reflect on unmet objectives, and give yourself permission to dream about the future. It's definitely a to-do list worth writing. ♥

Page Starters:
Recording Precious Little Moments

by Allison Strine

Scrapbook how you spend your leisure time. *Page by Allison Strine.* **Supplies** *Patterned papers:* NRN Designs (green), Carolee's Creations (brown), Colors By Design (title); *Grass border:* Shotz by Danelle Johnson, Creative Imaginations; *Sticker:* Susan Branch, Colorbök; *Rubber stamps:* Uptown Design, Hero Arts (flower), Stamps by Judith (flowerpots); *Stamping ink:* ColorBox, Clearsnap, Inc.; *Computer fonts:* Bolide (title) and CAC One Seventy (journaling), downloaded from the Internet; *Fibers:* Rubba Dub Dub; *Pressed flowers:* Golden Flower Co. *Idea to note:* Allison stamped polymer clay to create the clay pots and flower accents.

Often, we're so busy leading our complicated 21st-century lives that we forget to stop and smell the roses (or, in my case, the chocolate chip cookies!). As a scrapbooker, I want to make sure I record as many precious moments as possible, from the sight of my one-year-old blowing out her first birthday candle to the feeling of peace that overcomes me as I sit beneath the lofty pine trees in my backyard.

For me, Saturday mornings in the backyard help define who I am, what's important to my family, and how we choose to spend our time. Creating a "leisure time" layout is a great way to preserve this aspect of our lives. Wouldn't you love to know how your great-grandmother spent her spare moments (or if she ever had any spare moments)? Wouldn't it help make her more real to you? Spark your imagination with these questions:

◆ What did you do to relax this week? Did you pamper yourself every day?
◆ Is there typically one time of the day or week when the whole family gets together to just do nothing?
◆ What does "doing nothing" mean to you? Is it acceptable to do nothing, or is there a stigma attached to it?
◆ Where do you most like to spend your free moments?

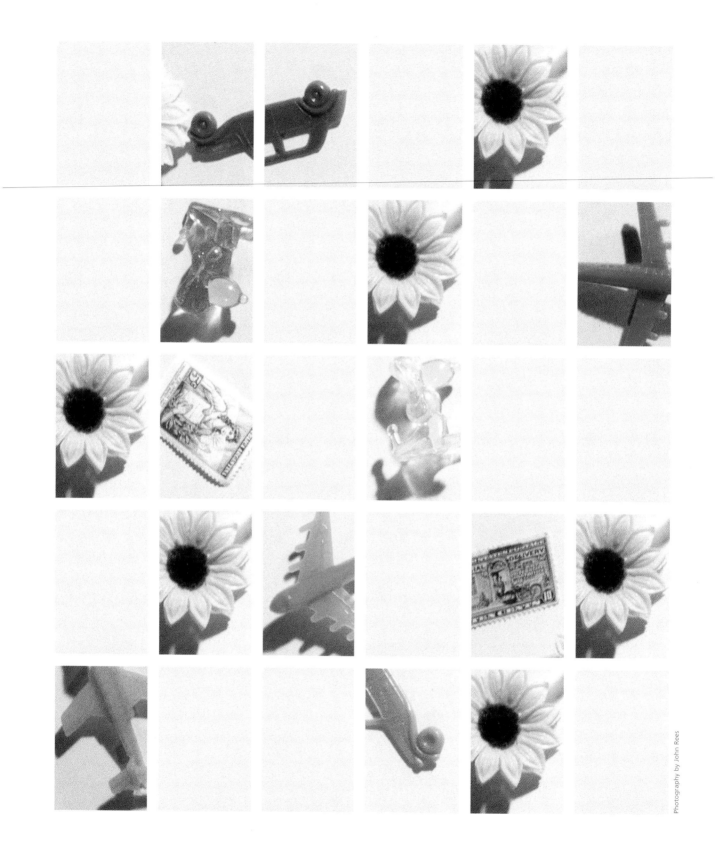

Photography by John Rees

Little Details

Close your eyes and picture your childhood home. How good is your memory as you visually walk through the rooms? Do you recall the things you touched and used every day? Was the kitchen equipped with the latest conveniences? Were the floors covered with carpet, wood or linoleum? Can you remember the furniture in your bedroom and how it was arranged?

As a teenager in the early 1970s, I redecorated my bedroom with trendy hanging beads, mood lighting and a bright-purple carpet. My kids would love to see my "groovy" room, but I have nothing to show them. While I have special-occasion photos from my childhood, I have few that show the home I grew up in or the things that were part of my daily life.

by Julie Turner

> Photograph and scrapbook life's "bits and pieces"

As I thought of this, another idea came to me. I decided to create a "home page" layout for my kids. It would include small photos of the details that give our home its character and personality. The layout would also give future generations a glimpse of the past.

I was so happy with the results, I extended the same concept to other pages as well. Here's a quick rundown of how I (and my friend Kelly) took a similar approach on home, vacation, boy and girl pages! →

Figure 1. Show your home, the people in it, and the little details you'd like to remember. *Pages by Julie Turner.* **Supplies** *Stamping ink:* VersaColor, Tsukineko; *Rubber stamps:* PrintWorks; *Embossing powders:* Clear Embossing Powder, Gary M. Burlin and Co.; Ultra Thick Embossing Enamel (white), Suze Weinberg; *Rectangle punch:* NanKong; *Ribbon:* Midori; *Pop dots:* All Night Media; *Other:* Jute. *Idea to note:* Julie's layout originally appeared in the *2001 Scrapbook Hall of Fame* idea book.

The Turner Home Page

Planning a layout about our home was as much fun as looking at the finished product (Figure 1). The entire project was done as a family, from selecting which details to photograph to arranging the tiny photos on the page.

Some of the photos and journaling were incorporated into small, accordion-fold books that can be untied and opened. Imprinted letters across the covers of the books spell "home." (I made the impressions by pressing a rubber-stamp letter into several layers of heated embossing powder.)

While I chose a highly visual approach for my layout, I wanted future generations to know the importance of each of the items depicted. To accomplish this, I tucked a handwritten page behind the layout that gives a description of each photo.

This project was so satisfying that we plan to document Grandma's house. We also want to document the mountain cabin my husband's side of the family has owned and enjoyed for the past 25 years.

What to Include on a "Home Page"

Wondering which details to include on your layout? Here's what I photographed:

- Things that are a structural part of our house, such as the front door, wood flooring, light fixtures or hand-finished fireplace mantel
- Things that we touch and use everyday, such as furniture, kitchen appliances, dishes or the telephone
- Things that reflect how we spend our time at home, such as our music collection and piano, our home-school books and papers, a computer keyboard or the children's toys
- Things that remind us of family traditions or family events, such as the bust of George Washington we purchased on a family trip to the East Coast
- Things that have sentimental value, such as roses from the bush my husband gave me for Valentine's Day
- Things that are family favorites, such as comfort foods, the kids' "blankies," or the tree in our front yard that kids love to climb
- Things that make a statement about our values, such as an open Bible or the corner of an old family photo

Figure 2. Include representative sections from the hundreds of photos taken at your house over the years. *Pages by Kelly Ettenborough.*
Supplies *Memorabilia pockets:* 3L Corp.; *Computer fonts:* CK Journaling and CK Script, "The Best of Creative Lettering" CD Combo, *Creating Keepsakes.*

A Home-Page Variation

Scrapbooker Kelly Ettenborough of Peoria, Arizona, created her own variation of a "home page." After living in her house for eight and a half years, Kelly had hundreds of photographs and dozens of scrapbook pages of associated people and events. When it was time to sell the home, Kelly created the pages in Figure 2 to capture its history, from the young couple excited about building their first home to the clouds painted on the nursery ceiling.

The photos are in roughly chronological order. Kelly included small samples of the tile, carpet and granite used. Under the large house photograph are larger pictures of the house's back and side yards, people pictures, and journaling about the fun times in the house.

Kelly also tucked the floor plan, elevation information and MLS listing in the pocket under the flap.

While Kelly's layout took time to plan and create while packing, she loves having these pages now that owning the house is just a memory.

Tips for Capturing Home Details

Ready to photograph your home in all its glory? Consider the following:

- Involve your entire family in a brainstorming session. Let each person contribute ideas to the list of details to document.
- Look through all your unused photos. You may already have pictures of things you want to remember.
- Shoot photos of the remaining items on your list. Remember to shoot a little further back than usual since the photos will be cropped very small.
- Use a square or rectangle punch to quickly crop your photos into uniform shapes. Set the punch upside-down on the table so you can easily line up your photo in the punch opening. Remember, the details don't need to be in the center of each punch. Be creative with your cropping to create more visual interest.
- Include a "hint" of relationships in your detail photos. A hint can include things such as fingers on a musical instrument, a smile between family members, or two people holding hands.
- Cut an opening in the top layer of your page's sheet protector so people can access any interactive embellishments (such as a little book or flap). The cutout should be the same size and shape as the book or flap.

Figure 3. Document the journey to your destination. Include sights along the way, how you passed the time, gas prices and more. *Pages by Julie Turner.* **Supplies** *Handmade paper:* Memory Lane; *Computer font:* Garamouche, P22 Type Foundry; *Square punch:* Family Treasures; *Embossing powders:* Clear Embossing Powder by Gary M. Burlin and Co.; Ultra Thick Embossing Enamel (black), Suze Weinberg; *Metal ring tags:* American Tag Co.; *Eyelets:* e-z set, Coffee Break Designs; *Circle paper clip:* Cavallini & Co.; *Fibers:* Rub-a-Dub-Dub Fibers; *Small envelopes:* Hero Arts; *Other:* Road map from trip, mat board (for popping up photos), wheel from a toy car, button.

Road Trip

While looking through a vacation album one day, I found that I have numerous layouts of destinations but nothing to remember the time spent getting there. That's why I adapted the "home page" concept to the road trip we took recently to California (Figure 3). Not only does the layout include small photos of sights we saw along the way, it also documents things we did to pass the time, plus details of things that will change over time, such as gas prices and car styles.

I used our actual road map, with the destination circled, to make the cover for a road trip journal I attached to the page. Inside the book are photos of our family, lists of games we played, music we listened to, books we read and the restaurants where we ate. The book is tied together with black elastic and decorated with a wheel from a toy car. It has a button closure.

Moonstone Beach

At times, small-detail photos can be combined with memorabilia, like the polished stones and shell used in Figure 4. The small photos are arranged in a more playful pattern, with window openings cut into the page to show off our beachcombing treasures.

To create this window effect, I lined up two pieces of cardstock and cut identical openings through both pieces. Next, I trimmed a sheet protector so it was slightly larger than the cardstock opening. I put my memora-

bilia inside the cut piece of sheet protector, like a pocket, and sealed the edges with archivally safe adhesive tape. I sandwiched the sheet-protector pocket between two pieces of cardstock to form the memorabilia window, then I adhered all the layers together.

Figure 4. Combine small photos with memorabilia in a playful pattern. *Pages by Julie Turner.* **Supplies** *Handmade paper:* Memory Lane; *Metal ring tags:* American Tag Co.; *Computer font:* Garamouche, P22 Type Foundry; *Other:* Stones from the beach, scraps of sheet protector to make the windows, mat board to pop up the photos.

Boys' Toys

As my boys have grown older, their taste in toys has changed. Gone are the action figures and toy trains, and here to stay are building sets, computer games and sports. The layout in Figure 5 shows their changed interests by picturing them with their current favorite playthings. I tied a tiny tag through eyelets on each detail shot to identify the toy. Behind one of the photos, I tucked a larger pullout tag with some additional journaling.

Figure 5. Whether the boys in your life are young or old, show their current toys. *Page by Julie Turner.* **Supplies** *Computer font:* Garamouche, P22 Type Foundry; *Tags:* American Tag Co.; *Eyelets:* e-z set, Coffee Break Designs; *Fibers:* Source unknown.

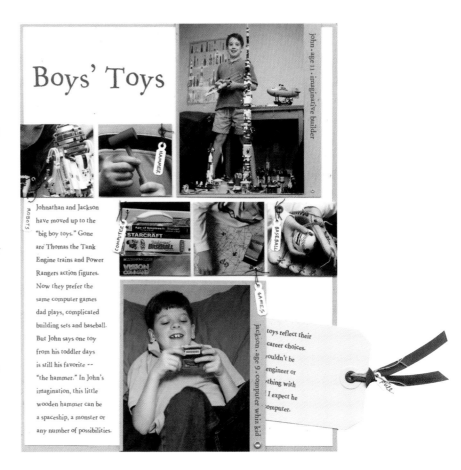

Jillian

My daughter, Jillian, makes me smile when she comes out of her room all decked out in fancy dress-up clothes and jewelry. I love her sweet lips smeared with lipstick, her little arms lined with rhinestone bracelets, and her tiny toes peeking out from pink-feathered shoes. Someday Jillian will be all grown up, but I'll remember my "little princess" whenever I look at the detail photos on this layout (Figure 6).

To create a soft, feminine look, I mounted the photos on squares of thin mat board wrapped with a pretty patterned paper. Next, I lined them up along a piece of organdy ribbon and adhered them. Silver beads tied with white thread add a subtle, elegant touch to the page.

As you scrapbook the "big" events in life, don't forget to capture the little details as well. They may be small, but they'll help you remember some of life's finest memories! ♥

Figure 6. Give your "little-princess" memories and photos the royal treatment. *Page by Julie Turner.* **Supplies** *Patterned paper:* Anna Griffin; *Square punch:* Family Treasures; *Pen:* Antique HyperJell, Zebra; *Beads:* Westrim Crafts; *Ribbon:* Midori; *Fiber:* DMC; *Silver frame:* Memory Lane.

"Little Details" Page Starters

Love the little-details concept but need help knowing where to begin? The following can get you started.

Baby
- The tiny toes we love to kiss
- Chubby fingers wrapped around a favorite toy
- Everyday items like pacifiers, bottles or diapers
- Close-up details of a crib or rocking chair
- A corner of a special blanket
- A favorite outfit or shoes
- Sleepy eyes or a tiny ear
- A first smile or tooth
- Nursery decorations
- A swirl of hair

Wedding
- Buttons, bows and lace
- Collars and cuffs
- Rings and other jewelry
- The door to the church
- The altar, candles or a stained-glass window
- Reception decorations, table settings and glassware
- Food, drinks and wedding cake
- A kiss, holding hands, an embrace
- Dancing feet and swirling skirts
- A father's proud look or a grandparent's face
- The flower girl's hands holding a basket
- The ring bearer's hands holding the pillow

Pets
- Close-ups of paws, face, ears or tail
- Collar and tag
- Favorite toy
- Feeding dish

Sports
- Gear (fishing, hockey equipment, etc.)
- Clothing (special shoes, uniforms, etc.)
- Location (gym, lake, track, etc.)
- Action (a foot kicking or skating, a golf swing, etc.)

Teens
Send a disposable camera to school with your teen to capture the following:
- Current fashions (shoes, shirt logos, jewelry, accessories)
- School bus or other transportation
- Textbooks, notebooks, pencils
- Inside and outside of locker
- Lunchroom and food
- Hall, gym, library, computer room
- Faces of favorite teachers or friends
- Classroom (desk, clock)
- Sports equipment
- Band instrument
- School mascot

caught on film?

Photo or not, you can still scrapbook the memories

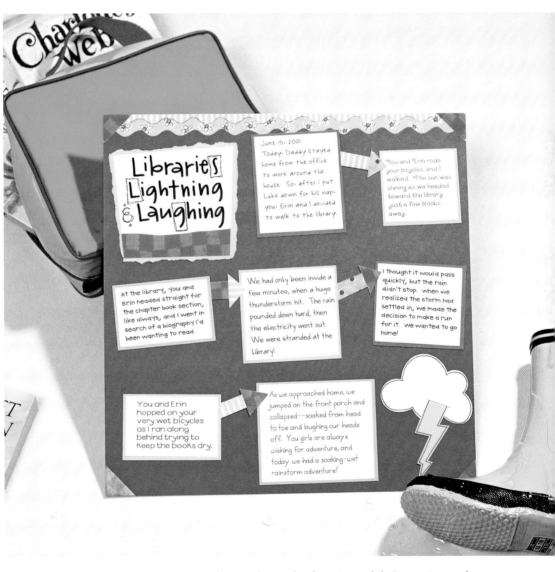

Figure 1. Even without the photos, you can creatively preserve a memory in your scrapbook. *Page by Rebecca Sower.* **Supplies** *Stickers:* me & my BIG ideas; *Pen:* Zig Writer, EK Success; *Computer fonts:* CK Handprint, CK Penman and CK Primary, "The Best of Creative Lettering" CD Combo, *Creating Keepsakes; Cloud and lightning:* Rebecca's own designs. *Idea to note:* Rebecca cut arrows from border stickers.

ONE LAZY SUMMER AFTERNOON, my daughters and I decided to visit the local library a few blocks from home. Mom on foot and daughters on bicycles, we headed down the sidewalk toward the library. When we arrived, the girls made a beeline for the chapter-book section, while I went in search of the biographies.

We hadn't been there 10 minutes when a huge thunderstorm struck, pelting down rain and shutting down the electricity in the whole neighborhood. After waiting almost

ARTICLE BY REBECCA SOWER

Figure 2. Make use of an entire page to creatively display a journaling list. *Page by Rebecca Sower.* **Supplies** *Patterned paper:* Making Memories; *Pen:* Zig Writer, EK Success; *Craft wire:* Artistic Wire Ltd.; *Jar and other accents:* Rebecca's own designs.

Figure 3. Capture your family's light-hearted memories, even though they may not have representative photos. *Page by Rebecca Sower.* **Supplies** *Patterned paper:* Carolee's Creations (checked) and Colorbök (stars); *Eyelets:* Dritz Corporation; *Pens:* Zig Writers, EK Success; *Other:* String.

an hour, we decided the rain wasn't going to stop—we had to make a run for it! The girls screamed and squealed the whole way, while I tried to walk fast, then faster, then run, then run faster (all the while trying to keep the books dry).

When we all collapsed safely on the front porch, soaked from head to toe, we laughed and laughed and carried on and on about our library adventure. It wasn't until a couple of days later that I could've kicked myself for not taking photos of our rain-soaked selves— what a great scrapbook layout that would've made. Rats! Another missed opportunity.

Then my mind started going back to other terrific memories we'd shared as a family, most of them not on film. I had to ask myself two questions: "Are my scrapbooks *only* for the memories for which I have photographs? What about all the other moments I wanted to capture but didn't have 'proof'?"

Also, beyond the not-captured-on-film *events* I wanted to preserve, what about the *feelings*, *dreams* and *emotions* that told the story of my family? Could I really say that scrapbooks full of photographs with basic journaling would best tell the story of my family to future generations?

That's when I sat down at my computer and gave my best shot at putting down on paper all the memorable moments my mind could remember about our family. I knew I didn't come close to capturing them all, but I hoped I'd remember more over time. I made a little vow with myself—when a past memory for which I didn't have a photograph came to mind, I'd make every attempt to get it down on paper.

I'm proud to say I've done just that. In fact, if I printed out all the memories, it would be the beginnings of a book. My first intentions were to print these memories onto acid-free cardstock and include them randomly in my existing albums. But as I pictured this, I saw line after line of words that might be interesting to the author (me!), but could get long and boring for anyone else.

As I thought about it, I asked myself, why shouldn't I treat these mini-stories the same way I do my photographs? Why shouldn't I embellish them with fun scrapbooking products and display them creatively as if they were photos? (See Figure 1.) Boy, that's when I really tore into things! I printed out all the memories I'd been capturing on my computer, dragged out all my scrapbooking supplies, and went to town!

I didn't stop there. If these *happenings* from my family's lives were important to capture, so were the *feelings, sayings, hopes and dreams, lessons learned, favorites, quirks* and *personalities* that didn't have a photo to back them up.

How could I have been so silly? I thought of all the times I'd raced like a madwoman to catch up on scrapbooking box after box of photos, all the while letting precious little memories of life risk

Figure 4. Effective journaling doesn't have to be written in complete sentences. Add catchwords or highlights bookmark-style to existing layouts that lack journaling. *Page by Rebecca Sower*. Supplies *Rubber stamps:* Close To My Heart (animal prints, wildflower, sun, pine bough), PSX Design (leaf), Stampin' Up! (bugs); *Punches:* McGill (rectangle) and The Punch Bunch (leaf); *Safety pins:* Source unknown; *Pens:* Zig Writers, EK Success; *Eyelets:* Dritz Corporation; *Watercolors:* Sakura; *Stamping ink:* Creative Beginnings.

being forgotten as I told myself, "I wish I could capture that in my scrapbook, but I forgot to take a picture!"

Take the time to go back through your finished scrapbooks. Are there any "stories" missing? Have there been meaningful moments you've shared that didn't get caught on film? It's not too late to retrace your steps and include more memories in your albums. Here, we've shown you some creative ways to make these

additions to your scrapbooks fit in nicely without missing a beat.

10 Powerful Ideas

No-photo *events* (like getting caught in the rain!) are wonderful stories to add to your scrapbooks, but include some of these, too:

❶ What I would like my children or grandchildren to know about me that they might not know unless I tell them

❷ Your hopes and dreams for your children (putting them down

It's not too late to retrace your steps and include more memories in your albums.

Figure 5. Turn an existing single-page layout into a double-page layout by utilizing an entire page for creative journaling. *Pages by Rebecca Sower.* **Supplies** *Sun paper-piecing patterns:* BumperCrops; *Pens:* Tombow; *Fibers:* thecardladies.com; *Handmade paper:* Source unknown; *Craft wire:* Artistic Wire Ltd.; *Square and hole punches:* McGill; *Stamping ink:* Creative Beginnings; *Mulberry paper:* PSX Design.

on paper will help your child never forget what you wished for his or her future)

❸ What each member of your family loves about your home, your yard, each other, your pet and more (see Figure 2)

❹ Each family member's most embarrassing moment, proudest moment, saddest moment, happiest moment, scariest moment, funniest moment

❺ Funny sayings, mispronounced words and each child's quirky habits (see Figure 3)

❻ "Had to be there" moments and private family jokes

❼ Each family member's favorite sleeping position, favorite outfit, favorite ice cream flavor, and on and on and on (then, document the least favorites too, such as household chores)

❽ Lessons learned the hard way (you could take a serious or light-hearted approach on this one)

❾ Think of all the senses—sight, touch, sound, smell and taste. It's fun to add catchwords or highlights bookmark-style to an existing layout (see Figure 4).

Do you or your family members have particular feelings based on any of the senses? For instance, whenever I smell a rose, my mind drifts back to my grandfather's backyard full of beautiful roses and how he tirelessly cared for them. Or, is there a particular song, quote or poem that seems to express your feelings or trigger a memory? (See Figure 5.)

❿ In addition to the "deeper" issues above, remember to capture the less serious, more light-hearted side of your family as well. The dreams you have for your daughter's future are important, but so is the cute way she pronounces certain words as she learns to master the English language.

Think about it! Your family is chock-full of characteristics, personalities, emotions and stories unique only to your family. It's time to stop fretting over the boxes of photographs yet to be scrapbooked. A *lot* of other moments deserve to be preserved in your scrapbooks as well. ♥

I made a little vow—when a past memory for which I didn't have a photograph came to mind, I'd make every attempt to get it down on paper.

Journaling Ideas:
Documenting the Love of Sports

by Denise Pauley

Dig a little deeper for in-depth journaling that documents the love of the game. *Page by Denise Pauley.* **Supplies** *Patterned paper:* The Crafter's Workshop; *Maruyama papers:* Magenta; *Computer font:* Cheapskate, downloaded from the Internet; *Stickers:* Treehouse Designs; *Tags:* American Tag Co.; *String:* The Robin's Nest; *Pen:* Zig Millennium, EK Success; *Brads:* American Pin & Fastener.

If you have a child who competes in several sports, love to participate in them yourself, or simply know an armchair athlete who is riveted to ESPN, do some in-depth journaling that documents the love of the game.

When journaling on your sports layouts, be sure to include pertinent facts, such as achievements, goals, setbacks, coaches, teammates or favorite professional teams or players, but dig a little deeper to get more meaningful details as well. Here are some questions you can ask your sports fan:

◆ When were you first introduced to this sport?
◆ Why do you enjoy it so much?
◆ How do you feel while playing (or watching) it?
◆ Who is your sports role model or hero?
◆ What's your ultimate sports-related goal or dream?

Who could ask for anything more?

* These Are the Moments

by Lisa Bearnson

A child's words of love can make a world of difference. *Page by Lisa Bearnson.* **Supplies** *Patterned paper:* Provo Craft; *Buttons:* Magic Scraps; *Button ties:* Twistel, Making Memories; *Button adhesive:* Glue Dots, Glue Dots International; *Chalk:* Stampin' Up!; *Computer fonts:* CK Handprint, "The Best of Creative Lettering" CD Combo; CK Bella and CK Single Serif, "The Best of Creative Lettering" CD Vol. 3; CK Fun Boxes, "The Best of Creative Lettering" CD Vol. 4, *Creating Keepsakes.*

That day, I wouldn't have been voted as mother of the year. Both of my sons had left for the bus stop bawling. Kade, my oldest, and I'd gotten in a huge debate over the timing of "She'll Be Coming Around the Mountain" while he practiced the piano. Eight-year-old Collin was mad because I'd made him wear a coat when the ground was covered by *only* six inches of snow.

As if tensions weren't high enough, our new black Lab got worked up over the commotion and left a pool of excitement for me to clean up. As I took care of this and other tasks that morning, I fought back tears. I thought about how mean my kids must think I was, and I wondered why I'd let myself get so upset. As I sat there, feeling like a failure, four-year-old Brecken grinned at me and said, "Mom, I *like* the way you're growing up!"

For several minutes, time stood still. I cradled my little girl in my arms and cried—this time for joy. Even while I doubted myself, my sweet child liked the way I was growing up, and that's all that mattered. Ever since then, Brecken's simple statement has echoed in my mind, giving me confidence. Her words remind me that a misty morning doesn't signify a cloudy day.

Open your ears and your heart, and you'll discover that life's simplest moments are often the most meaningful. They help us remember what's right with the world. Read on, and discover the simple moments that have touched other scrapbookers' lives.

 "Cherish the Moment"
by Toni Houlobek
Rockford, IL

Toni's Thoughts

"It's not always easy getting a two year old to sit and pose, which is why this is one of my favorite pictures of my son Michael. As I thought of this day, I thought about how I'll never be able to relive this age or all the things that make Michael 'my little man.' I decided to record how I cherish the moments he says, 'I love you, Mama' and I say, 'I love you more.' Children grow up too fast, and I loved scrapbooking these memorable moments between parent and child."

SUPPLIES
Specialty paper: Books by Hand
Computer fonts: Kayleigh (title), downloaded from the Internet; Script MT Bold (journaling), Microsoft Word; CK Journaling (journaling), "The Best of Creative Lettering" CD Combo, *Creating Keepsakes*
Brads: Impress Rubber Stamps
Craft wire: Artistic Wire Ltd.
Gold pen: Sanford
Tags: Toni's own design

Cut out a fancy title with an X-acto knife. Cut leaves from paper and add them to tags and a journaling block.

Mary's Thoughts

"My oldest son took this picture of me feeding the twins when they were just a few weeks old. Sometimes I felt like I needed more than two hands to get the job done, so one day I just sat down on the floor and propped the twins up in my legs. They seemed content, and I felt in control for the first time. It was a great feeling.

"When I created this page, I used a large heart to symbolize my heart, with two smaller, connected hearts symbolizing my babies' hearts. In the title, I faded the word 'moment' to suggest a sigh of contentment at being a mother."

SUPPLIES
Computer fonts: Kaufman (journaling and "A Mother's Precious") and Charlemagne ("Moment"), downloaded from the Internet
Stamping ink on hearts: Dauber Duos, Tsukineko
Heart punches: Emagination Crafts
Other: Fibers

Create a fade-out title by typing the same word several times. Leave the original word black, then change the color to gray on each word that follows. Do a lighter shade on each version until the last word is barely visible.

 "A Mother's Precious Moment"
by Mary Larson
Chandler, AZ

Janelle's Thoughts

"My sister snapped this picture during a brief lull in the rowdy football game I was playing with my three-year-old nephew. He had just tackled me, and we lay in the grass and looked at the sky and the clouds and the trees above us. I felt so intensely how good it is to be alive and to really see the world around me.

"My thirtieth birthday came two days after this picture was taken. There's nothing like turning 30 to make a woman really think about her life! When I thought about what I'd like to take into my next 30 years, this sweet moment stood out: a quiet spot in the middle of our running and laughing, a moment of contentment and awareness with a child I love. I'm so glad I have a picture of it!"

SUPPLIES
Patterned paper: Provo Craft
Punches: All Night Media (flower), EK Success (egg for leaf), Family Treasures (circle)
Computer font: Tempus Sans, Microsoft Word
Lettering template: Blocky, Provo Craft
Pen: Zig Writer, EK Success
Title and quote: From the song "My Next Thirty Years" by Tim McGraw

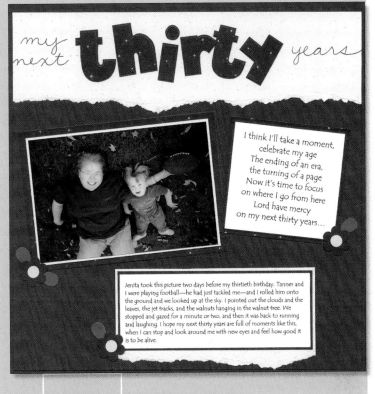

I think I'll take a moment,
celebrate my age
The ending of an era,
the turning of a page
Now it's time to focus
on where I go from here
Lord have mercy
on my next thirty years...

Jenita took this picture two days before my thirtieth birthday. Tanner and I were playing football—he had just tackled me—and I rolled him onto the ground and we looked up at the sky. I pointed out the clouds and the leaves, the jet tracks, and the walnuts hanging in the walnut tree. We stopped and gazed for a minute or two, and then it was back to running and laughing. I hope my next thirty years are full of moments like this, when I can stop and look around me with new eyes and feel how good it is to be alive.

"My Next Thirty Years"
by Janelle Clark
Westerville, OH

"One Moment's Proof"
by Jennifer Ditz
Cincinnati, OH

One
moment's
PROOF of
heaven's
EXISTENCE.

Audrey (3) enjoying a perfect moment from the front of the boat. Hot Springs – July 2001

Jennifer's Thoughts

"I'll never forget this moment! My little friend Audrey was unknowingly displaying her love for life as she stood on the front of the boat with her arms open wide.

"I wanted to create a layout that would bring back the feeling of the moment just by looking at it. I chose gold and red colors to represent the rich warmth of the sun that day. Using thin fiber and an embroidery needle, I stitched a sun directly on my background paper. I softened the bright background with brown chalk."

SUPPLIES
Mulberry: Black Ink
Chalk: Craf-T Products
Computer fonts: 39 Smooth, Double Topple, International Playboy, Mandingo, Riverside, Yippy Skippy, downloaded from the Internet
Other: Fiber

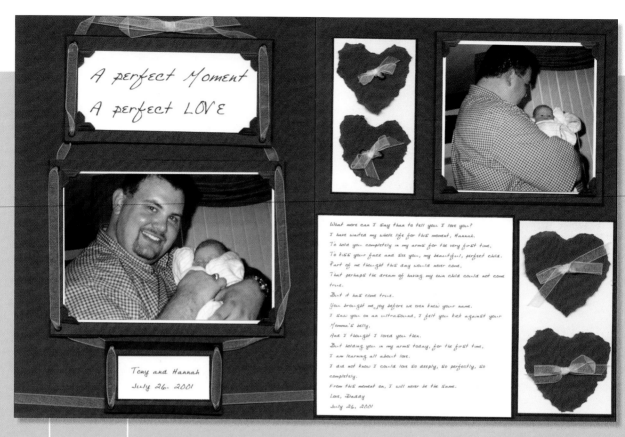

 "A Perfect Moment, A Perfect Love"
by Dece Gherardini
Mesa, AZ

Dece's Thoughts

"This is a layout of my husband, Tony, holding our baby Hannah for the first time. We'd been trying to have a baby for 11 months when I finally became pregnant. We were so happy—the news was a dream come true.

"When I showed the layout to my dear husband, he had tears in his eyes. He told me the journaling expressed exactly what he had felt while holding Hannah for the first time, even though he said he did not have the words to express those feelings. I am thrilled at how tenderly and perfectly my husband loves Hannah."

SUPPLIES

Computer font: Bethany's hand, downloaded from the Internet
Ribbon: The Robin's Nest Press

Photo corners: Canson
Hand-torn hearts: Dece's own designs
Other: Black eyelets

Thread ribbon through black eyelets for a classy touch.

Journaling to Note

What more can I say than to tell you that I love you?
I have waited my whole life for this moment, Hannah.
To hold you completely in my arms for the very first time,
To kiss your face and see you, my beautiful, perfect child.
Part of me thought this day would never come,
That perhaps the dream of having my own child
could not come true.
But it has come true.
You brought me joy before we ever knew your name.
I saw you on an ultrasound; I felt you kick against
your Momma's belly,
And I thought I loved you then.
But holding you in my arms today, for the first time,
I am learning all about love.
I did not know I could love so deeply, so perfectly,
so completely.
From this moment on, I will never be the same.

Love, Daddy

Just Stopping to Take a Look

Madison and Alex were so cute during our walk to the Livonia Spree fireworks. It was about a mile from the car to the park and Madison and Alex had been holding hands on the way. But when we stopped at a gas station to get some pop it was so cute that they continued holding hands while checking out the roller-pollies in the flowerbed. I thought it was hilarious how all three (Mom, Aunt Renee, and myself all ran for our cameras).

Madison loves her cousin Alex so much. It's probably because they're so close in age and alike in so many ways. I'll never forget how sweet Alex was when he first met her soon after we arrived home from the hospital. They've had a special bond from the very start.

Summer 2001

"Hand in Hand"
by Kimberly Stone
Westland, MI

Kimberly's Thoughts

"My daughter Madison and her cousin Alex have always been such great friends. Since they were little, they have held hands wherever they go. They always look so cute together.

"On this day, we were on our way to a fireworks display when Madison and Alex stopped to look at some bugs crawling in a flowerbed. They had no idea that the crowds of people walking by were looking at how cute and sweet they were. I'm glad I had my camera with me since Madison and Alex are growing up so fast and these little moments won't last forever."

SUPPLIES
Patterned paper: Provo Craft
Large daisy punch: Family Treasures
Baby buttons: Impress Rubber Stamps.com
Computer fonts: Scrap Brother (title) and Zachary (subtitle), downloaded from the Internet; CK Journaling (journaling), "The Best of Creative Lettering" CD Combo, *Creating Keepsakes*
Other: Green thread

Jennifer's Thoughts

"In the two years I've known little Audrey, we've developed a wonderful relationship and friendship—despite our 22-year difference in ages! She really gives the most powerful hugs, as if she never wants to let go. I was thankful my boyfriend was able to capture one of those hugs on film.

"I wanted to draw attention to Audrey's gorgeous blue eyes, so I did the layout in a blue, monochromatic color scheme. To create the torn heart in the background, I traced a large heart shape onto blue paper, then tore where I'd drawn my lines. After attaching the heart to patterned background paper, I poked holes in the heart with a needle. The needle helped guide the string as I wove it into the layout."

SUPPLIES
Patterned paper: Bryce & Madeline, Creative Imaginations
Computer font: FanciHand, downloaded from the Internet
Embroidery floss: DMC

For the best results, trace over your heart shape with a wet cotton swab before proceeding with any tearing.

"Hold on to This Moment"
by Jennifer Ditz
Cincinnati, OH

Hold on to this moment

Audrey gives the best hugs in the world. I wish I could hold her forever.

Hot Springs July 2001

"A Moment Captured"
by Melanie Pontius
Ogden, UT

Melanie's Thoughts

"My sister took the picture of her daughter Sierra at a park while the family was waiting for a dinner reservation. During the wait, my niece blew dandelion seeds to help pass the time. She called the dandelions her 'wishing flowers.'

"I wanted the layout to have the same clean look as the picture, so I embroidered the title with the same colors as those in the picture. I also chose three background papers that repeated colors from the photo.

"Although the photo on the left-hand page captures the moment, I added more meaning by including descriptive words about Sierra on the facing page. I added a dandelion to help the layout continue to 'flow' visually."

SUPPLIES
Embroidery floss: DMC
Craft wire: Fibrecraft
Buttons: Hillcreek Designs
Pen: Zig Writer, EK Success
Poem: From *www.two-peasinabucket.com*
Computer fonts: Bradley Hand, Microsoft Word; CK Flower Power, CK Fun, CK Pretty, CK Roses, CK Swirl, CK Stars, "The Art of Creative Lettering" CD; CK Cursive and CK Italic, "The Best of Creative Lettering" CD Combo, *Creating Keepsakes*

Give the "dandelions" a soft, fluffy look with tulle. Create "stems" with thread-covered wire.

Sequence Shots

Tell a story through a series of photos

TEXT BY CATHERINE SCOTT

PHOTOGRAPHY BY JOHN REES

*D*oes this scene sound all too familiar? You're busy attending to a daily routine when something catches your attention. You turn your head and see one of those "picture-perfect" scenarios. You run for your camera, look through the viewfinder, then wait for the ideal second to snap the picture.

Before you can decide what the "peak" moment is, the opportunity is gone. Drats! You missed it. You watched the whole thing pass and didn't get one photo. Why is it hardest to take pictures when you recognize that the rare moment happening before your eyes is one you may never witness again?

Some memories—like a genuine hug between a father and son—only last moments and lead to prized photographs if you're ready. But what about the memories that last a little longer? What about the memories that are actually "moments"—times when people aren't standing still or posing for the camera? How do you capture them on film?

Reader Mechelle Felsted of Flagstaff, Arizona, recently sent us a series of photographs and asked, "If a picture is worth a thousand words, what will three in a row be worth?" My thoughts exactly. For memories that last longer than a moment, a series of photographs can help tell the whole story and make a lasting impression. →

Figure 1. Help your pictures tell the story behind an action by taking "before," "during" and "after" shots instead of just one photograph. *Photos by Alisa Muriano.*

Getting Started

Ready to put the "series" technique to the test? Depending on your camera type and the moment you're trying to capture on film, you've got two options: use your camera's "continuous shooting" feature or shoot spaced photographs during the activity.

■ *Continuous shooting.* This camera feature is perfect for ultra-fast moments—for example, your daughter's surprised reactions at seeing a new car sitting in the driveway on her sixteenth birthday.

To get know-how quickly, review your camera manual. Most newer cameras (especially SLRs, which offer more control than point-and-shoot cameras) incorporate continuous shooting in multiple modes (such as portrait or sports). To activate the feature, all you do is press—and hold—the shutter release button.

■ *Spaced shooting.* If your camera doesn't offer continuous shooting, or if the moment you're photographing occurs repeatedly or lasts an extended period of time,

consider taking multiple photographs spaced out through the experience you're trying to capture.

Take more shots than you'll need, and don't worry about whether you're capturing the perfect photograph or not. Taking extra pictures increases your chances of getting the best, most telling photographs possible.

A reminder: As you press the shutter release button, you'll experience a slight delay before the camera actually takes the picture. Even if the scene you see while pressing the button isn't perfect, what your camera captures in the next instant could be!

5 Suggestions of What to Capture

Now that you know how to take a series of photos, you're ready to consider the events and moments you'd like to capture. Following are my five suggestions:

1. CAPTURE ACTION. Reader Alisa Muriano of Virginia Beach, Virginia, observed her son, Jack, curiously examining a hole in the

ground at an amusement park (see Figure 1). She grabbed her camera and got a picture of him peeking down into the hole. Seconds later, when a stream of water shot out of the hole, Alisa was ready. After the event was over, she snapped a picture of Jack's reaction to the discovery.

With their ability to show the "before," "during" and "after" of a moment, photo series offer a fun way to record action on film. Use a photo-series approach to capture the action of:

• Participating in sporting events
• Building a snowman (or anything else!)
• Playing on a playground

2. CAPTURE A RELATIONSHIP. Photo series can help capture activities and moments that demonstrate the essence of a relationship. Says Sandy Watrous of Sandy, Utah, "I always try to take several photographs so I can tell a story with my photos. I avoid taking posed shots, and instead try to capture subtle interactions between loved ones."

SCRAPBOOKING YOUR PHOTO SERIES

You've got a wonderful series of photos that tell a story. What next? Scrapbook them! Consider the following:

❶ Mat the photos on the same photo mat in a vertical or horizontal line (in order, of course!). Use the rest of the space to record details and the pictured event's significance.

❷ Number each photograph in order of occurrence. Use corresponding numbers to create meaningful journaling for each picture.

❸ Create a flipbook of photographs on your layout. Include corresponding journaling on the back of each picture.

❹ Enlarge the last photograph of the series to emphasize what happened at the end of the series. Explain the significance in your journaling.

❺ Connect the series of photos with playful arrows to show the progression of events. Journal inside the arrows, or include journaling beneath each photo to help explain why you included the series of photos in your scrapbook.

To create a "tiled" look for her background and photo frame, Lee Anne scanned and reduced an octagon shape, then used it as a template. To make realistic-looking acorns, she punched acorn shapes in two different colors of brown cardstock. After cutting the bottoms off the darker-brown acorns, Lee Anne glued the tops to the lighter-brown acorns.

Capture the "thrill of the chase" through a photo series on your page layout. *Pages by Lee Anne Russell.* **Supplies** *Lettering template:* Whimsy, ScrapPagerz.com; *Punches:* EK Success (acorn), Family Treasures (square); *Octagon template:* Creative Memories; *Eyelets:* Impress Rubber Stamps; *Pop dots:* All Night Media; *Computer font:* CK Sketch, "The Art of Creative Lettering" CD, *Creating Keepsakes.*

Figure 2. Capture a relationship's essence by taking a series of photos during a shared moment. *Photos by Sandy Watrous.*

In Figure 2, Sandy's photo series shows her grandson, Zane, being taught to skip rocks across water by his grandfather. Although we don't see their faces, the body language between grandpa and grandson shows the closeness of their relationship, the trust, and the togetherness these two share. Moments that capture the essence of a relationship and are well-suited for a photo series might include:

- Learning to cook a family recipe from another family member
- Sharing a favorite hobby with a relative or friend
- Reading a story together

3. CAPTURE PERSONALITY.

As Jeff Scott of Bountiful, Utah, watched his daughter and wife through the lens of his camera, he was amazed at how animated his daughter's facial expressions were. Over a 30-minute period, he managed to snap 20 photographs of different expressions without being detected.

At the end of his "photo session," Jeff called out his daughter's name. He got two of his favorite pictures as his daughter became aware of his presence. When the photos came back from the developer (Figure 3), Jeff selected his favorites and created a photo collage for his wall.

"The photographs are especially meaningful now that my daughter is older," says Jeff. "They show so much of her personality, and it's amusing for us to look at her and realize that she makes the same facial expressions today that she made as a toddler. Her animation is such a core part of her personality."

Other moments that reveal an aspect of someone's personality and are good photo-series candidates include:

- The person displaying a strong emotion, such as exuberance, stubbornness or sadness
- A person conversing with a friend or a loved one (either face to face or over the phone)
- A person trying something new or approaching a new situation

4. CAPTURE AN ACCOMPLISHMENT.

Mechelle Felsted was overjoyed at the opportunity to photograph her son, Corbin, performing his first dive (see Figure 4). She sat across from the pool, watching Corbin through her camera's zoom lens, as he worked up the nerve to tip headfirst into the water.

Advises Mechelle, "Ask your subject to perform the action a few times, then shoot pictures at different times every time the action is performed. It all pays off in the end—I now have an adorable photo sequence that shows a major accomplishment in the life of my son. It will help me remember it forever."

Figure 3. Facial expressions caught on film in a series of photographs can reveal much of a person's personality and disposition. *Photos by Jeff Scott.*

Figure 4. Accomplishments caught on film in stages capture treasured moments to be remembered forever. *Photos by Mechelle Felsted.*

Other accomplishments you might want to capture through a photo series include:

- A child tying his or her shoes for the first time
- Someone receiving an award or other positive recognition
- A person completing and admiring a project

5. CAPTURE THE PASSAGE OF TIME.

Photo series are also great for showing the passage of time. Think of all that changes as the days, weeks, months or years pass. Photo series can span these time periods and connect them into one meaningful event or record for you to treasure. Here are a few examples of "passage of time" sequences:

- Planting a garden in the spring, watching it grow, then harvesting the fruits and vegetables in late summer

- Showing your house at the peak of each season—in the spring with the buds and blossoms, in the summer with the deep greens and vivid flowers, in the fall with the colorful leaves, and in the winter, when everything's covered with snow
- Photographing someone in the same setting each year to show his or her growth and progression

While you can capture some memorable moments in one shot, others benefit from being photographed in a series.

Whenever you find yourself struggling to capture an event, press that shutter button resolutely (if your camera has "continuous shooting") or start clicking. You won't use every picture you take, but by choosing the best of whatever you capture, you'll create a series that will tell a story and capture those priceless memories. ♥

How does your family play?

Capture the fun times

Monday night is family time in our household. We take the phone off the hook, and one family member (this changes every week) lets us know what we'll be doing.

Sometimes the kids climb on their dad's back and play "Bucking Bronco" on the trampoline. Other times we go on an "I spy" walk around the neighborhood. I like to blindfold the kids, then have Steve drive us on a "wild goose chase" with a destination known only to the two of us. Sometimes the Bearnson family ends up at an ice-cream parlor, other times at a park. It's fun to hear the kids say, "I know exactly where we are" only to find they're way off course.

One of my favorite excursions? One we took to a huge new candy store in a neighboring town. Steve and I led our kids into the candy store, handed each child a five-dollar bill, then told the child to remove his or her blindfold. "Buy whatever you want with the money," we said. The kids were so excited they acted like . . . well . . . kids in a candy store!

How does your family play together? Have you captured these moments on film? See how seven scrapbookers shared their fun memories on the following pages.

by Lisa Bearnson

family play

Pages by Lisa Bearnson. **Supplies** *Patterned paper:* American Crafts; *Ribbon:* Making Memories; *Computer fonts:* LBLisaB and LBLoni, "Scrapbooking with Lisa Bearnson" CD, *Creating Keepsakes.*

Pages by Lindsay Teague. **Supplies** *Textured cardstock:* Bazzill Basics; *Stamping ink:* StazOn, Tsukineko; *Cut-out letters:* FoofaLa; *Label tape:* Dymo; *Patterned paper and black clip:* 7 Gypsies; *Epoxy letter stickers:* Shotz, Creative Imaginations; *Letter stamps:* Ma Vinci's Reliquary; *Pen:* Zig Millennium, EK Success; *Square punch:* EK Success; *Silver frame:* Polly & Friends, Leeco Industries; *Ribbon, jump ring and "2003" charm:* Making Memories; *Letter stickers and brads:* Doodlebug Design; *Letter tags:* DieCuts with a View.

Although he liked playing on the beach, Michael loved to be in the pool as long as someone in the family was holding him!

Together is a wonderful place to be.

He loved for Daddy to hold him and splash. Grandaddy was fun too, and Aunt Anne played with Michael every chance she got. But Michael's favorite person to play with in the pool was, by far, cousin Andrew. Michael's face would light up every time Andrew got into the pool. Andrew would do everything he could think of to make Michael smile and laugh. Michael just loved when Andrew played peek-a-boo with him by swimming under his baby boat. He would ask, "Where is?" and hold out his hands when Andrew dunked down, and his face would break out in a grin as soon as Andrew's head popped out of the water. Michael sure was a lucky boy to have all his family around him for vacation.

Coleman Family
Vacation

Page by Heather Coleman. **Supplies** *Textured cardstock:* Bazzill Basics (blue) and My Paper Garden (white); *Vellum:* Paperbilities; *Page pebble:* Making Memories; *Computer fonts:* 2Peas Just Plain Little (journaling) and 2Peas Flea Market (title), downloaded from *www.twopeasinabucket.com.*

Pages by Candi Gershon. **Supplies** *Patterned paper and square accents:* KI Memories; *Rubber stamps:* Ma Vinci's Reliquary and PSX Design; *Stamping ink:* Clearsnap and Ranger Industries; *Buttons:* EK Success; *Computer font:* 2Peas Typo, downloaded from *www.twopeasinabucket.com*; *Number stickers:* Sticker Studio.

Pages by Candi Gershon. **Supplies** *Patterned paper:* Chatterbox; *Tag:* Words 2Dye4; *Date stamp:* Making Memories; *Stamping ink:* Ranger Industries; *Label:* Dymo; *Computer fonts:* 2Peas Typo, downloaded from *www.twopeasinabucket.com*; Toxica and Stamp Act, downloaded from the Internet. *Idea to note:* Candi used photo-editing software to type captions on each photo.

Pages by Ali Edwards. **Supplies** *Textured cardstock:* Bazzill Basics; *Printed transparencies:* Narratives, Creative Imaginations; *Label stickers:* Pebbles Inc.; *Epoxy stickers:* Shotz, Creative Imaginations; *Leather "M" charm:* Inspirables, EK Success; *Rubber stamps:* Turtle Press and PSX Design; *Stamping ink:* Hero Arts and Ranger Industries; *Computer font:* Myriad Roman, downloaded from the Internet; *Other:* Staples.

Editor's note: For instructions on how to alter a coin book (and view another example by Ann), see page 97.

Album by Ann Pelke. **Supplies** *Patterned papers:* Karen Foster Design and PSX Design; *Acrylic paint:* Delta Technical Coatings; *Rub-on words, definition stickers and metal frame:* Making Memories; *Other:* D-rings, seam binding and studs.

Pages by Erin Lincoln. **Supplies** *Patterned paper:* KI Memories; *Computer fonts:* 2Peas Tubby (journaling), downloaded from *www.twopeasinabucket.com;* Bookman (title), Corel WordPerfect; *Rub-on letters and embroidery floss:* Making Memories; *Stitching template:* Li'l Davis Design; *Other:* Brads.

Word Collage Tip

In Microsoft Word, use the text box feature to create a word collage.

Here's how:

1 Determine the size of your word collage. Create a text box to use as a "frame."

2 Create a text box for each letter in your title. To eliminate the line and overlapping white space around each letter, click once on your text box, choose "Format" in the menu bar and click on "Text Box." Under the "Colors and Lines" tab, select "No Fill" and "No Line."

3 Size and move each letter within your "frame" until you like the way it looks. *Tip:* When you click on each text box, a menu bar will pop up. Click the "Change Text Direction" button to turn a letter on its side.

4 Print in reverse on cardstock, then cut out the letters with an X-acto knife. Or, print on typing paper and adhere the print to your cardstock with temporary adhesive. Cut the letters out, peel off the typing paper, and rub off the adhesive.

—*Erin Lincoln, Frederick, MD*

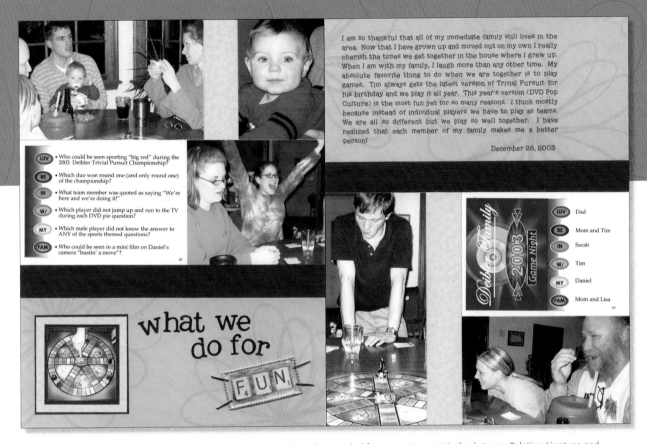

Pages by Erin Roe. **Supplies** Computer fonts: 2Peas Typo (journaling), downloaded from www.twopeasinabucket.com; Palatino Linotype and Trebuchet MS, Microsoft Word; Easy Street EPS (script on trivia card), downloaded from the Internet; Textured cardstock: Bazzill Basics (blue) and WorldWin (lime); Patterned papers. KI Memories (blue floral) and EK Success (Scrabble tiles in title); Charm: Maude and Millie; Letter stickers: Doodlebug Design; Staples: Making Memories.

Game Card Tip

I created my own Trivial Pursuit question-and-answer cards and printed them on photo paper for a glossy look. Microsoft Publisher software made the cards look very similar to actual cards. I changed the words in the logo to "Deibler Family Game Night 2003" and also changed the categories to "LUV," "BE," "IN," "W/," "MY" and "FAM." Questions relate to funny things about each person in my family from that night of game playing.

Questions include:

- Who could be seen sporting "big red" during the 2003 Deibler Trivial Pursuit Championship?

- Who won round one (and only round one) of the championship?

- What team member was quoted as saying, "We're here and we're doing it"?

- Which player did not jump up and run to the TV during each DVD pie question?

- Which male player did not know the answer to ANY of the sports-themed questions?

- Who could be seen in a mini film on Daniel's camera "bustin' a move"?

—Erin Roe, Hampton, VA

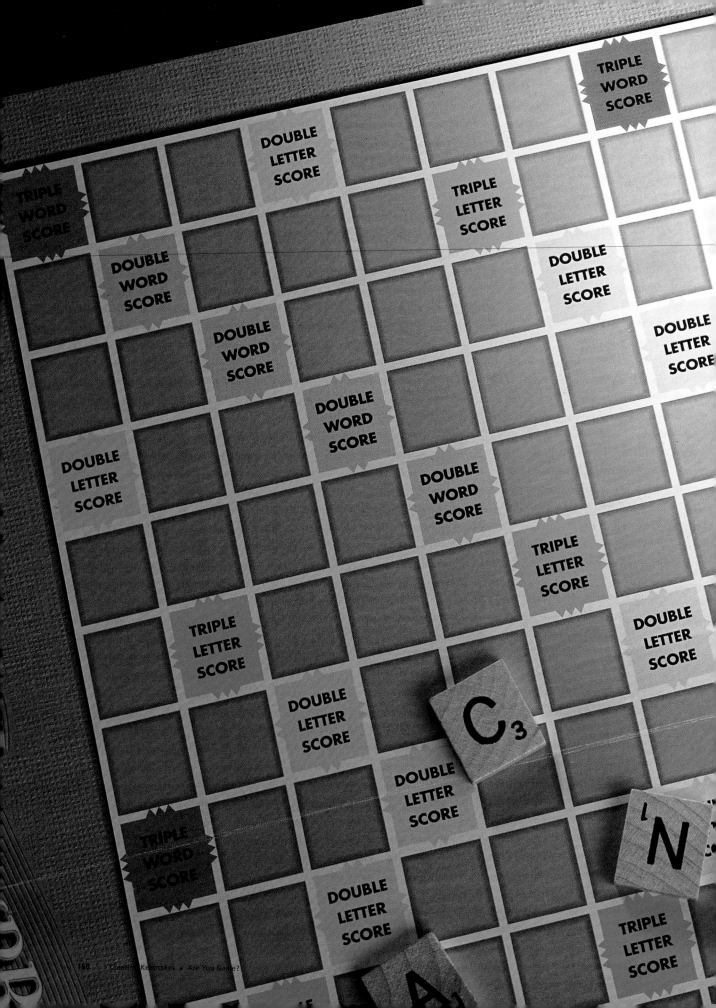

Get winning ideas for board-game layouts

HERE'S A RIDDLE: What takes concentration, strategic thinking, sportsmanship, patience and a sense of humor? What gives laughter, achievement, satisfaction, entertainment and togetherness? A board game! From classics like chess and Scrabble to new favorites such as Cranium and Pretty Pretty Princess, board games will always have a place in our hearts and homes, giving us time to relax and reconnect with family and friends.

Whether you feel nostalgic about the games you played as a child, hope to create new memories with your own children, or simply love to unwind with friends on game nights, bring your photos of the festivities and come to play.

Following are six layouts created by "game" scrapbookers that are sure to give you winning ideas and inspiration!

BY DENISE PAULEY

"Pretty Pretty Princess"
by Jennifer Ditz
Cincinnati, OH

SUPPLIES

Rubber stamps: Impression Obsession, Judikins and Robber Moon
Embossing powder: Judikins
Computer fonts: Lasagna and Piano Recital, *www.twopeasinabucket.com*
Craft wire: Artistic Wire Ltd.
Embroidery floss: DMC
Watercolor pencils: Sanford

Stamp and emboss

subtle images on

background paper

to reinforce your

theme.

"A Knight to Remember"
by Lee Anne Russell
Brownsville, TN

SUPPLIES
Computer fonts: Daniel (title), downloaded from the Internet; Doodle Basic (journaling), "PagePrintables" CD, Cock-A-Doodle Design, Inc.
Flat-topped eyelets: The Stamp Doctor
Eyelets: Impress Rubber Stamps
Chalk pencils: Faber-Castell
Chalk: Craf-T Products
Fiber: On the Fringe
Punch: McGill
Title idea: From the movie "A Night to Remember"

Play up the "knight" theme on a chess layout with knight-piece accents and a twist on your title.

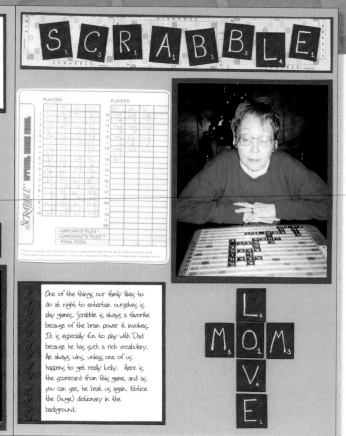

Sometimes, when you get really, really desperate, and you have all I's and E's or other bad letter combinations, you have to make up a word and hope that it is in the dictionary. Occasionally you will get lucky, such as QUIN (a scallop), but most of the time you will not, such as JONT (?). Dad makes interesting faces when he thinks you might be using this tactic.

One of the things our family likes to do at night to entertain ourselves is play games. Scrabble is always a favorite because of the brain power it involves. It is especially fun to play with Dad because he has such a rich vocabulary. He always wins, unless one of us happens to get really lucky. Here is the scorecard from this game, and as you can see, he beat us again. Notice the (huge) dictionary in the background.

"Scrabble"
by Nicole Keller
Rio Hondo, TX

SUPPLIES
Computer font: Tall Paul, downloaded from the Internet
Scissors: Dragonback edge, Fiskars
Chalk: Craf-T Products
Pen: Uniball Gel Tropical, Sanford
Ideas to note: Nicole created the letter tiles by cutting pieces of burgundy cardstock to the size of actual Scrabble tiles. She then chalked the edges with black chalk to create dimension, and added the letters and point values with a white gel pen.

Scan the back of a scorecard and use it to back title letters. Or, include your score-card on the layout.

CHECKERS

"aUNt loNi,

will you play a

GaME of CHECKERS

WitH ME?"

WARNING:

CHOKING HAZARD: Excessive fun
while playing this game may lead to
laughter, or even, shortage of breath.
Worse case scenario- choking.

SB
STEVENS
BROOKSBY

AGES 6 & UP
For 2 Players

"Checkers"
by Loni Stevens
Gilbert, AZ

SUPPLIES
Computer fonts: Downloaded from the Internet
("Aunt Loni"); Arial Black ("Warning") and Abadi MT
Condensed Light ("Choking Hazard"), Microsoft Word
Punches: Family Treasures (square) and Marvy Uchida (circle)
Lettering template: Upper Block, EK Success
Vellum: Paper Adventures
Thread: On the Surface
SB logo: From game box
Date stamp: Staples
Other: Nailhead, eyelet and key tag

Use punched squares

to create a checker-

board look for

your border.

"Goodnight Moon"
by Denise Pauley
La Palma, CA

SUPPLIES
Textured paper: Black Ink
Vellum: Paper Adventures
Computer font: Annifont, downloaded from the Internet
Brads: American Pin & Fastener
Fibers: On the Surface
Idea to note: Denise included lines from the book *Goodnight Moon* beneath her matted photo.

"Sew" a photo mat to your page with fiber to create a "flip" photo with text beneath.

Include accents that play up—and extend—your page theme.

"Snakes and Ladders"
by Renée Senchnya
Sherwood Park, AB, Canada

SUPPLIES
Lettering template: School Days, EK Success
Computer font: CK Toggle, "The Best of Creative Lettering" CD Combo, *Creating Keepsakes*
Ladders and snakes: Renée's own designs
Idea to note: As a playful touch, Renée added three-dimensional eyes to her snakes.

hugs, kisses and family time

Celebrate special relationships with these ideas

Supplies *Patterned paper:* 7 Gypsies; *Computer font:* Garamouche, P22 Type Foundry.

"nosey"
kisses
March 2003

"Nosey Kisses"

by Tracy Miller
Fallston, MD

What started as a photography class assignment turned into an affectionate moment between sisters, says Tracy.

◆ Tracy kept accents to a minimum so the emphasis would remain on her strong photo.

◆ Torn cardstock and exposed patterned paper lend a touch of texture to a streamlined design.

◆ Save time and cardstock by printing your photo with a white border. Or, ask your photo developer to print a border.

ARTICLE BY LANNA CARTER

Supplies *Patterned paper:* 7 Gypsies; *Decorative paper:* Making Memories; *Vellum:* Paper Adventures; *Textured cardstock:* Bazzill Basics; *Letter stamps:* Printers Type, Hero Arts; *Stamping ink:* Clearsnap; *Computer fonts:* Problem Secretary and Lipstick Traces, downloaded from the Internet; *Ribbon:* Jo-Ann Crafts; *Heart plaque:* Making Memories.

"Kisses for My Brother"

by Jlyne Hanback
Biloxi, MS

For Jlyne, it's hard to tell from the photo which child is more delighted—the one giving or the one receiving the kisses.

◆ To create the lips, Jlyne downloaded a dingbat character, then printed several color copies on vellum. She cut the images out with a craft knife, then ran them through her Xyron machine before adhering them to the layout.

◆ On a black-and-white page, add a slash of bright color for visual interest.

"Family Time"

by Tammy Lombardi
Rico, FL

Saturdays in the Lombardi house mean family time. Sam and Tammy take their kids out for lunch and a field trip.

◆ Create a photo grid. Fill in some spaces with strong shapes and journaling subtitles.

◆ Wrap your layout with fibers, then run a journaling block over them.

◆ Make a layout about simple family traditions.

Supplies *Computer font:* Willing Race, downloaded from the Internet; *Circle and square punches:* Marvy Uchida; *Tag:* Tammy's own design; *Other:* String.

"Trial and Error"
by Gillian Nelson
Gilbert, AZ

As her eldest child, Kyle is often a "learning tool," says Gillian. She created this layout to remind her son that he is loved.

◆ Customize a metal-rimmed tag by replacing the center with the paper, vellum or fabric of your choice.

◆ Include hand lettering as well as computer fonts. Your writing will serve as a remembrance for future generations.

◆ Write a letter to your child.

Supplies *Patterned paper:* Made to Match, American Crafts; *Metal-rimmed tag:* Making Memories; *Brad:* American Tag Company; *Pen:* Le Plume, Marvy Uchida; *Computer font:* Calisto MT, Microsoft Word.

"Love to Argue"
by Patricia Anderson
Selah, WA

Patricia and her son, Christian, love to argue—about how much they love each other. Luckily, they both win the argument.

◆ For an attractive journaling block, paint the center of a patterned-paper block with acrylic paint. After it dries, print your journaling on it.

◆ "Age" a metal accent by painting it with acrylic paint. Wipe off most of the paint before it dries.

◆ Create strong page design with "visual triangles" of color and the principle of thirds.

Supplies *Patterned paper:* Magenta; *Computer fonts:* Cezanne Regular (title), P22 Type Foundry; Times New Roman (journaling), Microsoft Word; *Alphabet charms, frame and heart eyelet:* Making Memories; *Charm:* Scrap-Ease; *Acrylic paint:* Plaid Enterprises; *Other:* Thread and ribbon.

Supplies *Stickers:* Sonnets, Shotz and Rustic Bottle Caps, Creative Imaginations; Nostalgiques, EK Success; SEI; *Rub-ons, eyelet letters, clear 3-D stickers and metal-rimmed tags:* Making Memories; *Chalk:* Stampin' Up!; *Walnut ink:* 7 Gypsies; *Stamping ink:* StazOn, Tsukineko; *Ribbon:* C.M. Offray & Son; *Label:* Dymo Label Maker; *Other:* Paper clips, staples, pins, washer, thread, cardboard and cork.

"It Used to be about the Flowers"

**by Renee Villalobos-Campa
Winnebago, IL**

Before having children, says Renee, "my Valentine's Day was for flowers and cards. Now it's even sweeter because my husband and I get hugs, kisses and love from our kids."

◆ To create a background "folder," cut cream cardstock to a file folder shape, then stain the cardstock with walnut ink.

◆ To create custom "typewriter key" accents, rub tan paint into engraved eyelet letters. After the paint dries, tap each letter in black solvent ink.

◆ Experiment with fonts and lettering techniques. Renee used paper clips to form the "N" in "Now." She used "stitched" stickers for each "about."

"Sweet Tenderness"
by Cari Locken
Edmonton, AB, Canada

Nothing gives Cari more joy than to see her sweet children playing happily together.

◆ Use initials on a tag to represent the people in the picture.

◆ Layer a variety of patterned papers and cardstock blocks to create a mat for a focal-point photo.

◆ Thread your tag with fibers, then hang it from a ribbon border.

Supplies *Patterned papers:* Karen Foster Design (orange); KI Memories (striped); 7 Gypsies (print); *Textured cardstock:* Bazzill Basics; *Stickers:* Sonnets, Creative Imaginations; Nostalgiques, EK Success; *Pen:* Zig Millennium, EK Success; *Computer fonts:* Arial ("Sweet") and Chaucer ("Tenderness" and journaling), downloaded from the Internet; *Ribbon:* Michaels; *Fibers:* Adornaments, EK Success; *Button and tag:* Making Memories; *Other:* Button.

"Sweethearts on the Slopes"
by Jenna Tomalka
Battle Creek, MI

Says Jenna, "My sweet husband made all the arrangements—including childcare—for this surprise getaway."

◆ To output a screened photo with photo-quality text, select the "Draft" setting on your printer and print the photo. Next, select the "Photo Quality" setting and run the paper through your printer again for the title and journaling.

◆ Print a photo on a transparency, then layer it over a tag for a subtle accent.

◆ Use nature (such as the tree here) to frame an outdoor photo.

Supplies *Patterned paper:* Club Scrap; *Heart charms:* Making Memories; *Bookplate:* Magic Scraps; *Tags:* Sizzix; *Transparencies:* 3M; *Computer fonts:* CK Hustle (title, tags and journaling) and CK Constitution (bookplate), "Fresh Fonts" CD, *Creating Keepsakes; Fibers:* Adornaments, EK Success; *Other:* Eyelets.

Supplies *Patterned paper:* Karen Foster Design; *Vellum:* The Paper Company; *Computer font:* Selfish, downloaded from the Internet; *Fibers:* Fibers By The Yard; *Charms:* The Card Connection; *Wax seals:* Hampton Arts; *Wax stamps:* Embossing Arts; *Letter stamps:* PSX Design; Hero Arts; Anita's ("H"); *Vellum tags and eyelets:* Making Memories; *Ribbon:* C.M. Offray & Son; *Embroidery floss:* DMC; *Chalk and metallic rub-ons:* Craf-T Products; *Other:* Beads and craft wire.

"Once Upon a Time"

**by Jeniece Higgins
Northbrook, IL**

Jeniece created a layout that celebrates years of happiness by commemorating some of the highlights.

◆ Create a frame by threading fibers, ribbon, thread or embroidery floss through eyelets around a photo.

◆ Use tags to tell a story that spans many years. Jeniece cut slits in her page protector so the tags can easily be removed to read the journaling on the back.

◆ Add an authentic love-letter look with wax seals.

"Love is a Gift"

**by Jill Cummins
Lexington, KY**

A friend snapped this endearing photo of Jill and her boyfriend, TJ, at a sorority dance. "This photo captures a perfect moment between us," she says.

◆ Create a faux photo mat with acrylic paints. Determine the size of your "mat," then paint swashes of color in that area. You can also paint the mat, then tear out the center and mount your photo from behind for a more dimensional look.

◆ Stamp letters onto clay, then bake it according to the package directions. After the clay cools, paint each letter with acrylic paint.

Supplies *Patterned paper:* Sarah Lugg (love postcard), The Paper Company; 7 Gypsies; NRN Designs; *Acrylic paint:* Palmer; *Polymer clay:* Prēmo, Sculpey; *Typewriter stickers:* Nostalgiques, EK Success; *Letter stamps:* Hero Arts; *Gold eyelets and heart clip:* Making Memories; *Computer fonts:* 2Peas Sonnets Script, downloaded from *www.two-peasinabucket.com*; Garamond, Microsoft Word; *Other:* Jute and vellum.

"Favorite Memories"
by Jennifer Bester
Reading, MA
SUPPLIES

Textured paper: Books by Hand
Computer font: Garamouche,
Impress Rubber Stamps
Letter charms:
Twopeasinabucket.com
Idea to note: The heart accents
were inspired by gift wrap.

TRY THIS TECHNIQUE: Cut
a plain heart sticker, die cut
or punch into four different
pieces for an interesting
mosaic accent. Adhere the
pieces to various rectangles
of cardstock and chalk the
edges. Split your layout into
sections with wavy lines of
cardstock for a whimsical
look.

Favorite Memories

The day you surprised me at the airport in
Vienna with a single red rose. I didn't know
you had it in you!

The night you threw me my first and only
surprise birthday party before we even started
dating.

The housewarming party in our first home.
Once we'd finished all that work with our own
hands, I realized that together we'd be able to
accomplish anything we'd set our minds to.

The moment I saw you cradle Franny in your
arms for the first time. I just knew you were
going to be a wonderful father.

The first time I listened to the song you wrote
for me...that was a moment I will NEVER
forget!

The afternoon we couldn't control our laughter
as we were carrying our heavy luggage to the
train station in Paris. I haven't laughed so hard
since that day.

The day we graduated from UMass together. I
feel as though our dreams for the future were
born on that day.

looking back photo tips

- Take a picture of the two of you every year on
  your anniversary—in the same place, if possible. It will give you a priceless treasure to look
  back on.

- For a professional-looking picture, use a solid-
  colored background, such as a photo cloth, a
  piece of fabric or a blanket; it will keep the
  focus on your faces. Dress in the same color as
  the background and your faces will stand out.

Photo ops: The possibilities are endless!
—*by Barbara Carroll*

10 ideas *for celebrating your relationship*

Seven years, six homes, five jobs and four children ago, Jeff and I were married. We've been together since high school, so add that up to make 10 years of knowing each other.

In those 10 years, so many things have happened to strengthen us and reaffirm us, to challenge us and make us grow. Like the child unexpectedly born with developmental issues. The personal success of graduating from college or achieving a dream. Little surprises like a card in my suitcase during a girls-only trip. Even the quiet times at night when we can just be together.

These are the moments I want my children to know about someday. Moments, in fact, I myself don't want to forget. That's why I include them in my scrapbook. My album is filled with these small remembrances of our life together.

You and your husband are the core of your family. While it's easy to leave the two of you out of your scrapbook and focus only on the little ones, it's important to record the small moments that make your relationship what it is. The 10 ideas below will help you get started creating pages that celebrate your marriage and your unique relationship.

❶ Journal about how you anticipated life would be after your wedding, and compare it to what you know now. I thought that by the time we were 30, we would be millionaires, have six adorable, well-behaved children, and be living in our dream home on the beach!

❷ Take photos or journal your favorite thing about your husband. It could be his eyes, the way he tells a joke, how he cooks every night, or the way he holds a baby.

❸ Record each other's idiosyncrasies—even the personality traits that drive you crazy. Adults have funny little quirks, just like kids do. We wouldn't hesitate to create a layout based on a child's manner of eating. Why do we leave our husbands out? Or ourselves for that matter?

❹ Create scrapbook pages to display cards, love notes, date night movie tickets and more. Jeff surprises me all the time with little mementos. That's something I want my children to know about. Hopefully, it's something they'll carry on in their own marriages, too.

❺ Get your feelings down. What is it about your husband that drew you to him? What does he do for you that you just couldn't live without?

❻ Journal about a time in your life when you really had to come together to overcome a problem. How did you strengthen each other? How did the two of you work together?

❼ Scrapbook your traditions and rituals, like date night every Friday or backrubs every Sunday.

❽ What do you do to make each other laugh?

❾ What are your similarities and differences—physically and emotionally?

❿ What are your hopes and dreams for the future? For your family?

Your marriage is the center of your life. Why not give it the place it deserves in your scrapbook? With these ideas, you'll be off to a great start.

—by Tara Whitney

"Jeff Surprises Me"

by Tara Whitney
Valencia, CA
SUPPLIES
Vellum: The Paper Company
Alphabet rubber stamps: Hero Arts
Stamping ink: Source unknown
Brads: Making Memories
Other: Swirl clips
Idea to note: Tara included cards and envelopes from her husband on her layout.

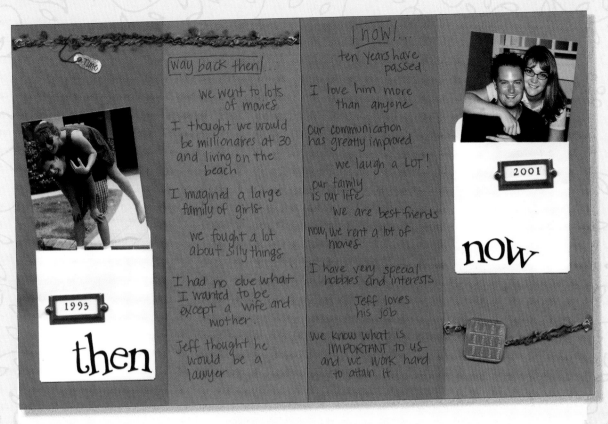

Way back then!...

We went to lots of movies

I thought we would be millionaires at 30 and living on the beach

I imagined a large family of girls

We fought a lot about silly things

I had no clue what I wanted to be except a wife and mother.

Jeff thought he would be a lawyer

now!...

ten years have passed

I love him more than anyone

Our communication has greatly improved

we laugh a LOT!

our family is our life

We are best friends

now, we rent a lot of movies

I have very special hobbies and interests

Jeff loves his job

we know what is IMPORTANT to us and we work hard to attain it

then

now

1993

2001

"Then and Now"
by Tara Whitney
Valencia, CA
SUPPLIES
Letter stickers: Sonnets, Creative Imaginations
Rubber stamps: Hero Arts
Stamping ink: Tsukineko
Bookplates and library pockets: Animaldesigns.com
Fibers: Rubba Dub Dub
Tag: Avery
Conchos: Scrapworks
Pen: Pigma Micron, Sakura
Other: Charm

"Love Is You"
by Tara Whitney
Valencia, CA
SUPPLIES
Computer fonts: Architect, downloaded from www.twopeasinabucket.com; Gill Sans Light, downloaded from the Internet
Brads: Making Memories
Ideas to note: Tara adapted the idea for her layout from a Hallmark card. She created a window for the arrow and placed a sheet protector over the top of it.

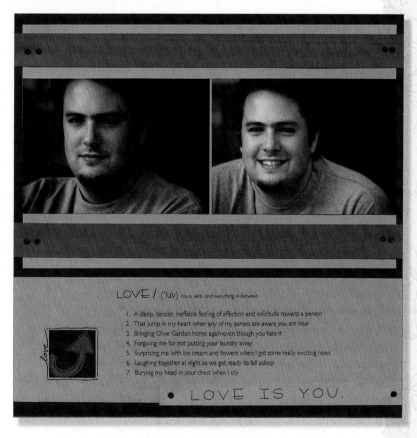

LOVE / ('luv) *noun, verb, and everything in-between*

1. A deep, tender, ineffable feeling of affection and solicitude toward a person
2. That jump in my heart when any of my senses are aware you are near
3. Bringing Olive Garden home again–even though you hate it
4. Forgiving me for not putting your laundry away
5. Surprising me with ice cream and flowers when I get some really exciting news
6. Laughing together at night as we get ready to fall asleep
7. Burying my head in your chest when I cry

• LOVE IS YOU.

love

"Eight Years"

by Jennifer Wohlenberg
Stevenson Ranch, CA

SUPPLIES

Textured paper: Memory Lane
Alphabet rubber stamps: Hero Arts
Stamping ink: Stampin' Up!
Computer font: Garamond, downloaded from the Internet
Heart brads: Source unknown
Idea to note: To bring out the natural texture of the cardstock used for the photo mat, Jennifer swiped an inkpad over it several times in uneven motions.

Two weeks before moving into our first home, we were quite anxious about finances and the general stresses of relocation, but we knew we would definitely want to celebrate our eighth anniversary while we still had Elizabeth available for babysitting. We didn't exchange gifts, but that didn't matter, just having the chance for a quiet dinner alone, especially when we knew those dinners were coming to an end, was enough present in itself. We chose Super Mex -- Brad's favorite Mexican restaurant, and one we wouldn't be able to visit once we lived in Stevenson Ranch -- and had a wonderful dinner there. Afterwards, we went to Borders and browsed through the books, just enjoying the quiet time. We talked a lot about our mixture of excitement and anxiety at finally reaching our goal of home ownership, and I remember feeling so grateful that I would have him by my side as we embarked on this new adventure. It was a really low-key way to mark our eight years of married bliss, but for us, it was the perfect celebration.
August 14, 2001

"28 Years Together"

by Barbara Carroll
Tucson, AZ

SUPPLIES

Rubber stamps: Hero Arts
Stamping ink: ColorBox, Clearsnap, Inc.
Computer fonts: Comic Sans, Microsoft Word; Gilde, downloaded from the Internet
Fiber: Rubba Dub Dub
Tag: Memory Lane

28 years

It is almost impossible to believe we have been together for such a long time. It doesn't seem that long ago that a shy boy took my hand as we stood Christmas caroling with all our friends. I remember being surprised and filled with a glow. A wedding, two college graduations, a house, two amazing children later and here we are. We have stood strong in good times and bad. Through it all, we have remained each other's best friends, confidantes and anchors. I am proud we have been married for 28 years but even more, I am thankful.

together

ten years have gone by and things just get better and better... really! I have four great children and a husband I grow closer to each day. When you first get married you think, "how could I possibly Love him more?", but I've found through all of the ups & downs you grow closer and really appreciate the other person more and more. Whenever I see Chad walk through the door my heart still skips a beat... and I hope I will have that feeling for a long, long time! Sure... we sometimes have disagreements, but you Learn to work through them and come to a solution good for both of you. Every year we've been together has been such an adventure and I can't wait to see what the future has in store for us. I just know I'm with the right person... it becomes clearer to me every day...

Chad & Christina est. 1992

"10 Years Later"

by Christina Cole
Salt Lake City, UT

SUPPLIES

Patterned papers: Rebecca Sower, EK Success (red); Provo Craft (lime)
Computer font: Butterbrotpapier, downloaded from the Internet
Tag: Making Memories
Pen: Zig Millennium, EK Success
Embroidery floss: DMC
Other: Ribbon
Ideas to note: To create the page, Christine cut along one of the ripples on the red patterned paper and adhered it to the white paper. She left spaces when printing out the journaling, then used the same font in a larger size to go back and fill in the spaces.

"Soul Mates"

by Karen Brutschy
Pasa Robles, CA

SUPPLIES
Patterned paper: K & Company
Rubber stamp: Stampabilities
Stamping ink: ColorBox, Clearsnap, Inc.; VersaMark, Tsukineko
Embossing powder: Stampendous!
Eyelets: Emagination Crafts
Brads and clear stone: Making Memories
Square punch: EK Success
Key charm: Embellish It!
Foam: Darice
Chalk: Craf-T Products
Computer fonts: Davinci, Times New Roman and Courier New, Microsoft Word
Poem: Downloaded from www.twopeasinabucket.com
Other: Ribbon

IDEA TO NOTE: Try making your own scrabble letters for unique titles and photo captions. Here's how: ❶ Print the letters on tan cardstock and punch them out with a small square punch. ❷ Adhere them to the page with adhesive foam tape. ❸ Rub the letters with a watermark ink pad, then apply light-brown chalk.

"You"

by Jennifer Wohlenberg
Stevenson Ranch, CA

SUPPLIES
Textured paper: Memory Lane
Computer font: Jayne, downloaded from the Internet
Leather rubber stamps: Midas Alphabet Set
Stamping ink: ColorBox, Clearsnap, Inc.
Fibers: Rubba Dub Dub
Eyelets: Making Memories
Other: Leather heart

"Thoughts on Us"

by Marissa Perez
Issaquah, WA

SUPPLIES
Vellum: The Paper Company
Computer font: Bernhard Fashion, downloaded from the Internet
Stickers: Jolee's Boutique, Stickopotamus

As I look at this picture of you taken on our honeymoon I wonder if you knew what you were in for when you said "I will." Six years later, I love you more than I can even begin to describe with words. All I know is that when I sit in the dark and think about you and me and us that I get this big swell in my heart, and I feel this small smile creep across my face as my eyes well up with tears—occasionally one even escapes and slides down my usually cheek. My sweetheart, I know that I do not often tell you that I love you and more often than not I even forget to show you, but please know that I do. Please know that it has always been you. From the moment I first laid eyes on you, I knew. From that moment I knew that you were my gift. That you would be strong enough and kind enough to be mine. I remember when we were dating that I could completely collapse in your strength. You would hold me and let me be me. And you still do. You still do.
Husband
When we were first married, I knew immediately that life was good. You picked up your dirty clothes, you kept gas in the car, you did dishes and laundry. You liked movies and you liked to eat out at all my favorite restaurants. You went to church with me, you were honest with me, you tried hard to be good to me and to keep our relationship alive. You sacrificed your friends and family to make my drive shorter though that made yours longer. You worked and went to school without complaint. You carried your Victoria Secret's lunch bag with pride. You told all your friends that marriage was good. You were patient with my insecurities and kept me laughing when the money was tight.
Father
When Nigel was born, I again realized how fortunate I was. You changed diapers, you stayed up at night, you could put him to sleep, you tried to make me feel pretty when I really wasn't. Your willingness to stay home and take care of Nigel will never be forgotten. You jumped in and helped whenever you could, even though you may have only had a couple hours sleep. You would change linens in the middle of the night when Nigel was sick, you would offer to stay up and keep us both company when he couldn't sleep. You told your friends I was a good mother. You were patient with my learning how to adapt to this stage.
Companion
And then I had my stroke. Two weeks before you were to start grad school. Two weeks before you were finally to get a break. While I lay in that hospital bed wondering what was happening to me, I never had to worry that you would be anywhere but by my side. You cried in the hall so that you could be strong for me. You told me everything would be alright even though we really weren't sure that it would be. You were the strong one, again, while I lay helpless in a bed not mine. When they told us that I might never walk again, you didn't walk away but rather, held my hand and cried with me. You helped me home and held us together while I rested and got well. You would leave school early so that you could help. You sacrificed your grades, your esteem, your time, and your pride so that you could help our family. You told your friends you didn't mind. You were what kept us going. It didn't go unnoticed.
Always
Richard, I wanted for you and for us a life that was comfortable and worry free. But that was not to be. For whatever reason, we have had to face trials that have tested our limits. What I wanted most on the day we were married was to be there for you, always. To take care of you and of us. But instead, you have taken care of me. With you I can cry or complain or be mad or be happy. You get the parts of me that no one else does. Somehow you let me be me. And I give you the real deal. Not the shiny happy me that everyone else gets, but the real me that is sometimes funny, sometimes goofy, sometimes scared, sometimes lonely, sometimes strong, sometimes stubborn, sometimes sensitive, sometimes cranky, sometimes silly, but always in love with you. I am sorry that you have had to work so hard. I am grateful that you think that we are worth it. Thank you for loving me and for putting up with me and for meaning what you said on that long ago day that we married. I love you sweetheart. It's always been you. It still is. And always will be.

"Six Years Later"

by Marnie Flores
Madison, WI

SUPPLIES

Computer font: Scrap Cursive, "Lettering Delights" CD Vol. 3, Inspire Graphics

"We Are Still Heaven"

by Jennifer Wohlenberg
Stevenson Ranch, CA

SUPPLIES

Specialty paper: Memory Lane
Computer font: CAC One Seventy, downloaded from the Internet
Dog tags: Chronicle Books
Fibers: Rubba Dub Dub
Metal alphabet stamps: Pittsburgh Metal Stamps
Stamping ink: ColorBox, Clearsnap Inc.

we
are
still
heaven
March 31, 2002

"At the Moment"
by Christina Cole
Salt Lake City, UT
SUPPLIES
Computer font:
Monkey Chunks,
downloaded
from the Internet
Hearts, trees and arrows:
Christina's own designs

AT THE MOMENT...

NOVEMBER 2000

CHRISTINA OF COURSE LOVES TO SCRAPBOOK! SHE IS TRYING TO JUGGLE EVERYTHING WHILE RAISING FOUR AWESOME KIDS. SHE IS ALSO ANXIOUS ABOUT WHERE WE MAY BE MOVING TO!

KADEN HAS THREE GREAT LOVES AT THE MOMENT. THEY ARE #1 HIS BLANKET #2 WINNIE THE POOH/ELMO AND #3 ANYTHING TO DO WITH GOLF!

EMILY IS DEFINITELY THE SERIOUS ONE IN THE FAMILY! SHE ALSO LIKES TO DRESS UP WITH ELISE AND PLAY BARBIES. SHE IS GOING TO PLAYSCHOOL AND LEARNING SOME FUN STUFF!

CHAD IS WAITING TO HEAR WORD ON WHAT MED SCHOOL HE WILL BE GOING TO. HE IS DOING CANCER RESEARCH RIGHT NOW THAT IS VERY EXCITING AND IS THE BEST HUSBAND IN THE WORLD!

KYRIL IS IN GRADE TWO AND LOVES POKEMON AND ANYTHING ASSOCIATED WITH POKEMON. HIS BEST FRIEND IS ALEX WHO ALSO LOVES POKEMON... THEY GET ALONG VERY WELL! KYRIL ALSO LOVES TO DRAW AND PLAY GOLF.

ELISE LIKES ANYTHING GIRLY... ESPECIALLY JEWELERY! SHE LOVES TO DRESS UP AND PLAY PRETEND. SHE GOES TO KINDERGARTEN AND IS STARTING TO READ AND WRITE.

Journaling Idea:
At the Moment

❖ ❖ ❖

Add meaning to scrapbook pages with
family photographs by including captions of
what each family member was involved in when
the photograph was taken. Save time by sending
color copies of the completed scrapbook
page as your holiday newsletter!

QUOTABLE QUOTE:

"Where we love is home,
home that our feet may leave,
but not our hearts."

—OLIVER WENDELL HOLMES

Playing Barbie in the front hall

Riding my bike to the corner store
Waiting for the school bus at the corner
Neighborhood kickball games

The swingset dad built
Sleepovers in the attic
Sharing a room with my new baby sister

The blizzard of '78
My best friend right around the corner

home

is *where* your

story begins...

Watching Franny play on the front stairs of my mother's house brought back a flood of memories from my childhood. We moved frequently when I was a kid, but we spent the longest time together as a family here at Lewis Road. From age 4 to 10, those years when everything seems so special and almost magical, we lived in the second floor apartment. I met my first best friend at the bus stop while nervously awaiting my first day of kindergarten. My father taught me how to ride my bike by attaching a broom stick to the back, and running down the street behind me as I tried to balance. Most of the pictures from my childhood were taken on the front lawn or inside the walls of this house. After my parents divorced, my mother stayed here and Jill and I went to live with Dad. Now that my mother has passed away, Jill and I have inherited this house that holds most of my fondest memories. There is something so powerful about watching Franny jump off the bottom step the same way I did so many times. This IS where my story began—right here on this front porch. I can't wait to be able to tell her all about it...

"Home Is Where Your Story Begins"

by Jennifer Bester
Somerville, MA
SUPPLIES
Computer fonts: Typist and Carpenter, downloaded from the Internet; Times New Roman, Microsoft Word
Eyelets: Impress Rubber Stamps
Door embellishments: Trimmed from a greeting card by Crane Stationers
Idea to note: The doors open up to reveal individual letters that spell the word "home."

"Our House of Many Colors"

by Alycia Alvarez
Cabot, AR
SUPPLIES
Patterned paper: Paper Adventures
Computer fonts: Lucida Handwriting ("Colors") and Enviro (all other), downloaded from the Internet
Paint-can clip art: Microsoft Picture It!
Other: Paint swatches

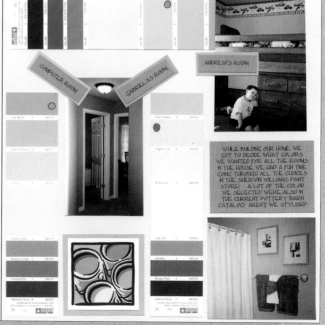

"Siblings"

by Kim Heffington
Avondale, AZ

SUPPLIES

Patterned paper: Scrapbook Wizard
Computer fonts: Dragonfly, downloaded
from *twopeasinabucket.com*; Tempus Sans,
Microsoft Word
Heart punch: EK Success
Idea to note: Kim printed the title
backward and cut it out using an
X-acto knife.

"Cody and Steph"

by Joy Uzarraga
Hinsdale, IL

SUPPLIES

Patterned paper: Making
Memories
Vellum: Paper Accents
Letter stickers: me & my BIG ideas
Letter punches: ABC Punches, EK
Success
Flower punch: Marvy Uchida
Leaf stickers: Stickopotamus

Rubber stamps: Stamps by Judith
Stamping inks: Stamps by Judith;
Ancient Page, Clearsnap, Inc.
Fibers: Cut-It-Up
Eyelets: Doodlebug Design
(round), Stamp Doctor (scalloped)
Tag: DMD Industries
Crocheted appliqués: Freckle
Press
Chalk: Craf-T Products
Pen: Zig Writer, EK Success

"Child of My Child"

by Dee Gallimore-Perry
Griswold, CT

SUPPLIES
Chalk: Craf-T Products
Pen: Zig Millennium, EK Success
Buttons: Hillcreek Design
Computer font: CK Sketch, "The Best of Creative Lettering" CD Vol. 4, *Creating Keepsakes*
Poem: Downloaded from *www.two-peasinabucket.com*

Dee's mother took these photos one day when Dee's son, Brendan, was spending time with his "Mimi and Poppy." "I've always loved these photos," relates Dee, "but they sat in a box for five years while I was waiting for the perfect inspiration. I wanted to create a wonderful keepsake for my parents and son. When I came across the poem 'Child of My Child,' I immediately knew I wanted to use it with these photos."

Child of my child,

Heart of my heart,

Your smile bridges the years between us—

I am young again discovering the world

through your eyes.

You have the time to listen

And I have the time to spend.

Delighted to gaze at familiar,

loved features, made new in you again.

Through you, I'll see the future

Through me, you'll know the past

In the present we'll love one another

As long as these moments last.

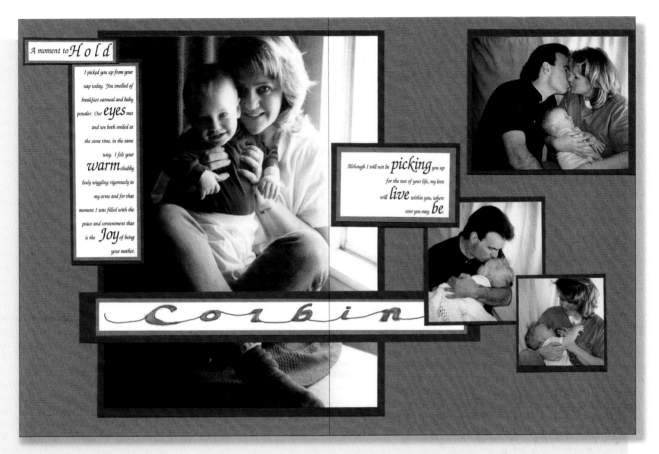

"A Moment to Hold"
by Mechelle Felsted
Flagstaff, AZ

SUPPLIES
Pens: Glitter Gel Pen, American Crafts; Zig Writer, EK Success; Pigma Micron, Sakura
Colored pencils: Prismacolor, Sanford
Computer font: Zapf Chancery, Adobe Systems, Inc.

Mechelle wanted to capture the precious moments shared each day with her son, so she spent a few days recording every smell, touch and look. "I wanted to scrapbook what we experience," shares Mechelle. "The simple tasks of caring for Corbin bring me such joy."

JOURNALING SPOTLIGHT

A MOMENT TO HOLD

I picked you up from your nap today. You smelled of breakfast oatmeal and baby powder. Our eyes met, and we both smiled at the same time, in the same way. I felt your warm, chubby body wriggling vigorously in my arms, and for that moment I was thrilled with the peace and contentment that is the joy of being your mother. Although I will not be picking you up for the rest of your life, my love will live within you, wherever you may be.

"Time"

by Leslie Lightfoot
Stirling, ON, Canada

SUPPLIES

Patterned paper: Scrip Scraps
Vellum: Hot Off The Press
Computer font: Courier New, Microsoft Word
Tags: Source unknown
Letter stickers: me & my BIG ideas
Leaf stickers: Kathy Davis, Colorbök
Eyelets: Impress Rubber Stamps
Other: Checkered fabric

"Time Well Spent"

by Nicole Gartland
Portland, OR

SUPPLIES

Computer fonts: PP_Hips 20s (title) and
Andale Mono (journaling),
downloaded from the Internet
Brads: Premier Grip
Fibers: On the Surface
Stamping ink: Fresco, Stampa Rosa
Pens: Le Plume II, Marvy Uchida;
Pigma Micron, Sakura
Colored pencils: Prismacolor, Sanford
Other: Beads

"Lessons from Granny"

by Jennifer Wohlenberg
Stevenson Ranch, CA
SUPPLIES
Patterned papers: Magenta,
Carolee's Creations
Computer font: Brandywine,
downloaded from the Internet

"Great-Grandfather"

by Kristi Barnes
Bountiful, UT
SUPPLIES
Vellum: The Paper Company
Wood border: Shotz by Danelle Johnson,
Creative Imaginations
Computer fonts: Garamouche, Impress
Rubber Stamps; Spring, Microsoft Word
Chalk and embossing powder: Stampin' Up!
Other: Jute and brads

Lessons from Granny

Granny has always tried to be involved in the lives of her grandchildren in any way she can. Living with Pam and Mike, it's easy to help Mallory with her homework every day. She'll sit with her for hours each night, helping her determine the answers to each question. During her summers living with Coco, she always has a plan to teach Brady something new. She sends weekly letters to Brenna and Allie with stickers and little gifts inside. Even her Alaska girls aren't far from her thoughts. When Granny went up to Alaska in '97, she taught Charli how to read, and worked with her to prepare her for Kindergarten. Though she's too ill to visit Alaska any more, she still tries to make the most of the girls' visits to Las Vegas. While Charli visited this time, Granny spent a great deal of time with her on her journal assignment and other schoolwork. While she appears at times to be a bit of a taskmaster, we think it's more that this is what Granny does best. Though she may not be the type to participate in games of pretend or other childhood silliness, she is a good teacher, and by teaching them, she gives them the longest-lasting gift of all — the gift of knowledge. We know that Mallory and Charli have treasured these times with her, and as the rest of her grandchildren grow, we hope they will come to appreciate them too, because these truly are precious lessons from Granny.   March 16, 2002

As we look to the future as Husband and Wife, we are fortunate to have examples of long-lasting marriages to look to for guidance: Our Parents.
My parents married in 1962 and Tony's parents married in 1970. As in all relationships, some days have been better than others, but the bond that brought them together is stronger than the hard times. Love endures beyond disagreements about finances and child rearing, changing jobs and moving, illness and grief.
Thank you, Mom and Dad, for giving us an example of what it is to marry, to grow, to be committed to one another, to love.

"Kinder-Gardener"

by Cheryl McMurray
Cardston, AB, Canada
SUPPLIES
Patterned paper: Provo
Craft
Sticker letters: Ready-To-
Make, Stickopotamus

Pen: Zig Writer, EK Success
Punches: Darice (mini
flower), EK Success (medium
flower, leaf and hole)
Small envelopes: Impress
Rubber Stamps
Chalk: Craf-T Products

"Grandma's Garden"

by Cindy Knowles
Milwaukie, OR
SUPPLIES
Patterned paper: PrintWorks
Scissors: Mini-Pinking and
Victorian edges, Fiskars
Rectangle punch: Fiskars
Flower enhancements:
O'Scrap!, Imaginations!
(large); Stickopotamus (small)
Computer fonts: DJ Bumble
and DJ Crayon, "Fontastic!"

CD Vol. 1, D.J. Inkers; Scrap
Katie, "Lettering Delights" CD
Vol. 2, Inspire Graphics; First
Grader, Print Artist
Lettering template: Block, ABC
Tracers, Pebbles for
EK Success
Pop dots: Stampa Rosa
Other: Seed packet
Idea to note: Cindy cut the
title from photos of her moth-
er's flower garden.

❋ journaling ideas: Providing Insight Through Association

Spring will always remind my kids of my mother. She has *two* green thumbs and loves to work in the garden (see above). For me, I will forever associate summer with my dad hauling hay in the twilight. When you think of a season or holiday does it remind you of someone special? If so, why not try journaling by association?

Just like word-association games, jour-naling by association can help you make

connections you may not have thought of otherwise. It often results in random memories that will help you capture char-acteristics and moments shared with those you love.

Journaling by association is easy. Take a few minutes and jot down some words that remind you of your topic. Then, sit down with a family member or friend and go through your list, asking him or her to

recall what memories each word evokes. When journaling by association, push your family members to uncover the reasons behind the immediate association.

Let journaling by association help you capture the essence of those you cherish, while providing future generations insight into the lives of those who touched you.

—by Cindy Knowles

"Spring"

by Tracy Kyle
Coquitlam, BC, Canada
SUPPLIES
Patterned paper: Jill Rinner
Vellum tulip: Cut from a Hallmark card
and sprayed with Archival Mist
Computer font: Scriptina, downloaded
from the Internet
Sticker: Flavia, Colorbök
Chalk: Craf-T Products
Idea to note: Tracy sliced a section from
the middle of the sticker so she could
fit the swirls on both ends of the page.

"Blossoms"

by Annie Wheatcraft
Frankfort, KY
SUPPLIES
Vellum: The Paper Company
Tags: American Tag Co.
Computer font: Angelina, downloaded
from the Internet
Brads: Boxer Scrapbook Productions
(small), source unknown (large)
Craft wire: Artistic Wire Ltd.
Chalk: Craf-T Products
Beads: Gick Crafts

Blossoms are scattered by the wind
and the wind cares nothing,
blossoms of the heart no wind can touch.

"Rain"

by Pamela Kopka
New Galilee, PA
SUPPLIES
Vellum: Paper Adventures
Computer font: CK Journaling,
"The Best of Creative
Lettering" CD Vol. 2,
Creating Keepsakes

Lettering template: Block, ABC
Tracers, Pebbles for EK Success
Idea to note: Pamela used an
enlarged copy of her photo
as background paper. She
trimmed the ends of the photo
to fit the 12" x 12" paper.

"Mud Fights"

by Lee Anne Russell
Brownsville, TN
SUPPLIES
Computer fonts: McBooHMK,
"Hallmark Card Studio" CD
Vol. 2, Hallmark; Garamouche,
Impress Rubber Stamps

Punches: The Punch Bunch
(splat), Family Treasures
(square)
Fiber: On the Surface
Buttons: Hillcreek Designs
Chalk: Craf-T Products

Supplies *Textured cardstock:* Bazzill Basics; *Patterned paper:* Paperbilities; *Recipe cards:* Downloaded from *www.cutecolors.com*; *Letter stamps:* Close To My Heart; *Stamping ink:* Archival Ink, Ranger Industries; *Fruit labels:* Downloaded from *www.alteredpages.com*; *Mesh:* Magic Mesh, Avant Card; *Fibers:* Fibers By The Yard; *Buttons:* Making Memories; *Paper clips:* ACCO; *Other:* Charm and pen.

"Taste Tester"

by Maureen Spell
Carlsbad, NM

A baby's first introduction to solid foods is a great photo opportunity. Maureen photographed her daughter sampling a variety of new foods.

◆ Mat photos memorably with collaged papers.

◆ Use baby-food labels as page accents. Or, download the images from a web site, such as *www.alteredpages.com*.

◆ What does your child like to eat? Document it on "Thumbs Up" and "Thumbs Down" lists.

"Sisters"

by Sharon Laakkonen
Savannah, GA

Big sisters can be the best of friends, and Bethany and her brother have a special relationship. Despite the age difference, they make great playmates.

◆ Capture a close relationship on film, then on a layout.

◆ Use buttons, brads or eyelets as punctuation accents.

◆ Enlarge a dramatic photo for visually pleasing effects.

Supplies *Patterned paper:* Karen Foster Design; *Textured cardstock:* Bazzill Basics; *Charm and buttons:* Doodlebug Design; *Lettering template:* Wordsworth; *Fibers:* Adornaments, EK Success; *Other:* Brads and transparency.

baker in training

See how three scrapbookers captured the fun

Baking may be a chore for a mother with a busy schedule, but it's no burden for a "baker in training." As soon as Michele Corbeil of Brooklin, Maine, gets out the mixing bowls, her daughter Mia is right by her side, "ready to crack eggs, sift flour, knead or roll out pie dough."

Michele couldn't resist snapping pictures of a flour-dusted Mia as the two prepared to make crust for a blueberry pie. Although *Creating Keepsakes*

generally asks for three or more photos for this column, we thought it would be helpful to see how top scrapbookers handle a layout when only two photos exist. We gave the pictures in duplicate sizes to Cori Dahmen, Denise Pauley and Anita Matejka.

Check out the resulting layouts that follow, along with the scrapbookers' explanations of why they chose the approaches they did! ❤

"Baking Memories"

by Cori Dahmen
Gresham, OR

SUPPLIES

Patterned paper: Daisy D's and Mustard Moon

Computer fonts: CK Cursive, "The Best of Creative Lettering" CD Combo; CK Fun, "The Art of Creative Lettering" CD, *Creating Keepsakes*

Buttons: Theresa's Hand-Died Buttons

Die cuts: Based on some by Cut-It-Up

Wood paper: Paper Adventures

Embroidery floss: DMC

Other: Spices and small baggies

CORI'S APPROACH

Cori loved Michele's photos and knew she had several good options for a page title. "I went with 'Baking Memories' because of the visual image it evoked," says Cori. "I also liked the way 'Baking Memories' tied in with the photos. Not only were mom and daughter 'baking' blueberry pie, they were creating memories that will be 'baked' into their hearts for a lifetime."

Cori sewed her background pattern to reinforce the image of ties that bind, while her buttons hold the spice bags in place to "further cement that relationship." Adds Cori, "I chose flower-patterned paper and spices to remind the viewer that Mia is a little girl having fun. I included the die cuts to help reiterate the baking feel."

ARTICLE BY ERIN KEMP

"Flour Child"

by Denise Pauley
La Palma, CA

SUPPLIES

Patterned cardstock: Club Scrap
Computer font: Annifont, downloaded from the Internet
Fiber: Rubba Dub Dub, Art Sanctum
Muslin bags: Impress Rubber Stamps
Metal flowers: Making Memories
Brads: American Pin & Fastener
Chalk: Craf-T Products

DENISE'S APPROACH

The photos of Mia are adorable," says Denise. "Because she's such a beautiful child, I chose to design a simple layout to keep the photos the center of attention. Since Mia and the counter are covered in flour, I made flour the 'theme' of the layout and used a play on the words 'flower child.' "

Mia's orange T-shirt and the brown cabinets in the background give the photos a fall feel, so Denise chose a dark color palette that featured harvest-like dark browns, oranges and beige.

To further the flour motif, Denise used small pieces of muslin to create a "flour sack feel." She brushed chalk on the dark surfaces to simulate flour, and incorporated silver flowers to bring out the silver-looking workspace on which Mia is rolling the dough.

"I really loved Michele's journaling and how it captures Mia's early love of baking," notes Denise. "More importantly, it also shares how Mia has such fun making a mess in the kitchen!"

Take a pretty girl, a powdery mess, and you've got the perfect ingredients for a baking layout.

"Mia C.: Baker in Training"

by Anita Matejka
Lincoln, NE

SUPPLIES

Patterned paper: Mustard Moon
Vellum: Karen Foster Design
Pigment ink: Brilliance, Tsukineko
Lacquer: Crystal Lacquer, Sakura
Clip art: Microsoft Clip Gallery
Computer fonts: Tangerine ("Mia C."), Tall Paul
(journaling) and Teen Light ("Baker in Training"),
downloaded from the Internet
Jump rings: Crafts Etc.

ANITA'S APPROACH

Anita wanted to re-create the look of the flour on the table, so she took turquoise vellum and placed it over another paper to match the table in the picture. To make her "sprinkled" flour, Anita sponged and smeared pigment ink on her paper.

"The title 'Baker in Training' inspired me to create a replication of the name badges you see at stores or fast-food restaurants when an employee is being trained," says Anita. She didn't have any black, glossy 12" x 12" paper on hand, so Anita created her own by applying Crystal Lacquer over black cardstock.

"He Has a Leg Up on Us All"

by Lee Anne Russell
Brownsville, TN

SUPPLIES

Patterned paper: Making Memories
Computer font: Yippy Skippy, downloaded from the Internet
Punches: Emagination Crafts (leaf), Family Treasures (square)
Button: Impress Rubber Stamps
Chicken feet: Lee Anne's own design
Embroidery floss: DMC
Pen: Zig Writer, EK Success
Idea to note: Lee Anne designed the layout's background to look like her son's napkin.

page starters: scrapbooking dinner traditions

Fall means the kids are back in school, and with homework, sports and other extra-curricular activities, the family schedule is probably hectic. Amidst all the busyness, it feels good to reconnect around the dinner table with good conversation and your family's favorite comfort foods. Consider creating a layout that captures important aspects of your family life by answering the following questions:

◆ What foods do your kids ask for most often? What is each family member's favorite meal? What sounds good to eat after you've had a rough day? Do you have any recipes you prepare just when the weather is cold outside?

◆ What is your typical mealtime routine? Do your family members take turns cooking? Do you eat early or late? Do you sit together as a family, or is everyone going in different directions at dinnertime?

◆ Who sets the table? Have the dishes been in the family for years? Do the kids like to drink from a special glass? Do you rotate who does cleanup?

◆ Do you pray before meals? Do you say the same prayer at each meal, or is each prayer unique?

◆ What do you talk about over dinner? Do you catch up on what's going on in each other's lives, regroup and plan for the next day, or discuss world events?

—by Julie Turner

"What did we used to say, mom?"

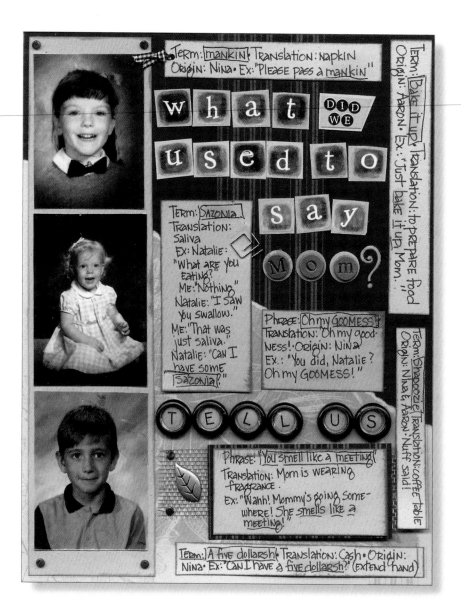

Figure 1. To help you recall the cute things your kids said, scrapbook the words before you forget. *Page by Lynne Rigazio Mau.* **Supplies** *Patterned papers:* Club Scrap; *Eyelet letters, metal eyelet, leaf and square clip:* Making Memories; *Stamping ink:* Ancient Page, Clearsnap; *Letter stickers:* Sonnets; *Rub-ons:* Bradwear, Creative Imaginations; *Mesh:* Scrapworks; *Typewriter stickers:* Nostalgiques by EK Success; *Disks:* Rollabind; *Glaze:* Diamond Glaze, JudiKins.

Cute Quips

Reading "A Good Laugh" (page 7) made me wonder if we realize just how quickly we forget the adorable and precocious things our children say. When I completed a layout on the topic (Figure 1), my husband and I remembered enough additional incidents to create at least three more layouts. Thanks, as always, for the inspiration!

—*Lynne Rigazio Mau*
Channahon, IL

family sayings

Share what's heard around your household

Figure 1. Capture what
you say to your kids to
help you remember
and relive your times
together. *Page by
Denise Pauley.* **Supplies**
Patterned paper: Penny
Black; *Lettering tem-
plate:* Type,
ScrapPagerz.com;
Letter stamps: PSX
Design; *Rubber stamps:*
Rubber Stampede
(large clock), PSX
Design (compass and
heart) and Hero Arts
(small clock and
postage stamp);
Stamping inks:
Clearsnap, Stampin'
Up! and Tsukineko;
Pens: Zig Writer,
EK Success; Slick Writer,
American Crafts; *Chalk:*
Craf-T Products;
Metallic rub-ons:
Craf-T Products;
Craft wire: Making
Memories; *Spiral clips:*
7 Gypsies; *Other:* Shrink
plastic, jewelry pin
and safety pin.

GROWING UP, did your mother ever say some-thing for the umpteenth time, then add, "I sound like a broken record"? (You remember. It was about the time you vowed that if you ever had kids of your own, you would never utter that phrase.) Well, the other day I suddenly realized that I *am* that mother and I am, indeed, that broken record!

With a toddler and a preschooler, I'm over-whelmed with noise. Some are good (infectious giggles, adorable off-key singing, barely intelli-gible but completely cute conversations). Some are not so good (squabbling, whining, and a host of mysterious sounds coming from the refrigerator I suspect will break soon).

In response, I'm constantly lobbing back such phrases as "We *share*," "No, put that back," and the ever-popular "Shh." One day, amidst the chaos, I realized that I repeat three phrases a hundred times a day, and they all

Figure 2. Showcase family phrases alongside family photos to create a meaningful memento. *Pages by Barbara Carroll.* **Supplies** *Computer font:* Garamond, Microsoft Word; *Leaf punch:* EK Success; *Pewter frames:* Making Memories.

hinge on the word "just."

One example is my response to the requests flying at me while I'm on the phone, driving the car or in the bathroom: "Just a minute." Not that it's always effective against "More juice," "Let's watch Dora" and "Open this," but for the one-in-ten times that it works, it's worth it. And though I'm frazzled now, I know the sad day will come when I realize I don't need to say "Just a minute" to my kids anymore. For this reason, I've decided to periodically create a sayings layout to record the different phases of our life together (Figure 1).

What words do you repeat throughout the day? Are they for a purpose, to be silly, or just because you can't get them out of your head? Has your family created its own expressions that you routinely say to one another? Including them on a layout is a wonderful way to capture a piece of family history for future generations to share. Gather inspiration from the following examples, then prepare to notice what phrases commonly float around your household!

Family Familiarity

Over the years, families begin to develop their own language. They use phrases that might not mean much to you and me, but which illustrate their ties and the times the family has shared.

Scrapbooker Barbara Carroll created her "Family Connections" layout in Figure 2 around five sayings that started out small but came to hold special significance for her family.

Record the phrases that have taken on great meaning and will eventually become woven into your family folklore. This is a great way to journal on pages featuring annual family photos.

Meaningful Slang

And then there are cases where family phrases become such common utterances they turn into slang! If you're not a Bangerter, for example, the sayings "What a graxie," "Shred 'em up" and

A picture is worth a thousand words, but sometimes your words are equally important.

Figure 3. When family sayings become slang, it's time to record their meaning for posterity. *Pages by Alisa Bangerter.* **Supplies** *Lettering template:* Wacky Upper, EK Success; *Computer fonts:* CK Constitution and CK Typewriter, "Fresh Fonts" CD, *Creating Keepsakes*; Arial, Microsoft Word; *Stamping ink:* Stampin' Up!; *Adhesive:* Glue Dots International; *Fibers:* On the Surface and Cut-It-Up; *Embroidery floss:* DMC; *Buttons:* Making Memories (large brown) and other. *Idea to note:* To create a textured look for the border, Alisa sponged ink over a piece of mesh ribbon.

"Who needs a goggle?" will probably leave you scratching your head.

Says Alisa, "The phrases are so common in our home that when others ask what we're saying, it takes us a moment to realize that we probably sound really silly at times to those outside our family."

In her "Say What?" layout in Figure 3, scrapbooker Alisa Bangerter reveals not only what these phrases mean, but tells how they came to be. The result is a layout that future generations will see and say, "Oh, that's when that started!" Illustrate your family favorites with photos or create a layout that adopts the style of a dictionary entry!

Other Ideas

Need more help getting started on a "phrases" layout? Focus on each member of your family and think of what you always hear him or her say. Jot the phrase down and explain the meaning behind it or why it suits this person's personality. Or, try brainstorming about one of the following questions to determine what's repeated in your house:

◆ Do you have a favorite movie with memorable lines that you can't help but quote?
◆ Have your children made any cute statements that you constantly repeat?
◆ Does your family have unusual ways to say "hello," "goodbye," "good morning" or "goodnight" to each other?
◆ Do your nicknames for family and friends have humorous or sentimental explanations?

◆ Is there anything you say that your children love to mimic?
◆ What are some inside jokes you have with friends?
◆ Which song lyrics do you constantly sing?
◆ What are some of your teen's most popular expressions?
◆ Have your kids ever mispronounced a word or changed a common phrase that you now say a "new" way?

A picture is worth a thousand words, but sometimes your words are equally important. By taking the time to create a few silly, serious or sentimental layouts that put the spotlight on what your family said, as well as what they did, you can add another dimension to your albums that will be cherished for years to come. ♥

what mom *does while i'm in school*

It's back-to-school time for my kids, which means the whirlwind begins at about 6:45 a.m. It's no easy task getting five boys out of bed, dressed, fed and off to school. (Oops, we forgot to comb the hair!)

As my sons rush out the door, backpacks flying behind them, I realize the real whirlwind is just beginning for me. Each day is usually packed with writing articles, participating in conference calls, doing laundry, volunteering at the school, planning meals, shopping for birthday gifts, driving my children to lessons, responding to e-mails and doing more laundry. Before I know it, those five backpacks are in a pile by the front door and five hungry mouths are asking, "What's there to eat?" (Oh yeah, I forgot to add "make dinner" to the list!) →

What does your mom do when you're at school?
1. Talk on the phone.
2. ...
3. Jumps on the bed.

~ by Deanna Lambson ~

Figure 1. Who wouldn't want to stay home and play all day? A child's expression may be the perfect title for your layout. *Pages by Katherine Brooks.* **Supplies** *Patterned paper:* O'Scrap!, Imaginations!; *Computer fonts:* Problem Secretary, downloaded from the Internet; CK Journaling, "The Best of Creative Lettering" CD Combo, *Creating Keepsakes; Punch:* Family Treasures; *Chalk:* Craf-T Products; *Button:* Hillcreek Designs; *Fibers:* Rubba Dub Dub; *Stamping ink:* VersaMark, Tsukineko; *Craft wire:* Artistic Wire Ltd.; *Eyelets:* Impress Rubber Stamps; *Rubber stamp:* Stamp Antonio; *Lettering templates:* ScrapPagerz.com; *Tags:* Katherine's own design; *Other:* Jute.

I was delighted when my kindergartner came home from school recently with a creative essay on "What Mom Does While I'm in School." I smiled. I couldn't wait to see what he had written.

Wait a minute! Mom talks on the phone? Jumps on the bed? Plays Nintendo? I don't know *where* he got those ideas. I rarely even pick up the phone, and I haven't jumped on the bed for at least a week. (I bumped my head last time.)

If you haven't asked your kids what they think you do all day, you may be in for a surprise! But whether their responses are on target or way out in left field, you'll get a glimpse into the personalities of your children. You might even get ideas for activities on those "long, boring" days!

6 Fun Approaches

Think the theme is fun but not sure where to begin? Consider the following approaches:

1. **Use your child's comment as the title for your layout.** Katherine Brooks of Gilbert, Arizona, works as a professional childcare provider. One day, as her five-year-old daughter, Meghan, walked out the door to school, she turned and said, "I don't want to go to school. I want to stay home and play with the babies like you, Mom!"

Katherine had to laugh. "Meghan was convinced that my days consist of playing 'Ring Around the Rosies,' singing baby songs and eating picnic lunches out in the grass. While I do some of those things, she doesn't see the bottles, the diapers or the crying. Taking care of my son Matt and three other children each day can get pretty hectic!"

Katherine came up with a layout that gives Meghan and others a more realistic view of her day (see Figure 1). The layout includes custom "Let's Play . . ." tags with messages that say it all:

- Let's Play . . . "Time to pick up the toys"
- Let's Play . . . "Who can cry the loudest?"
- Let's Play . . . "What's that smell?"

Figure 2. Once a year is "Mother's Day," but every day is "Mom's Day." Record the perspective of each of your children in a handy vellum envelope. *Page by Cori Dahmen.* **Supplies** *Computer fonts:* Libby Script, downloaded from the Internet; CK Handprint and CK Script, "The Best of Creative Lettering" CD Combo, *Creating Keepsakes; Lettering template:* Grade School, ScrapPagerz.com; *Vellum:* Close To My Heart; *Pen:* Zig Millennium, EK Success. *Idea to note:* Cori made each vellum pocket by folding the paper into an open-ended envelope and using a large circle punch for the half circle.

To make mini notebook paper like that used on Cori's layout, follow five quick steps:

1. Print your list from the computer onto plain white cardstock.

2. Use a ruler and a .01 tipped blue pen to make horizontal lines.

3. Make the wider vertical line along the left margin with a .08 red pen.

4. Use a mini hole punch to make the three holes along the left side of the page.

5. To create larger notebook paper, simply substitute wider pen tips and a larger hole punch.

Figure 3. Try writing out your to-do list for a typical week. You may need several sheets of paper! *Pages by Cindy Knowles.* **Supplies** *Patterned paper:* Making Memories (background), Lasting Impressions for Paper (maroon dots); *Letter stickers:* Colorbök and Stickopotamus; *Pen:* Pigma Micron, Sakura; *Computer fonts:* Garamouche, P22 Type Foundry; PC Goofy, "Poems for Posterity" HugWare CD, Provo Craft; *School, heart and to-do list:* Cindy's own designs; *Pop dots:* Stampa Rosa; *Chalk:* Craf-T Products; *Craft wire:* Artistic Wire Ltd.; *Other:* Vellum envelope. *Idea to note:* Cindy created her torn heart enhancement, then scanned and resized it to use alongside her captions.

Figure 4. Use simple lift-up photo cards to record the responses of your own child and his or her friends. *Page by Allison Strine.* **Supplies** *Patterned paper for blue background:* Paper Patch; *Paper raffia and buttons:* Making Memories; *Stamping ink for journaling-box accents:* Colorbox, Clearsnap; *Fibers:* Filatura Di Crosa; *Computer fonts:* CAC Krazy Legs (journaling) and Hecubus (title and child journaling), downloaded from the Internet; *Pop dots:* All Night Media. *Idea to note:* For a fun "handle" on a flip-up page element, use buttons, either single or stacked.
Photo tip: While your little child is wearing her huge backpack, ask her to stand backward or sideways and turn her head toward you for the photo. You'll capture her facial expressions and her backpack in one shot.

• Let's Play . . . "Quiet time"
• Let's Play . . . "Time to clean the bottles"

While creating her tags, Katherine chalked the edges and created faint daisy watermarks with a flower stamp and an inkpad. "Every time I look at this layout," says Katherine, "I remember how blessed I am to be there for these children and my own."

2. Have a friend interview your children. Cori Dahmen of Gresham, Oregon, asked a friend to talk to Cori's children about what she does at home and at work (see Figure 2). "I'm not sure my kids learned anything," says Cori, "but I sure did. Amy thinks I have to talk to really annoying people, and Timmy's sure I make cookies while they're gone so they're not in my way in the kitchen!" Cori slipped each child's response sideways into a vellum pocket. Each card can be removed by pulling it to the left.

Little do Cori's children know her fantasy to-do list. As noted on the layout, it includes:
• Sleep in
• Go out for a mocha
• Chat on the computer
• Read tabloid magazines
• Get a manicure
• "Do" lunch
• Lounge in a bubble bath
• Watch talk shows
• Eat bon-bons
• Have hair done
• Get a massage
• Go shopping
• Give the maid her chores
• Play tennis
• Plan tomorrow's activities

3. Tell it like it really is. When Cindy Knowles of Milwaukie, Oregon, wrote her actual to-do list for a typical week, it numbered over 150 items and was 15 feet long! She created a scrapbook spread (Figure 3) to document a very important part of her life—volunteering. At the elementary school, Cindy has spent thousands of hours doing everything from creating flyers to teaching computer lessons to compiling the school yearbook.

"Contrary to what my son Taggart thinks," says Cindy, "I volunteer because I love kids. My own four children are at the top of my neverending to-do list. Volunteering at their school is one way to help make a difference in their lives."

When creating her layout, Cindy included samples of the many newsletters and flyers she's done for the school over the years. She reduced them to 40 percent of their original size and inserted them in a vellum envelope.

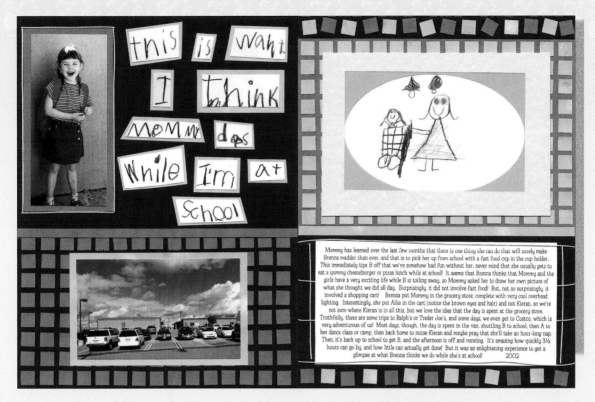

Figure 5. Many times a child can express himself or herself better through a drawing than through words. Ask for a picture! *Pages by Jennifer Wohlenberg.* **Supplies** *Patterned paper:* Karen Foster Design; *Computer font:* CAC One Seventy, downloaded from the Internet; *Colored pencils:* Prismacolor, Sanford; *Other:* Mizuhiki cord, Wonder Tape by Suze Weinberg and Hermafix Tabs.

4. **Ask your kids yourself.** "One day, my daughter Olivia told me her dad just looks at pictures of her all day and talks to his friends," says Allison Strine of Atlanta, Georgia. "After that, I couldn't help but wonder what she thought I did each day. So I asked! Her answer? Shop for scrapbooking stuff. Scan in layouts. . . . Sheesh! It sure bugs me when a four year old is right on target!"

Allison thought parents of other little friends in the neighborhood might be equally entertained by their child's perspective. So, whenever a child came over to play, Allison asked two questions: "Why do you go to school?" and "What does your mom do while you're at school?"

Allison's layout (Figure 4) includes the children's responses inside of four small photo cards at the bottom of the page. Two buttons are affixed to the lower edge of each photo with glue dots to create a mini handle. Allison changed the friend photos to black and white to maintain continuity and avoid the distraction of color.

5. **Have your child draw a picture.** When Jennifer Wohlenberg of Stevenson Ranch, California, tries to get a response from her six-year-old daughter, Brenna

generally answers, "I don't know." To get a better response, Jennifer asks Brenna to draw a picture.

When Jennifer asked Brenna to draw a picture of what Mom does while she's in school, Brenna emerged with a detailed drawing of Mom pushing a shopping cart in the grocery store. She even matted the drawing herself! (see Figure 5)

"I like to use symbolism in my scrapbook pages," explains Jennifer. "The colored blocks laid in a predictable mosaic pattern represent the organized schedule of my day. The tipped blocks along the top and bottom of the page symbolize the crazy, mixed-up way the day often turns out!"

A quick photo tip from Jennifer? "To capture Brenna with a less posed look, I ask her to tell me a joke. She always starts laughing."

6. **Incorporate thought bubbles and vellum "clouds."** When Shannon Watt of Van Nuys, California, told five-year-old Hannah they'd be running errands after school, her daughter was terribly disappointed. "Can't you do that while I'm at school?" she complained.

Annoyed, Shannon began listing everything she had to do in a day, then suddenly realized that her daughter

Figure 6. Hmm, what could she be thinking? Thought bubbles and vellum "clouds" help viewers read a photo subject's mind. *Page by Shannon Watt.* **Supplies** *Patterned paper:* Sonburn; *Mulberry paper:* Paper Adventures; *Brads:* Deco Fasteners; *Vellum:* Making Memories; *Circle punch:* Family Treasures; *Computer fonts:* American Typewriter and CAC Leslie, downloaded from the Internet; CK Handprint, "The Best of Creative Lettering" CD Combo, *Creating Keepsakes; Stamping ink:* ColorBox, Clearsnap.

had no idea. So she decided to create a page to capture her daughter's perspective (Figure 6). Note how Shannon punched small thought bubbles from vellum and placed them on her page, leading from Hannah's head to the vellum "clouds" above.

A quick photo tip from Shannon? "To capture this uninhibited photo of Hannah, I began talking to her about various subjects. I asked rapid-fire questions, then snapped her expressions as she responded. It was one of the most 'true to life' photo shoots I've ever done!"

So, what do YOU do while your kids are in school? Do you manage a busy department? Pay bills? Scrapbook? (dumb question) Whatever is on your to-do list today, here's another suggestion. Ask your kids what they think you do while they're away and include their responses in your scrapbook. I'm going to do it myself—as soon as I finish this last game of Super Mario. I've just got a few minutes before the boys get home! ❤

"But i'm not a Mom"

You don't have to be a mother to use these ideas! The concept is simply to take others' perceptions and contrast them with reality. Consider these variations:

• Ask your spouse, your parents, a sibling or a friend "What do I do at work?" While some job responsibilities are easily understood, others are obviously not! Give Approach #2 or #3 a try.

• Ask a niece or nephew what they think you do for fun. Adapt Approach #5 or #6.

• Ask people what they think your typical day includes. Put their most interesting or revealing answers on lift-up cards you position on your layout. Add a few of your own if you'd like to be creative! Include a "yes" or "no" under each card.

A mother's love cannot be measured. My mom looks back and sees many things she would do over or run differently. I look at her with absolute admiration. I didn't fully understand what kept her going through all of the hard times. She would have sacrificed everything and probably still would for her children. I now know what that feels like. I am soo blessed, to have such a wonderful woman be my mom. I have the BEST mom in the whole world. Regardless of what she would say, she did the best she knew how and did a great job. And I love her all the more for it.

November 1979

Supplies *Patterned paper, tape measure and sticker:* Life's Journey, K & Company; *Vellum:* The Paper Company; *Metal letters and word eyelet:* Making Memories; *Nailheads:* Prym-Dritz; *Acrylic paint:* Delta Technical Coatings; *Pen:* Zig Writer, EK Success; *Watch parts:* 7 Gypsies; *Watch crystal:* Scrapworks; *Computer font:* CK Constitution, "Fresh Fonts" CD, *Creating Keepsakes;* *Stamping ink and chalk:* Stampin' Up!; *Other:* Cheesecloth.

"Love Beyond Measure"

by Ashley Gull
Farmington, CT

Ashley and her mom sat at the kitchen table to reminisce over happy memories and their special relationship.

◆ Don't limit your die-cut letters to just that letter. Ashley turned a "V" upside down to create the "A" in her title. She intentionally punched the "M" backwards.

◆ How do you measure love? Add a tape measure as a symbolic accent.

◆ Memorialize the passage of time with watch pieces on your layout.

◆ Create an aged, leather-like look by crinkling cardstock, then rubbing it with chalks and inks.

memories of Mom

Capture her *personality* on your pages

As a youngster, I was constantly told, "You're so lucky—you've got a great mother." While I loved my mom, the *only* things I felt stood out were Mom's prematurely gray hair ("Is that your grandma?" kids would ask at school), my super-early curfew each night, and a mom who always seemed to be helping at school.

As I got older, I understood people's comments a little more. My mom would never go to bed until all her children were safely home. She always had bread or cookies baking when we got home from school. When I got a bad grade on a test, Mom would give me a big hug and say how proud she was that I always gave my best effort.

Now that I'm a mother, I *really* know what people were talking about. I truly appreciate how wonderful my mother is. She's cried with me through the hard times, encouraged me to reach my highest potential in all that I do, and laughed with me at all the dumb mistakes I make. She's never grown tired of parenting and always does her best. Yes, I have one terrific mother.

Have you told your mother lately that you love her? Have you scrapbooked the qualities you admire most in her? The following pages will encourage you to dig out your mom's old photos and share with others the legacy your mother has left or is leaving you.

by Lisa Bearnson

I remember reading the statistics on children of single parent households. They were discouraging to say the least. Children of single mothers were more likely to suffer from emotional instability, to perform lower on academic tests, and were more likely to encounter behavioral problems. My future, according to the numbers, was not promising.
I was 23 when I gave birth to my first child, a baby girl. I was unmarried and terrified. But there was a part of me that wa eager and determined to make sure those statistics would no apply to the child I raised.
My daughter and I spent the next six years alone. There were struggles and sacrifices, heartaches and many long nights. But I discovered that loving another human being so deeply and selflessly gave me the courage to overcome just about anything. And we did.
My daughter is now a beautiful 12 year old, and a living example that statistics don't have to be right. She is kind hearted, studious, and is the most respectful, well mannered adolescent I know. And although I am constantly second guessing myself, as most mothers do, I look at her and know that somewhere along the way, I have done something right.
I have been blissfully married for the last six years, and am fortunate enough to have experienced the miracle of childbirth yet again with my son. I take great pride in being a wife and mother of two. But among my greatest accomplishments are those six years I spent as a single mother. When life was full of unexpected turns, and a few statistics determined the course of my future. It is because of those six years that I wake up every morning and truly appreciate the blessings in my life; that I am able to experience love and joy and true happiness without reservation. I find strength even in the memory of it. It is a stepping stone to who I have become, a reminder of where I have been.
And I have no regrets.
6 YEARS

"6 Years"

BY MELLETTE BEREZOSKI • CROSBY, TX

Be "real" in your scrapbooks. Describe the joys and obstacles of motherhood. Mellette tells about the struggles, sacrifices and satisfaction of being a single mom for six years.

Motherhood has many challenges. Don't forget to include the good times as well as the learning experiences.

Page by Mellette Berezoski. **Supplies** *Patterned papers:* Anna Griffin, Deluxe Designs, K & Company, Pebbles Inc., Sweetwater and Two Busy Moms; *Twill tape:* Magic Scraps; *Alphabet stamps:* PSX Design; *Buttons:* Junkitz; *Number sticker:* Creative Imaginations; *Key charm:* Lone Star Charms; *Computer font:* Times New Roman, Microsoft Word; *Other:* Ribbon.

"Definitions of a Mom"

BY KYRA HARRIS • PHOENIX, AZ

Surprise your mom on Mother's Day with a page of definitions you've made up about her. Keep the definitions personal and reflective of experiences the two of you have shared. For example, Kyra's definition 15 says, "Doer of many loads of laundry for poor college students, a.k.a. her daughters."

Two other definitions I loved? "A woman whose inner child is still very much alive" and "The adult who said that scrubbing the bathroom and eating broccoli would build character." Note how Kyra included the following synonyms at the end of her journaling: terrific, generous, beautiful, amazing, dazzling, caring and wonderful.

Write your own dictionary definitions of a mom.

Page by Kyra Harris. **Supplies** *Jute:* May Arts; *Computer font:* Times New Roman, Microsoft Word; *Charm:* Designs by Pamela.

moth•er (mʌðɚ) **1.** *n.* my female parent **2.** *n.* an excellent role model who has provided her two daughters with a deep appreciation of love for family **3.** *n.* a woman whose face reveals years of joy and happiness apparent with every smile **4.** *adj.* maker of the world's most succulent macaroni sauce **5.** *n.* a woman whose rough hands from years of hard work and sacrifice still provide gentle touches that reassure me that everything will work out for the best **6.** *n.* a determined and strong-willed female who expects only the best from herself and from her family **7.** *n.* a comic who has perfected about 23 different kinds of laughs **8.** *n.* an artist who provided me with my first sets of fingerpaints and Crayola markers so I could make my own world as colorful as I wanted it to be **9.** *n.* a woman whose inner child is still very much alive **10.** *n.* the person who taught me about my individuality **11.** *n.* the adult who said that scrubbing the bathroom and eating broccoli would build character **12.** *adj.* mesmerizing **13.** *n.* the one I could count on for moral support and confidence during my years of braces and acne **14.** *n.* partner in a thirty-two year marriage **15.** *n.* doer of many loads of laundry for poor college students aka her daughters **16.** *adj.* supportive as I attempted my hand as an entrepreneur and tried to sell T-shirts covered with fabric paint and ribbons and earrings made of paper **17.** *n.* believer and follower of family traditions **18.** *v.* to never miss an opportunity to tell me how proud she is of me **19.** *n.* provider of unconditional love **20.** *n.* someone who radiates style and grace **21.** *n.* one-of-a-kind ‖ **synonyms:** terrific, generous, beautiful, amazing, dazzling, caring and wonderful
carla harris • june 2002

"The Smell of Cinnamon"

BY SUSAN CYRUS • BROKEN ARROW, OK

It is impossible to reminisce about my mother without also remembering her cinnamon rolls.

Cinnamon roll day was an *event* at our house. Mom started measuring the ingredients the night before so that she could get an early start on baking day. By midday, there would be dough rising in every warm location in the house. And for dinner that night, a delicious pan of dinner rolls, fresh from the oven.

But the cinnamon rolls were the best. She must have at least tripled the recipe to make that many pans at one time, and it always came as a surprise and a disappointment to discover that only one or two were actually for us; Mom always had plans for the rest. Lucky friends received them at Christmastime or as thank you gifts. And when Mom donated them for school auctions, one pan would sell for up to $40.

In the minutes after her accident, Bill and I sat on the bumper of the pickup while Dad called for help. I can still hear Bill asking, "What about the cinnamon rolls?"

He was 14. I was 19.

They were mentioned during the homily at her funeral mass.

Beverly Odum once told me that she actually has Mom's recipe. She tried to make them once, but Elizabeth nearly chipped a tooth on the results.

At times I have been tempted to ask for a copy and give it a go myself. But I imagine it would be an exercise in futility.

I'm sure it's just one of those recipes that only tastes right when it's made by Mom.

The smell of cinnamon

Do you associate a certain smell with your mother? Perhaps it's lilac-scented perfume. Maybe it's freshly turned dirt from her vegetable garden. For Susan, it's the smell of freshly baked cinnamon rolls.

Reminisces Susan, "Cinnamon roll day was an event at our house. Mom started measuring the ingredients the night before so she could get an early start on baking day. By midday there would be dough rising in every warm location in the house…. Lucky friends received the rolls at Christmastime or as thank-you gifts. When Mom donated them for school auctions, one pan would sell for up to $40."

Don't forget to capture the smells that you associate with mom.

Pages by Susan Cyrus. **Supplies** *Patterned papers:* 7 Gypsies; *Computer fonts:* Dorchester Script (title) and Minion (journaling), downloaded from the Internet; *Heart clip:* Making Memories; *Stamping ink:* Rubber Stampede; *Other:* Ribbon.

Idea to note: Create "cinnamon sticks" from rolled cardstock.

"Being a full-time mother is one of the highest salaried jobs in my field, since the payment is *pure love*."

— Mildred B. Vermont

"The phrase *working mother* is redundant."

— Jane Sellman

"Mother in the Making"

BY JENNIFER GALLACHER • SAVANNAH, GA

Jennifer had always wanted to be a mom, but when it happened she found herself feeling a bit inadequate. In the layout here, she shares the doubts she faced, followed by the realization that motherhood is a process and she's growing and moving forward. Jennifer confides how she's a "mother in the making" and hopes she is showing her daughter what a good mother can be.

Record your thoughts and feelings about motherhood.

Pages by Jennifer Gallacher, photo by Becky Thaden Photography.
Supplies *Patterned paper:* K & Company; *Small snaps and square frame:* Making Memories; *Ribbon:* C.M. Offray & Son; *Title letters, music paper and bookplate:* Li'l Davis Designs; *Letter stamps:* PSX Design; *Stamping ink:* Memories, Stewart Superior Corp.; *Chalk:* Craf-T Products; *Walnut ink:* 7 Gypsies; *Computer font:* CK Fraternity, Becky Higgins' "Clips and Fonts" CD, *Creating Keepsakes; Other:* Corkboard, textured paper, buttons and leather fiber.

Idea to note: Place cork inside a metal frame to add dimension.

create a *"helping hands"* album

I love looking at my mother's hands. The wrinkles and age spots represent so much sacrifice, service and simplicity throughout her life. I want to remember them forever and the sweetness they represent in my life.

I took a picture of my mother's hands and have created a small album with pictures and quotes that represent how my mother's hands have helped me over the years. The inside cover and coordinating page numbers describe the significance of each page. I can't wait to give the album to Mom on Mother's Day!

A mini album is a simple yet effective way to celebrate your mother. Note the "mother's hands" theme here.

Album by Lisa Bearnson. **Supplies** *Mini album and pages:* Perspectives, Making Memories; *Vellum quotes:* Memories Complete; *Ribbon and charm:* Making Memories; *Computer font:* Univers, Microsoft Word; *Alphabet charms:* KI Memories; *Label stickers:* Pebbles Inc.

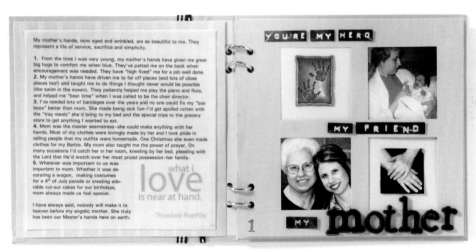

Your "mom" doesn't have to be a blood relative. Think outside the box—who were the other "moms" who helped raise you? They could have been people like a teacher, a spiritual leader or a friend's mother. Here, Lanna pays tribute to her many "moms." She includes personal journaling in envelopes she's attached to the layout.

Acknowledge other "mothers" who were also influential in raising you.

Pages by Lanna Carter. **Supplies** *Patterned papers:* Mustard Moon; *Vellum:* Provo Craft; *Die cuts:* Sonja, QuicKutz; *Nailheads and treble clef charm:* Jest Charming; *Buttons and brads:* Karen Foster Design; *Eyelets:* Creative Impressions (blue) and Chatterbox (white snaps); *Stamping ink:* Rubber Stampede; *Rubber stamp:* Hero Arts; *Library card and vellum envelope:* Lanna's own designs; *Fibers:* Fiber Scraps; *Tag templates:* Paper Pizazz; *Embroidery floss:* DMC; *Pen:* Pigma Micron, Sakura; *Other:* Hot glue stick, ribbon and charm.

Ideas to note: Lanna heated a hot glue stick, let it cool partially, then stamped it. She clipped the nailheads off the treble clef to create the charm.

("I remember *my mother's prayers* and they have always followed me. They have clung to me all my life.")

— Abraham Lincoln

"A Mother's Labor of Love"

BY ANGIE CRAMER • REDCLIFF, AB, CANADA

Choose one chore that binds three generations (you, your mother and grandmother). This will help you remember that some things never change! Angie found a photo of her grandmother in 1956, sitting on her front porch under a clothesline. A 1962 photo reveals a photo of Angie as a two year old, sitting in the snow with her mother's clothesline behind her. The large photo shows Angie's clothesline today.

Remember that some things never change—like chores!

Page by Angie Cramer. **Supplies** *Buttons, metal heart and tags:* Making Memories; *Letters:* Bradwear, Creative Imaginations; *Computer font:* Times New Roman, Microsoft Word; *Checkerboard stamp:* Art Gone Wild.

"Lessons Learned"

BY HEATHER MELZER • YORKVILLE, IL

Did Mom teach you to work hard through her example? Heather's mom showed how to be strong and independent, even while going through a divorce, raising three children and working a full-time job.

Describe the lessons learned from both Mom's mistakes and achievements.

Page by Heather Melzer. **Supplies** *Patterned paper:* Chatterbox; *Computer fonts:* P22 Cezanne Regular, P22 Type Foundry; Casablanca Antique and Day Roman, downloaded from the Internet; *Other:* Raffia, chiffon ribbon and heart charm.

"Beauty, Love & Respect"

BY ALLISON KIMBALL • SALT LAKE CITY, UT

Despite hardship, Allison's mother taught her to see past a person's exterior and look on the heart. Her mom's philosophy? Treat others with love and respect. Allison pays tribute to her mother's selflessness with pages that praise her example.

Share how your mother taught you to treat others with kindness and respect.

Pages by Allison Kimball. **Supplies** *Patterned paper:* Laura Ashley, EK Success; *Washer and heart:* Making Memories; *Letter stickers:* Chatterbox, me & my BIG ideas and Wordsworth; *Embossing powder and chalk:* Close To My Heart; *Transparency:* Pockets on a Roll, F & M Enterprises; *Brads:* HyGlo, American Pen & Fastener; *Other:* Ribbon and jewelry tags.

(*"sweater, n.:* garment worn by a child when its mother is feeling chilly.")

— Ambrose Bierce

"A suburban mother's role is to deliver children obstetrically once, and by car forever after."

— Peter De Vries

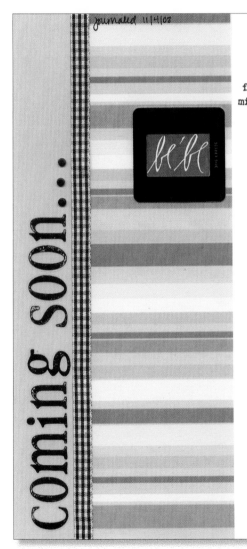

"Coming Soon... You"

BY AMY GRENDELL • SILVERDALE, WA

Looking forward, pregnancy seems like an eternity. Looking backward, only a fleeting moment. While the baby's still inside, write the words and phrases that describe your experience. Once the baby's here, you'll likely forget the heartburn, achy back and sleepless nights. Capture the memories like Amy did!

Write the words that describe your pregnancy. Remember, you don't always need photos to create a stunning page.

Page by Amy Grendell. **Supplies** *Patterned paper: Chatterbox; Letter stickers: me & my BIG ideas; Computer font: 2Peas Hot Chocolate, downloaded from www.twopeasinabucket.com.*

THE BEST FATHER'S DAY GIFT EVER

Pay tribute to an unsung hero

MY FAVORITE GIFT FROM MY FATHER? A star sapphire ring. If you wear it in everyday light, the stone shines a subdued brown. Hold it under direct light, and a brilliant star appears on the surface. I'm reminded of the power of light and hope.

The ring is a reminder of an even greater gift: how my father's life has touched my own. When I think of Dad, I think of his kindness and patience. I think of his "experience life to its fullest" attitude. I think of his support. He's a hero of mine, too often unsung.

Is a father in your life (either your own or your husband) an unsung hero, too? It's time to sing his praises. This Father's Day, surprise a truly great father with a tribute album or page that acknowledges how much he means to you and others. (We've included ideas to get you started.) It'll be his best Father's Day gift yet!

BY JANA LILLIE

"Definition of a Father"

BY JENNIFER DITZ (MCGUIRE)
CINCINNATI, OH

Supplies *Album:* K & Company (Jennifer decoupaged the cover with Perfect Paper Adhesive from USArtQuest and Sonnets paper from Creative Imaginations); *Papers:* Creative Imaginations and K & Company; *Stickers:* Sonnets and Mary Engelbreit, Creative Imaginations; *Rubber stamps:* All Night Media, Magenta and Uptown Design; *Embossing powders:* The Powder Keg (to bronze top layer); Ultra Thick Embossing Enamel, Suze Weinberg; *Computer font:* 2Peas Flea Market, downloaded from *www.twopeasinabucket.com. Idea to note:* Jennifer sponged brown ink over the paper for an aged look.

JENNIFER'S THOUGHTS

"After 35 years at General Electric, my dad retired on January 30, 2003. I knew I wanted to create a special album as a gift, but was unsure how to approach it. At his retirement party, I realized what my approach should be.

"Many of my dad's friends and colleagues spoke of his incredible qualities, such as generosity, intelligence, humor and devotion. The qualities that helped him be an excellent boss and friend also helped him be the best father. I decided to create a 'The Definition of a Father' album to highlight these qualities."

WHAT SHE WANTED THE ALBUM TO INCLUDE:

"I wanted to make the album a 'wonderland of photos and memories,' so I looked through old photos and found several special ones. Many weren't the best quality, but I wanted to include them anyway. I knew that as my dad flipped through the pages, he would be smiling at the photos and the memories behind them.

"I had my entire family help with this surprise gift. My mom helped pull together the photos, while my brother, Mike, and my fiancé, Ken, wrote some of their favorite memories. We all signed the first page of the album, making it even more personal."

WHY SHE CHOSE THE LOOK SHE DID:

"I wanted the overall look to be one that would appeal to my dad. Dad has collected gorgeous Rockwood pottery for many years, and his favorite pieces contain soft golds, blues and greens. I chose these colors to carry through the album.

"The rich yet soft colors of the paper lines I chose fit my needs perfectly, and they blended together nicely with the various stitched patterns. (Using a sewing machine to create unique stitches is a fast way to add class to a layout.) I added several embossing-enamel pieces with impressed stamped images for rich, unique embellishments. They reminded me of the bronze highlighting on many of my father's favorite Rockwood pottery pieces."

"10 Reasons I Love My Dad"

BY LISA BROWN
OAKLAND, CA

Supplies *Handmade paper:* The Art Store; *Fibers:* Rubba Dub Dub, Art Sanctum; *Pen:* Zig Writer, EK Success; *3-D white numbers:* Colorbök; *Letter stamps:* PSX Design; *Stamping ink:* Stampin' Up!.

LISA'S THOUGHTS

"My dad is a very special and important person in my life. His being a single parent to two girls has not always been easy, but he has always risen to the challenge. I made this album to give him as a thank-you for being such a great dad."

WHAT SHE WANTED THE ALBUM TO INCLUDE:

"My dad has a lot of characteristics that I love, and I wanted to showcase them in this album. I focused on 10 words that describe things I admire about him: friend, listen, duty, giving, funny, help, advice, time, travel and love.

"Finding pictures of my dad was challenging since he hates having his picture taken. I used pictures from various stages of his life and made copies in black and white to unify the album."

WHY SHE CHOSE THE LOOK SHE DID:

"Each page has a photo of my dad that flips up to reveal the journaling underneath. Each page also contains a single-word title that sums up one thing I love about him. It's the focus for the journaling beneath the photo.

"To create each page, I wet a piece of handmade paper, then tore it down to the size I wanted. I then stamped the title while the paper was still wet. This caused the ink to run slightly and gave it a worn, aged look. To create the background for my cover, I printed the title word repeatedly on a piece of white cardstock. I hand bound the album myself. The finished size is 7½" x 8½".

"By coming up with a page format I could use throughout the album for uniformity, I was able to create the album very quickly. The whole thing was completed in two evenings after work."

See More by Allison and Lisa

Love the artistry of Allison Strine and Lisa Brown? Innovative layouts and ideas by Allison Strine, Lisa Brown, Shannon Jones and Darcee Thompson are showcased in the CK book, *Scrapbooking with Style*. More than 200 page-layout ideas and step-by-step techniques. 164 pages. $14.95.

"My Dad, My Treasure"

BY ALLISON STRINE
ATLANTA, GA

Supplies *Album:* Canson; *Papers:* SEI; *Fibers:* On the Surface; *Pen:* Milky Lunar, Pentel; *Stickers, bradwear and metal heart frame:* Creative Imaginations; *Rubber stamps:* Juiciness (Kodachrome slide), Wordsworth (alphabet), Junque (smaller alpha) and Hero Arts (shadow square); textures by Junque, Planet Rubber, Stamp Oasis and Above the Mark; *Embossing powder:* Ranger Industries; *Numbers:* Making Memories; *Computer font:* 2Peas Flea Market, downloaded from *www.twopeasinabucket.com*; *Other:* Mesh. *Idea to note:* Allison created the cover by blending two colors of Sculpey polymer clay by Polyform, then flattening it and embedding foil by Amy's Magic Flakes. After curing the clay, she added prepared papers and ink by Krylon.

ALLISON'S THOUGHTS

"My dad and I shared a very rocky relationship for much of our lives. When I was a teenager, we butted heads more often than not. Today, as an adult and a parent myself, I have a much deeper realization of the complicated man my dad is. I created this album to celebrate the life lessons Dad has taught me.

"Interestingly, as I was working on this project, I noticed a very real shift in the depth of my understanding of my father. Carefully putting my loving thoughts on paper helped to solidify them. I couldn't help but crack a smile as I finished each page, imagining the reaction I knew he'd have. Big, strong dad would weep some big, soft tears!"

WHAT SHE WANTED THE ALBUM TO INCLUDE:

"I wanted to express my appreciation of Dad's many sides: his love of the land, his determination (okay, stubborn streak), and his thirst for knowledge.

"Fortunately, my father and I frequently exchange photographs over the Internet, and I was able to secretly request that he send me some favorites. For a guy whose lifelong love is photography, Dad appears in relatively few of his images. Noticing this has motivated me to get in front of the camera more often. My kids deserve it!"

WHY SHE CHOSE THE LOOK SHE DID:

"When you hold the album cover at different angles to the light, unique features of the design are highlighted. That's pretty much the way I see my dad: he's a complex guy who shows contrasting aspects of his personality at different times to different people.

"For the inside pages, I wanted a masculine, richly textured look, to represent the way I see my father. The shapes and colors in the papers worked well with the subtle yet strong mesh and fiber accents.

"Once I'd designed the format of the book, I created it in an assembly-line style. Even so, I was surprised at how quickly the album came together."

A TrIBUTe tO DAd

father's day 2003

LESSON THREE

Memories Matter.

Daddy, you have been behind a camera for longer than I've been alive. I remember being so frustrated as a kid, waiting impatiently for you to finish taking the darn picture so I could move on. At that time, I had no idea just how important and valuable those photographs would become to me. Now, as I look through my lens at Olivia impatiently rolling her eyes at me, I can't help but think of you with understanding and a little extra love.

Thanksgiving, 2001   Family Party

LESSON FOUR

Show a little love.

Dad, I love this picture of you and Ethan. You both look truly happy and relaxed. It makes me wish we didn't live a thousand miles away. Olivia frequently talks about how much she misses you, and that she wishes you lived in our house. I love to see you around the kids – you remind me of the way Grampa was with me when I was little.

Palm Beach, Florida, 2002

LESSON ONE
Don't Give Up

Daddy, when I look at this photograph I see someone I respect very much. I see a man who refuses to let his body win out over his mind. You have successfully battled leukemia, cancer and heart bypass surgery. And here you are, riding your bike again, just like you did before you got sick. You don't quit and I love you for it.

LESSON NINE
Think Big

Dad, you look awfully comfortable at the wheel here! It was always so exciting when you went down to the VI's. I was so proud to have a dad who was hip enough to go on weeklong sailing trips. It impressed the heck out of me that you, Teddy and Donald took gambles on property in the islands. Being a land owner sounded so cool, and even if it didn't pan out for the very best I know you guys had a lot of fun doing it. You were a bunch of big dreamers, and I learned that life is more exciting when you're thinking BIG.

LESSON SEVEN
The Power of Family

Daddy, to me Thanksgiving of 2001 was all about you. You were so happy all weekend because you had your entire family around you. The significance of that Thanksgiving for you was probably demonstrated by the tear in your eye during Olivia's blessing. Or was that just some errant gravy?

The family portrait was just plain fun. You had planned out the whole event, right down to the amount of time it would take you to run to your position from the camera. I love this picture and I love you.

LESSON EIGHT
Practice Makes Perfect

Dad, I love that forty odd years after your last lesson, you bought a piano for the Florida house. I remember when you told me about it, you were like a happy little kid with a new bike. I know you work hard at improving your skills, so it's funny that I always think of chopsticks when I see you at the piano. Your pride in accomplishment has taught me that hard work brings great personal rewards.

Daddy
you mean so much
to me. I love you,
and I'm glad you're
my Dad!
Happy Father's Day
2002

love,
allison lee

Journaling Ideas: Include "Other Voices"

by Denise Pauley

Add perspective to your scrapbook pages by asking loved ones to journal on them. *Page by Denise Pauley.* **Supplies** *Patterned paper:* Magenta (marbled blue); Susan Branch (green), Colorbök; *Textured cardstock:* Club Scrap; *Alphabet stickers:* Flavia, Colorbök; *Alphabet rubber stamps:* PSX Design; *Stamping ink:* Stampin' Up!; *Eyelets:* Stamp Doctor; *Other:* Glue Dots by Glue Dots International.

When future generations see the scrapbooks I've created, they'll learn all about me. Obviously, the photos will be of my family, documenting the milestones and events that transpired throughout our lives. But because I designed each page, the books will be colored with my memories and tinted with my emotions. Readers will know how much I loved my family, the warmth I felt during special times, and the hopes I had for my children … simply because my words are on each page.

Wouldn't it be nice to have other "voices" present in the album as well? Though love is the common thread, there's a world of difference between the feelings of a mother and those of a father (and sister, brother, grandparent or friend). To capture them all, I periodically turn over my journaling duties to others and ask them to express their emotions about the photos.

At family gatherings, bring along some cardstock and archival pens, and ask relatives to jot down a sentiment about the day. Before grandparents leave your child's birthday party, have them inscribe a note of congratulations. Ask wedding guests to offer bits of marital advice in a booklet that you'll include on a layout for the happy couple. Or ask your husband to write letters directly to and about your children.

If your ghostwriters are skittish about putting their feelings on "display," have them write on cardstock, fold it and tuck into a pocket … for only the recipient to see!

"Aaron"

BY HEATHER UPPENCAMP
PROVO, UT

Supplies *Patterned papers:* Mustard Moon (gray, green), Provo Craft (blue), Sprout in Botanical (green sprout); *Vellum:* Provo Craft; *Album:* Club Scrap; *Fiber:* On the Surface; *Chalk:* Stampin' Up!; *Envelope die cuts:* Accu-Cut Systems; *Eyelets:* Doodlebug Design; *Metal-rimmed tags:* Making Memories; *Charms:* Embellishments; *Other:* Embroidery thread and paper clips. *Ideas to note:* The photos at right on the "Rainy" page were a little grainy, so Heather covered them partially with vellum journaling. For her "Aaron's 35th" layout, Heather made up her own definitions. (For example, a father is "one who changes diapers, kisses boo-boos, reads stories, and scares away monsters. See also hero.")

HEATHER'S THOUGHTS

"One of my favorite quotes sums up the feelings behind this album: 'One of the greatest acts of love that my husband has bestowed upon me is the kindness and gentleness that he has bestowed upon our children.'

"As I looked through our family photos, I realized how many capture my husband in his main roles in life—as my best friend and sweetheart, and as father of our five children. Aaron's worked really hard to 'be there' for me and them, on special occasions and in everyday life. I wanted to celebrate all the time and love he has spent on us, and to remind him that he is loved in return!"

WHAT SHE WANTED THE ALBUM TO INCLUDE:

"I wanted to express how much I appreciate Aaron as my husband and how grateful I am that he's been so involved in raising our children. Aaron has changed diapers, given baths, read stories and chased away closet monsters for 13 years, and I want him to know that the children and I love him all the more for it.

"I included some special occasions like birthdays and family outings, but also some everyday pages of Aaron just playing with the kids or reading stories to them. I wanted him to remember how he's such an important part of their everyday lives."

WHY SHE CHOSE THE LOOK SHE DID:

"I chose a more masculine, classy look for this album. For inspiration on which colors and textures to use on the pages, I looked in Aaron's closet. I went with the blues, greens and reds he wears and that remind me of him.

"I used a lot of paper tearing and texture techniques to add richness to the overall theme. The album is masculine but warm, just like Aaron. The album was a labor of love, and such a joy to make! I know he will appreciate this reminder of the love that I and our children have for him."

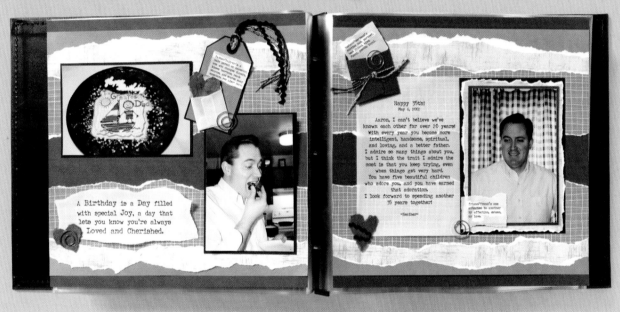

"My Father—
A Living Legacy"

BY NANCY MAXWELL-CRUMB
WHITMORE LAKE, MI

Supplies 8" x 8" album: Mrs. Grossman's; *Patterned papers:* Anna Griffin, K & Company and Rocky Mountain Scrapbook Company; *Gold heritage stickers:* me & my BIG ideas; *Key and button tags:* Fresh Cuts, EK Success; *Button and ribbon page accents:* Doo-Dads, Colorbök; *Emoticons:* Making Memories; *Brads:* American Pin & Fastener; *Fibers:* On the Surface; *Rubber stamps:* Anna Griffin and Stampabilities; *Stamping ink:* Ranger Industries; *Black photo corners:* Pioneer Photo Albums; *Computer font:* CK Extra, "Fresh Fonts" CD, Creating Keepsakes; *Leaf die cuts:* Deluxe Cuts; *Round tags:* Avery.

NANCY'S THOUGHTS

"My father was older when I was born, and I have been told throughout my life how much we are alike. He was a conservative parent when I was growing up, but my father has always had unconditional love for me. He has had very poor health (Parkinson's and leukemia) in recent years, and I wanted to create something to celebrate his life and his devotion to his family.

"Even with my father's health problems, he is always there for his children and grand-children. I wanted to make something to show how he has blessed not only my life, but the lives of my children."

WHAT SHE WANTED THE ALBUM TO INCLUDE:

"I wanted to show how loving my father is with his family. In many ways, he's been a father figure to my children. My sons (the 'boys he never had') have enjoyed spending time with my dad fishing, hunting for grasshoppers, going for boat rides, and stopping for treats at the gas station! He helps with homework, picks them up from after-school functions and more. He's always there if we need him."

WHY SHE CHOSE THE LOOK SHE DID:

"I wanted a masculine, heritage look for my album, so I chose browns, blacks and rusts for my main colors. I used rubber stamps with a 'Celtic' flair since my father is very proud of his heritage. Using the same papers and different accents helped reinforce my theme and helped me complete the album quickly."

CHILDHOOD

As a little boy you were the youngest of four (just like me) and your parents were immigrants settling into a new life. Growing up in Detroit was difficult at times, but your family always made the best of things. I look at this only early childhood picture of you, and can't help but see my own son's image. both my boy's have been blessed with so m traits that they have inherited from y

Stewart Maxwell - Detroit, Michigan

HERITAGE

You have taught me to be very proud of my heritage. Perhaps, this is what all true "Scots" believe, but you have always made sure from the time I was a little girl that I knew what my ethnic background was and the history behind it. Thank you for teaching me all about my ancestors and what I am made of!

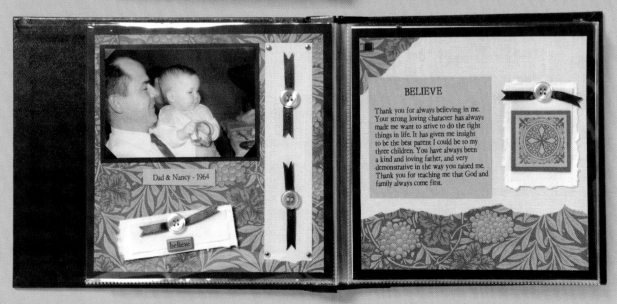

BELIEVE

Thank you for always believing in me. Your strong loving character has always made me want to strive to do the right things in life. It has given me insight to be the best parent I could be to my three children. You have always been a kind and loving father, and very demonstrative in the way you raised me. Thank you for teaching me that God and family always come first.

Dad & Nancy - 1964

believe

Ideas for Tribute Pages as Well

Prefer something faster? Create tribute pages for a father or husband instead!
Following are four layouts that are sure to please.

"Am I Doing It Right, Daddy?"

by Carrie O'Donnell
Newburyport, MA

Carrie's son, Christopher, doesn't like anything near his face, so Carrie knew getting him to brush his teeth would be a struggle. To her delight, once her husband, Chris, showed Christopher how to brush, their son just grabbed his little toothbrush and copied his father.

"My heart felt like it was going to explode," says Carrie. "I grabbed my camera and snapped pictures so Chris and I could remember the experience. These are my husband's favorite pictures with our son. It's a great reminder never to underestimate just how much boys learn from their daddies!"

Supplies *Patterned paper:* Making Memories; *Corrugated paper:* DMD Inc.; *Computer font:* 2Peas Nevermind, downloaded from *www.twopeasinabucket.com*; *Photo paper:* Glossy Premium, Hewlett-Packard. *Idea to note:* Carrie rolled the end of her journaling block to mimic a rolled-up toothpaste tube. She used corrugated paper for the cap.

"Meant for Each Other"

by Merryann Phillips
San Diego, CA

Merryann and her father have always enjoyed a close relationship, especially since her mother died of cancer 10 years ago. While Merryann scrapbooked layouts about her mother after her death, she feels strongly that it's important to do tribute-style layouts "while the important people in our lives are still living." She wanted her father to know how much it meant to be his adopted child.

When Merryann found this quote on the Internet, she decided to create this layout about her father. The results? Heartfelt tears and an even closer bond of love and friendship.

Supplies *Vellum:* Paper Adventures; *Rubber stamps and stamping ink:* Close To My Heart; *Beads:* Create-A-Craft; *Embroidery floss:* DMC; *Computer font:* Castellar, downloaded from the Internet; *Poem:* Author unknown, found on the Internet; *Other:* Silver eyelets.

"Fishing with Daddy"

by Martha Crowther
Salem, NH

Martha smiles every time she looks at this page. "My husband is an avid sportsman and loves fishing," she says. "During the annual fishing derby, my husband helped our son hook his very first fish. Brandon reeled the fish in all by himself, and you can see by the photo how excited he was to catch his first fish with his dad.

"This page means a lot because the day was filled with good memories, lots of laughs and a father and son bonding. I wanted to keep the page fairly simple, so I chose a green handmade paper for my background. I added slides of some smaller photos to help me remember the day. I added torn cardboard for a masculine effect."

Supplies Handmade paper: ArtisticScrapper.com; Computer fonts: CK Hustle, "Fresh Fonts" CD, Creating Keepsakes; 2Peas Fudge Brownies, downloaded from www.two-peasinabucket.com; Tags: Making Memories; Slides: Pakon; Screen: From Home Depot; Fiber: Adornaments, EK Success; Stones: Make It Mosaics, Plaid; Mosaic tiles: Magic Scraps; Other: Cardboard box and transparency.

Supplies Chalk: Craf-T Products; Computer font: Andy, downloaded from the Internet; Tags: Kelly's own pattern; Other: Eyelets and mesh netting. Idea to note: The "fiber" is actually a drawstring from an old sweatshirt.

"Dad"

by Kelly Jones
Tampa, FL

From the time Kelly's son was four, he spent two weeks each summer with Kelly's parents. "Dad would take Brandon to the golf course, movies, fishing, dinner, church activities, baseball games and more. When my parents visited us, Dad would eagerly anticipate going to Brandon's baseball games. Mom would always snap pictures of the two of them together."

Although the summer trips have ended, Kelly wanted to help Brandon remember the good times he'd experienced while visiting his grandfather. She created the layout here to help capture the fond memories. Kelly included what a wonderful dad her father was to her and how he'd helped Kelly be a better parent.

today's Grandparents

Scrapbook the special bond

IT'S HARD TO TELL WHO'S HAPPIER being a grandparent—Wayne or me. But don't chalk us up to the rocking chair set just yet. The only thick-soled shoes in our closet are hiking boots! We're part of the new wave of grandparents who are younger, healthier and more actively involved in the lives of their grandkids than in generations past.

Sure, we still read stories and bake cookies, but we're just as likely to be found playing sports, riding thrill rides at the theme park, and helping with homework on the Internet. There's just something about that skipped generation that makes it easy for grandparents and grandchildren to be special friends.

Being a grandparent is a serious job, you know. While parents may think we're spoiling their offspring, we grandparents know that the unconditional love we provide is helping shape our grandchildren, building self-esteem so they can grow to become loving, confident adults. We provide a connection to the past, share life lessons and pass along family traditions and values. And we're the best and most willing babysitters on the planet!

Celebrate a "grand" person in your life by creating a scrapbook page that will be as treasured as the relationship you share. We've showcased the work of seven scrapbook artists whose ideas are sure to inspire you.

BY BRENDA ARNALL

Supplies *Patterned paper:* Karen Foster Design; *Stickers:* AlphaWear, Creative Imaginations; *Rubber stamps:* Hero Arts; *Stamping ink:* ColorBox, Clearsnap; *Pens:* Zig Millennium, EK Success; *Computer font:* Adler, downloaded from the Internet; *Mini brads, photo turns, label holder and safety pin:* Making Memories; *Leaves:* Nature's Pressed; *Acrylic paint:* Liquitex; *Foam mounting tape:* Therm O Web; *Other:* Fabric.

"Shutterbugs"

by Brenda Arnall
Pace, FL

Journaling to note: "If you give a nine-year-old a camera, she will walk the length of the nature trail without complaint, and then ask to go around again. . . . If you let her photograph whatever she wants, she'll be intrigued by giant spider webs, a decayed tree filled with holes made by woodpeckers, and tiny ferns and flowers—even if she doesn't take a picture of them. If you sit patiently and smile while she gets set just right, she will take a surprisingly good photograph of you and beam with pride at the resulting print. And when it's all done, maybe, if you're lucky, you will have passed on to her an appreciation for the wonders of nature and a love for the art of photography."

IDEA TO NOTE:

Brenda applied an acrylic paint wash to the patterned paper to mute the color and design. She created an envelope from it as well.

Kayla's names for Grandpa have been a source of amusement over the years. When she was little and first talking, she called him "BadPaw." We'd all chuckle at "BadPaw" but soon fell in the habit of calling him that ourselves. As she got older the name became much more like Grandpa however. In Kayla's Georgia drawl, "Grandpa" comes out sounding like "Graaannnnnd Paaaw." And we mimic that, too. It doesn't matter to him how she says it. His heart melts when she calls him Grandpa and he'll do whatever she asks, even carrying her when she complains she's too tired to skate back up the big hill at the park.

Flat Rock Park · Columbus Ga. · October 2002

"Grandpa"
by Brenda Arnall
Pace, FL

Supplies *Patterned paper:* KI Memories; *Specialty paper:* Sam Flax; *Stickers:* Nostalgiques, EK Success; *Rubber stamps:* Hero Arts; *Stamping ink:* ColorBox, Clearsnap; *Pens:* Zig Millennium, EK Success; *Computer fonts:* 39 Smooth ("P"), Gunplay ("d"), Metacopy ("a") and McGannahan (journaling), downloaded from the Internet; *Mini brad, mini eyelet, and metal-rimmed circle tag and rub-on words:* Making Memories; *Heart frame:* Scrapworks; *Other:* Definition copied from Webster's Dictionary.

IDEA TO NOTE: To create a custom background for her title box, Brenda typed in golf terms, then reduced the opacity of the print in her software so the words appear as a watermark.

"Lessons in Golf"
by Brenda Arnall
Pace, FL

Supplies *Patterned paper:* Mustard Moon; *Stamping ink:* ColorBox, Clearsnap; *Pens:* Zig Millennium, EK Success; *Computer fonts:* Smash (title), downloaded from the Internet; Arial (title background), Microsoft Word; CK Higgins Handprint (journaling), Becky Higgins' "Creative Clips and Fonts" CD, *Creating Keepsakes*; *Alphabet eyelets, alphabet charms and metal-rimmed square tags:* Making Memories.

It is very difficult for Mimi that we live so far away from her. She misses you boys so much. So when we get together, she is anxious to get outside and play with you. She takes you fishing when we are in Texas and to the zoo and the aquarium and Six Flags. She is always looking for something fun to do with you. She plays soccer and basketball with you. She has so much more patience than Daddy and I do because she doesn't get to see you every day. In these pictures, we were vacationing in the Pocono Mountains. Mimi spent hours and hours tubing with you. She also rode snowmobiles and played games with you. Things were so different when I was a little girl. I loved my grandparents. They told me stories about my parents that made me laugh. Mammaw and Granny made the best meals imaginable. But, I remember them being so old and we didn't go out and do the things that kids like to do. I see the smiles and giggles on your faces and I am so glad that your grandparents are young, vibrant and interested in spending quality time with you. You are so blessed to have such a fun Mimi!

tubing in the Poconos 2·03

Mimi

Supplies *Patterned paper:* Daisy D's; *Transparency:* 3M; *Computer font:* CK Newsprint, "Fresh Fonts" CD, *Creating Keepsakes; Wooden frame and safety pin:* Li'l Davis Designs; *Definition stickers, staples and ribbon:* Making Memories; *Mini brads:* Karen Foster Design; *Embroidery floss:* DMC; *Pen:* Zig Millennium, EK Success; *Acrylic paint:* Americana; *Photo corners:* Kolo Photo Albums; *Other:* Denim, ripped fabric and vintage buttons.

"Mimi"

by Tracie Smith
Smithtown, NY

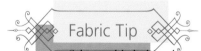

Fabric Tip

Salvage old clothing by reusing it on your scrapbook pages. All of the strips of fabric on this page came from my children's outgrown shirts and an old pair of jeans. Note the strip with the buttons sewn on. This piece was cut from an old shirt and placed directly on my page. No sewing necessary!

—*Tracie Smith*

"Horseplay with Grandma"

by Candi Gershon
Fishers, IN

Supplies *Patterned papers:* Carolee's Creations and Li'l Davis Designs; *Date stamp:* Making Memories; *Stamping ink:* Ranger Industries; *Coin holder:* 2Dye4; *Vellum:* Paper Adventures; *Computer fonts:* 2Peas Jack Frost and 2Peas Miss Priss, downloaded from *www.twopeasinabucket.com*; CBX Monument, "Journaling Fonts" CD, Chatterbox; *Other:* Gingham ribbon.

"Just One Day with You"

by Erin Lincoln
Frederick, MD

Supplies *Patterned paper:* Chatterbox; *Stamping ink:* ColorBox, Clearsnap; Stampin' Up!; *Letter stamps:* Fusion Art Stamps; *Hinges, frame, metal quote and buttons:* Making Memories; *Stickers:* Chatterbox and Pebbles Inc.; *Heart punch:* Emagination Crafts.

DO A CIRCLE JOURNAL FOR GRANDPARENTS

Sisters Karen Glenn, Kim Morgan and Bonnie Romney created a circle journal (see Figures 1–5) to thank their parents for the influence they've had on them and their children. They'll present this album to their parents on their 40th wedding anniversary.

Want to create something like this but your siblings don't scrapbook? Do what Karen, Kim and Bonnie did. Select your theme, then ask each family member to select a couple of photos, write down his or her thoughts, and choose a word to summarize the page. You can then scrapbook the page for your sibling.

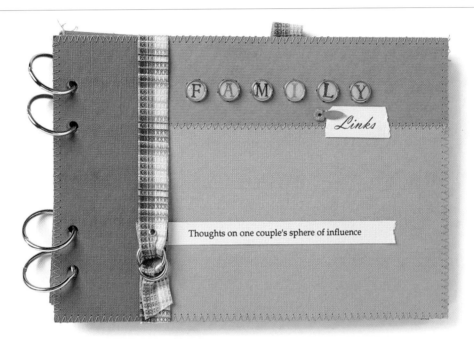

Figure 1. Present your grandparents or your children's grandparents with a circle journal created by family members. *Cover by Kim Morgan and Karen Glenn.* **Supplies** *Concho:* Scrapworks; *Metal rings and photo turn:* 7gypsies; *Letter stamps:* PSX Design; *Stamping ink and crystal lacquer:* Ranger Industries; *Computer fonts:* Garamond (subtitle), Microsoft Word; Links, package unknown; *Other:* Plaid ribbon.

Figure 2. Start your album with a dedication page. *Page by Bonnie Romney.* **Supplies** *Flat-top eyelet:* Making Memories; *Computer fonts:* Apoplex, downloaded from the Internet; FT38, package unknown.

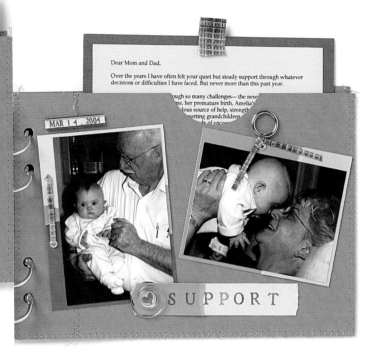

Figure 3. Share how much you appreciate qualities like calm, quiet confidence. *Page by Bonnie Romney.* **Supplies** *Oval swirl clip and bookplate:* Making Memories; *Computer fonts:* Georgia ("Chicago"), Microsoft Word; Remington (title), downloaded from the Internet; *Other:* Plaid ribbon.

Figure 4. Tell how much a grandparent's support has meant. *Page by Karen Glenn.* **Supplies** *Metal ring and date holder:* 7gypsies; *Eyelets:* Making Memories; *Stamping ink:* Ranger Industries; *Letter stamps:* PSX Design; *Other:* Circle clip.

Figure 5. Praise your loved ones for their good examples. *Page by Kim Morgan.* **Supplies** *Hinges and staples:* Making Memories; *Metal rings:* 7gypsies; *Letter stamps:* All Night Media ("Example") and Hero Arts ("dates"); *Stamping ink:* Ranger Industries; *Other:* Plaid ribbon.

Life Lessons FROM Grandpa

Today's Lesson: How to get lots of loot (candy) at a parade.

1. Stand in front of everyone else and try to look cute.

2. Wave and smile at all the pretty girls on the floats.

3. Smile some more – smile bigger, and keep waving.

4. Success – candy is coming your way!

yes, Dylan, the horse is nice, but he does not have candy. Stay focused.

2002

"Life Lessons from Grandpa"

by Christy McKay Gantt
Lugoff, SC

Supplies Textured cardstock: Bazzill Basics; *Patterned paper:* Chatterbox; *Transparency:* Hammermill; *Circle alphabet stamps:* PSX Design; *Stamping ink:* Ink It Up!; *Walnut ink:* Postmodern Design; *Other:* Candy wrappers.

Stitching Tip

I use machine stitching frequently on my layouts and have had several friends ask how I sew through multiple layers of cardstock. My first option is to sew only on the patterned paper, then adhere it to the cardstock. The patterned paper looks like it's sewn directly to the background cardstock but it's not.

When I have to machine stitch through several layers of cardstock, I've found that the key is to use a needle designed for sewing denim. It's sturdy enough to stitch through multiple layers of cardstock without breaking.

—*Christy McKay Gantt*

10 "Grand" Ideas for Grandparent Pages

BY DENISE PAULEY

Sometimes you'll snap the perfect shot of your child and your parents. In a single photograph, you'll capture all the love, friendship and family ties. But how should you scrapbook this treasure? What sentiment or story would you like to convey? For inspiration, consider the following ideas:

1 Do your children and parents share a special bond? Is your daughter "grandpa's girl" or your son the twinkle in your mother's eye? Document this connection—including journaling from both sides, if possible—with examples and anecdotes.

2 If anyone's going to spoil your children, it's your parents. In what outlandish ways have your kids reaped the benefits?

3 Being around kids can keep you young . . . especially if you're a grandparent. What activities do they share? Special games? Distinctive day trips? Simple walks in the park?

4 Grandparents are the teachers of life's lessons. What education and instruction have your children received?

5 Do relatives claim that your son is the spitting image of grandpa? What physical characteristics, qualities or traits have your children inherited?

6 Create a pre-heritage layout by interviewing your parents for a mini biography. Ask them to look back on their lives and discuss their most important milestones and memories.

7 Have your parents journal about what life was like when they were your child's age. What were their favorite pastimes? Family activities? Hopes for the future?

8 Are holidays extra special because the family gathers at your parents' house? Detail the ways they make their house a home.

9 Was your child named after one of your parents? Discuss the historical and familial significance of the name they share.

10 Do your kids not only have "great" grandparents, but also great-grandparents? Design a page showcasing all four generations and what you mean to one another.

NEIGHBORS & FRIENDS

SHOWCASE THOSE WHO LIVE CLOSE BY

by Lori Fairbanks

Remember the "I Love Lucy" TV show? Lucy Ricardo was forever getting into trouble—and trying to keep her husband, Ricky, from finding out about it. Their neighbors, Fred and Ethel Mertz, usually ended up involved as well. Without Ethel, who would have been Lucy's cohort in comic catastrophe? Without Fred, who would have tried to stop them?

As the Chinese proverb says, "A good neighbor is a priceless treasure." Hopefully, like Lucy and Ricky, you have the best kind of neighbors—friends who just happen to live close by. Take a look as 11 scrapbookers share the impact their neighbors have had on their lives.

Sisters, Neighbors, Friends"
by Lee Anne Russell
Brownsville, TN

SUPPLIES
Chalk: Craf-T Products
Leaf punch: EK Success
Mulberry paper: Memory Lane
Acorn charms and eyelets: Impress Rubber Stamps
Computer fonts: ChrisHmk Bold and JanieHmk,
"Card Studio 3" CD, Hallmark and Boys Are Gross,
downloaded from the Internet
Bricks, tree, bird and nest: Lee Anne's own designs
Buttons: Hillcreek Designs
Other: Jute
Idea to note: Lee Anne crumpled her punched
leaves to add dimension.

Use a paper trimmer to cut rectangular
"bricks" from cardstock, then chalk them
individually to create a weathered look.
Other options? Use brick-patterned paper
such as that by Hot Off The Press (Brick
Wall) or Provo Craft (Bricks). Or, chalk
your cardstock before cutting out the
blocks (the coloring will
be more random).

Serena Visits"
by Vivian Smith
Calgary, AB, Canada

Patterned paper: Provo Craft
Flower clip art: "Simple Folk"
HugWare CD, Provo Craft
Colored pencils: Prismacolor,
Sanford

Computer font: Coaster (title),
Fontographer 4.1, Macromedia;
PC Beach Front, "Little Images"
HugWare CD, Provo Craft

> Add visual interest with curved titles and playful flowers.

> Capture fun details (such as "Things We've Done Together" or "Things We've Borrowed") on creative measuring-cup journaling blocks. (You can help keep them in place with Velcro.) Create "sugar" with clear embossing powder and crystal ultra-fine glitter.

Can I Borrow a Cup of Sugar?"
by Cindy Knowles
Milwaukie, OR

SUPPLIES
Metallic paper: Memory Lane
Vellum: The Paper Company
Homespun yarn: Lion Brand Yarn Company
Clear embossing powder: PSX Design
Crystal ultra-fine glitter: Mark Enterprises
Computer fonts: CK Handprint, "The Best of Creative Lettering" CD Combo, *Creating Keepsakes*; Impact, Microsoft; Massive Headache, downloaded from the Internet
Measuring cups: Cindy's own designs
Craft wire and beads: Westrim Crafts
Other: "O" ring and Velcro

A hanging-tag title, distinctive buttons and torn borders can highlight fun photos.

"Won't You Be My Neighbor?"
by Sara Tumpane
Grayslake, IL

SUPPLIES
Patterned paper: Stamping Station
Lettering template: Sara's own design, based on the font "Disco Monkey," downloaded from the Internet

Chalk: Craf-T Products
Pop dots: All Night Media
Buttons: Western Accents
Paper glaze: Aleene's
Other: Circle tags, yarn and eyelets

Make flowers look more dimensional by overlapping the punches and bending some of the petals and leaves upward.

"The Boy Next Door"
by Jill Dickey
Pleasant Grove, UT

SUPPLIES
Patterned paper: Paper Patch
Punches: Family Treasures (daisy and leaf) and The Punch Line (circle)
Lettering template: Block Serif, ABC

Tracers, Pebbles for EK Success
Computer font: CK Journaling, "The Best of Creative Lettering" CD Combo, *Creating Keepsakes*
Other: Raffia

On the Street Where We Live"
by Janet MacLeod
Dundas, ON, Canada

SUPPLIES
Alphabet punches: EK Success
Lettering template: Curly Q (for word "live"),
ScrapPagerz.com
Letter stickers and letter frames: Provo Craft
Computer font: P22 Garamouche Regular,
downloaded from *www.impressrubberstamps.com*
Alphabet beads and craft wire: Westrim Crafts
Eyelets: Impress Rubber Stamps
Pop dots: All Night Media

Create custom
hearts from wire,
embroidery floss,
beads
and more.

Heartprints"
by Nichol Magourik
Dodge City, KS

SUPPLIES
Rubber stamps: "Little Letters" set,
Stampin' Up!
Stamping ink: Stampin' Up!
Computer fonts: CK Handprint, "The Best
of Creative Lettering" CD Combo, *Creating
Keepsakes* and Flowerchild, downloaded
from the Internet
Diamond glaze, Dollar Gold Roxs: Judi-Kins

Mini brads: HyGlo, American Pin & Fastener
Foam squares: Therm O Web
Chalk: Craf-T Products
Craft wire: Artistic Wire Ltd.
Beads: On the Surface
Embroidery floss: DMC
Hearts and swirl: Nichol's own designs
Other: Tags

Color in your title with the help of a paintbrush and a stamp pad. To "hold" small pictures, stamp pillars, then cut them out and position them on your pages.

"La Famiglia Architravo"
by Linda Mowery
San Diego, CA

SUPPLIES
Patterned paper: Debbie Mumm, Creative Imaginations
Vellum: The Paper Garden
Mulberry paper: Close To My Heart
Punches: All Night Media (swirl border) and Emagination Crafts (ivy leaves)
Ivy Wallies: McCall's

Rubber stamps: Italian Poetry Background, Hero Arts and Roman Pillar, Stampabilities
Stamping ink: ColorBox MetaleXtra, Clearsnap
Pen: Zig Writer, EK Success
Computer font: CK Bella, "The Best of Creative Lettering" CD Vol. 3, *Creating Keepsakes*
Lettering idea: Crooked Classic, *The Art of Creative Lettering*, Creating Keepsakes Books

"The Girls Next Door"
by Jennifer Blackham
West Jordan, UT

SUPPLIES
Lettering template: Blockhead Serif, ScrapPagerz.com
Computer font: CAC Pinafore, downloaded

from the Internet
Birdhouses and stone path: Jennifer's own designs

WORMS

After it had rained all day, the gutters were full of water & WORMS! The boys had a great time with the neighborhood kids, hunting for worms. (L - R) Rachel, Chase, Regan, Coleman, Kelsey, Lance, and Maren. April 2001

"Worms"
by Lori Houk
Lawrence, KS

SUPPLIES
Computer fonts: CK Handprint (journaling), "The Best of Creative Lettering" CD Combo, *Creating Keepsakes*; Doodle Summer (title), "PagePrintables")

CD Vol. 1, Cock-A-Doodle Design, Inc.
Textured paper: Solum World Paper
Pop dots: Stampa Rosa
Embroidery floss: DMC
Rope: Judi-Kins

Rope can be cute and casual on a layout. Tack the rope down every few inches with embroidery floss.

Our Favorite Neighbors.. The Danburgs

The Danburgs moved in across the street the same time we did 7 years ago. It has been fun to watch each others children grow and develop into fine young women and men. It seems like yesterday that they were delivering gifts to us for the delivery of our first child. He is now 7. He is the same age that Jennifer (their youngest) was when they moved in. Over the years they have been so generous with their time and gifts to us. I have enjoyed making goodies for them every Christmas. Almost as much as I enjoy receiving the goodies Debbie bakes every year and delivers on a beautiful glass Christmas platter. I was thrilled when Debbie gave me this picture of their kids 2 yrs ago. They will always have a special place in our hearts whether across the street or across the country (though I hope that never happens!)

FUN FACTS..

• They always buy our kids the COOLEST toys!

• They have all babysat our children

• They used to have A HUGE pine tree in their front yard (Until Uncle Wells cut it down!)

• They have 5 dogs (maybe more)

• They have chickens and pet turkeys (they live in the house!)

"Our Favorite Neighbors"
by Eva Flake
Mesa, AZ

SUPPLIES
Punch: EK Success
Pen: Zig Writer, EK Success
Mini brads: HyGlo, American Pin & Fastener
Computer fonts: Garamond, Microsoft Word 2000, Microsoft Corp.; Garamouche, Impress

Rubber Stamps
Chalk: Craf-T Products
Sunflower: Eva's own design
Pop dots: All Night Media
Other: Cotton string

Use thick cotton string to create fun tied looks.

Real Life Heroes

10 winning layouts about people who've touched our hearts

On September 11, 2001, our definition of heroism was changed forever. As the world reeled at shocking images of flames, twisted metal and terrified people running through the streets, ordinary men and women stepped forward to perform acts of incredible courage and mercy.

Rescue workers did the unthinkable, entering buildings to attempt rescues while everyone else was flooding out. Businessmen trapped in a hijacked plane called their families to say goodbye, then sacrificed themselves to keep the plane from reaching its ultimate target. People around the world stepped forward to donate blood, send money, do whatever they could to lessen the suffering. Each rose to the challenge.

The entries that poured in for our second "You're My Hero!" contest confirm that heroes can be found anywhere: in front of a classroom, behind the wheel of a police car, and often in our own homes. Read on to meet the heroes portrayed in our 10 winning layouts. →

BY MOLLY NEWMAN

Like many siblings, Christine and her brother Forrest had a rocky relationship as they grew up. She and her twin sister, Cindy, considered Forrest a pesky little brother, and they tormented him. Admits Christine, "Sometimes we were just plain mean."

The night before Christine and Cindy left home for college, 13-year-old Forrest changed their relationship forever. He quietly entered the girls' room, dropped a folded piece of paper on one of their beds, and left without saying a word. As the girls read the note, they began to cry. Forrest had written a poem about the "wall" that had grown between them over the years, dividing them with anger and arguments. He said the time had come to stop the arguing, noting, "And hopefully, now, the wall will crash down. Little, by little, by little."

Since that day 20 years ago, Forrest and Christine have grown to be each other's dearest friends and greatest supporters. Says Christine, "Now that Forrest is pursuing his lifelong goal to become a professional musician, I admire him more than ever for standing by his dreams!"

"Wisdom and Brilliance"
by Christine Brown
Hanover, MN

SUPPLIES
Corrugated paper: DMD Industries
Vellum: Paper Adventures
Computer fonts: Juice ITC, downloaded from the Internet; CK Journaling, "The Best of Creative Lettering" CD Combo, *Creating*

Keepsakes
Pen: Jel-Pop, EK Success
Chalk: Craf-T Products
Craft wire: Artistic Wire Ltd.
Fibers: On the Surface
Other: Star buttons, brads and liquid gold leaf

Christine made the photo frame at right by sponging liquid gold leaf over corrugated paper. She created shooting star accents with star-shaped buttons and vellum "tails." The poem on the left is a scan of Forrest's original verses.

Daxton Wilde was diagnosed with brain cancer when he was only four years old. For the next seven months, his life revolved around chemotherapy, doctors' visits, and outpourings of love from family and friends. Despite the pain and discomfort of his struggle, he never complained about any procedure or treatment.

As Daxton went through his treatments, he decided to create a book, *I'm a Super Hero,* to help other children with cancer learn what to expect. Starring Daxton as a valiant fighter against "the bad guy Cancer," this book was written and illustrated by Daxton with help from his mom.

Daxton lost his battle with cancer in January 2001. But the book he created and these photographs of his sweet smile remain as legacies of his indomitable spirit.

"Daxton, Our Super Hero"
by Nichole Burbank
South Weber, UT

SUPPLIES
Patterned paper: Colors By Design
Computer fonts: CK Cursive and CK Journaling, "The Best of Creative Lettering" CD Combo, *Creating Keepsakes*

After the terrorist attacks of September 11, Shelley sat glued to her TV as images of horror flashed across the screen. But in the days and weeks that followed, she realized that many of the rescue workers and others touched by the tragedies were heroes worthy of celebration. She created this layout to honor their selfless courage and unflinching determination.

Shelley downloaded photographs from the Internet, searching for images that represented those affected at the World Trade Center, the Pentagon, and the site of the Pennsylvania crash. She also included pictures of New York City mayor Rudy Giuliani and President Bush to commemorate their quick and decisive action.

Says Shelley, "I wanted to represent the everyday men and women who were touched by these events. I truly believe that there were hundreds, even thousands, of heroes on that day, and our country should be very proud. God bless America!"

"God Bless America"
by Shelley Clark-Glidewell
Charleston, SC

SUPPLIES
Vellum: Sonburn
Pens: Zig Scroll & Brush, EK Success; Gelly Roll and Pigma Micron, Sakura

Computer font: Arial, Microsoft Word
Craft paint: Tulip by Duncan
Other: Star brads

To create a background flag that "looked like it had been through a war," Shelley tore stripes from red cardstock and stamped rough stars with craft paint. She lettered the lyrics to "God Bless America" and the Pledge of Allegiance on vellum and layered them over the flag.

Caroline's grandmother Grace put faith, family and friends above all else. When Caroline was a child, Grace lived in an apartment at Caroline's home and spent precious hours teaching her granddaughter important lessons about love and courage.

Says Caroline, "She was always independent, yet she always had time for me. I remember spending Saturdays and Sundays playing Scrabble and card games with her. She loved to share stories about the past with me, too, and showed me the importance of preserving your memories."

Throughout Grace's life, she demonstrated her independent spirit. She raised six children while working on farms and as a nurse; she survived a bout of tuberculosis; and she drove cross-country by herself four times to visit friends and relatives. Her staunch Catholic faith was the core of her life, and the memorial service was the inspiration for Caroline's layout.

Caroline included prayers and readings from Grace's memorial service on her layout, printing them out on cardstock tags and inserting them into vellum envelopes. She chose subdued, elegant papers to flatter the heirloom, black-and-white photos of her grandmother.

"Amazing Grace"
by Caroline Davis
Mentor, OH

SUPPLIES
Patterned paper: K & Company
Velveteen paper and vellum: Paper Adventures
Computer fonts: Script MT Bold (title), Microsoft Word; Garamouche (journaling), source unknown
Eyelets and vellum envelopes: Impress Rubber Stamps
Leaf punch: The Punch Bunch

Dece's mother Linda had a traditional upbringing; she was raised to believe that a woman's role was to cook, clean, sew and mother her children. Although she filled these roles admirably, raising Dece and her brothers to be good citizens and keeping up her home, it was Linda's lifestyle changes later that made her a hero in Dece's eyes.

"In the 1970s, my mom realized she had a divine potential to do much more with her life," says Dece. When Dece started college in 1992, Linda returned to school as well. She and Dece studied hard together,

and Linda went on to earn her bachelor's degree while holding a full-time job. But even a college degree wasn't enough to satisfy Linda's drive and curiosity. Despite health problems and changes in her family life, she earned her master's degree in social work and began a new career.

Says Dece, "Mom has taught me to respect differences of opinion, but also to stand up for my own beliefs. She's shown me that I am in control of my life, and that I have the ability and responsibility to define myself. Mom is my hero, my example, and my friend."

"My Mother, My Hero"
by Dece Gherardini
Mesa, AZ

SUPPLIES
Computer fonts: Lucida Handwriting (title), source unknown; CK Journaling (journaling), "The Best of Creative Lettering" CD Combo, *Creating Keepsakes*

Adhesive for flowers and leaves: Glue Dots
Flowers and leaves: Dece's own designs
Chalk: Craf-T Products

For her rose accents, Dece crumpled cardstock to create a "distressed" look, tore the paper into circles, then twisted them into rose shapes. She used a similar approach for her leaves.

When Dawn was a little girl, her father was killed by a drunk driver. Her mother told her friends Abe and Judy, "If anything ever happens to me, I want you to take care of Dawn." They agreed. Less than a year later, their promise was put to the test when Dawn's mother was killed in a car accident.

Abe and Judy opened their home and their hearts to Dawn, welcoming her as if she were one of their own. Says Dawn, "Their children—both their birth children and I—were always their first priority. I have wonderful memories of growing up, although my early experiences could have traumatized me forever."

Through adolescence, college and her own experiences as wife and mother, Dawn has always been able to rely on Abe and Judy for support and love. She is quick to note, "They have served as great role models for us all."

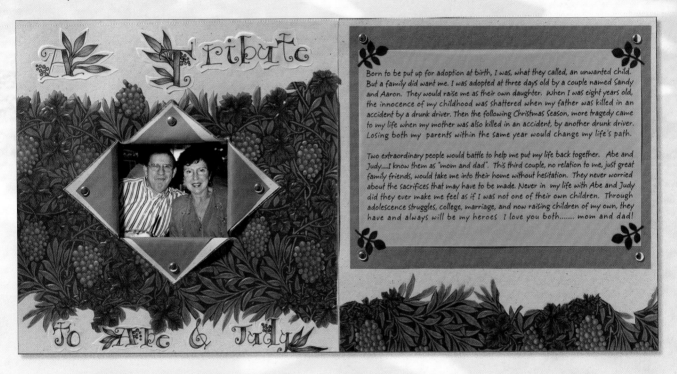

"A Tribute to Abe and Judy"
by Dawn Hinck
Englewood, FL

SUPPLIES
Patterned paper: Paper Adventures
Vellum: K & Company
Leaf punch: The Punch Bunch
Computer font: Starbabe, Print Shop Ensemble III, Broderbund
Lettering idea for title: Leafy Capitals, "The Art of Creative Lettering" CD, *Creating Keepsakes*
Brads: Impress Rubber Stamps
Colored pencils: Prismacolor, Sanford

To create her photo frame, Dawn layered sheets of paper, cut an "X" in the center, then folded down the resulting triangles. She attached them with brads (eyelets and stitching also work well).

Cindy's father-in-law has spent his life providing for his family. But when his wife's health began to decline, he needed to begin caring for her daily needs as well. As Alzheimer's disease has begun to affect her mind, she has needed more and more care, patience and love, all of which her husband has given without complaint.

Despite the demands of caring for his wife, Cindy's father-in-law still finds time to share with the rest of his family. Says Cindy, "He makes time to visit with his grown children, and he always attends special events for his grandchildren."

Cindy was inspired to create her unique journaling after taking a class by CK founding editor Lisa Bearnson. Cindy edited her text to include phrases from the traditional wedding vows "For richer or poorer, in sickness and in health, for better or worse." Each word is "buried" in the text and highlighted with an increased size and different typeface. Notes Cindy, "Using this technique, I could emphasize the wedding vows my father has honored so graciously."

"Love That Lasts"
by Cindy Knowles
Milwaukie, OR

SUPPLIES
Patterned paper: Paper Accents (black/gold speckled), Paper Adventures (vellum), source unknown (black/gold stripe)
Pens: Uni-Gel Medium, Sanford
Computer fonts: CK Journaling, "The Best of Creative Lettering Combo," *Creating Keepsakes;* DJ Sketched, "SuperFontastic!"

CD, D.J. Inkers
Lettering template: Smarty, Déjà Views, The C-Thru Ruler Company
Heart charms: Creative Beginnings (small), Darice (large)
Ribbon and cord: May Arts
Pop dots: All Night Media
Embroidery floss: DMC

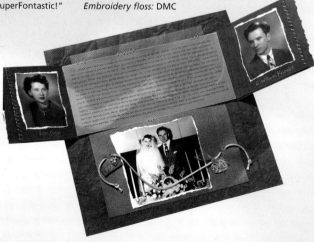

As Twyla created this layout, she thought about all the ways in which her husband, Rick, is a hero to her children, especially Shelby. Seven-year-old Shelby wrote the journaling on the pages, describing the important things her dad does for the family.

Says Twyla, "Shelby is eager for her father's helping hand with many of her little projects and calamities. She loves spending time with him because she gets to do such different things—such as setting up tents and making pirate ships—than she does with me."

A greeting card inspired Twyla to create her heart and hand accents. She drew the designs with an embossing marker, then embossed them with white powder to make them stand out. In her layout, Twyla used shades of gray to avoid competing with the subdued, black-and-white tones of her photos.

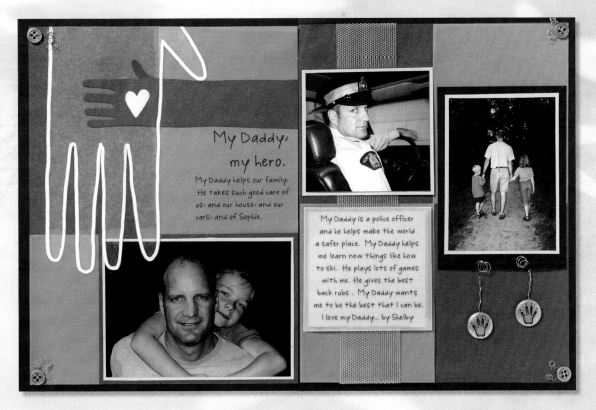

My Daddy, my hero.

My Daddy helps our family. He takes such good care of us, and our house, and our cars, and of Sophie.

My Daddy is a police officer and he helps make the world a safer place. My Daddy helps me learn new things like how to ski. He plays lots of games with me. He gives the best back rubs. My Daddy wants me to be the best that I can be. I love my Daddy... by Shelby

"My Daddy, My Hero"
by Twyla Koop
Surrey, BC, Canada

SUPPLIES
Vellum: Paper Adventures
Computer font: CK Jot, "The Art of Creative Lettering CD," *Creating Keepsakes*
Embossing pen: Marvy Uchida
Embossing powder: Hero Arts
Silver mesh: Source unknown
Buttons: Countess

WINNER YOU'RE MY HERO! CONTEST

When Angie had her son Ian at age 16, people all around her gave dire, discouraging warnings. "They said I was ruining my future," says Angie. Years later, her son Ian's incredible talents and personality have proved that his birth was the greatest blessing of her life instead.

Ian has accomplished much as a student, athlete and loving family member. "It makes my heart swell every time someone pays me a compliment about him," says Angie. She is also proud that since being diagnosed with diabetes at age four, Ian has learned to manage his disease himself, testing his own blood and giving himself insulin shots.

Notes Angie, "Every step of the way with Ian has been a learning experience. Somehow, our journey together has felt more like one of friends than of parent and child." Through watching Ian grow and shine, Angie has found encouragement for her own struggles. She takes honest pride in raising a heroic young man.

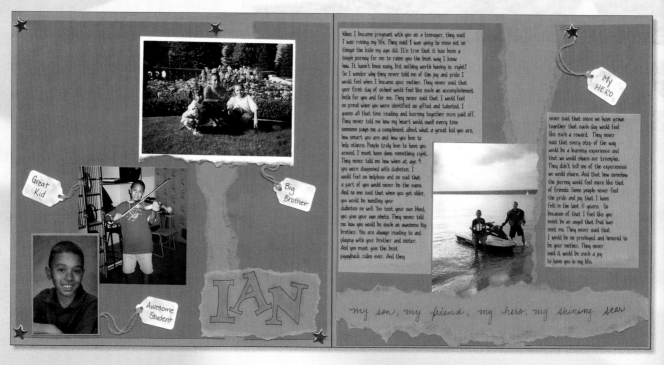

"Ian"
by Angie Morris
Colorado Springs, CO

SUPPLIES
Vellum: Making Memories
Lettering template: Party, ScrapPagerz.com
Star brads and tags: Sources unknown

Pen: Zig Writer, EK Success
Embroidery floss: DMC
Chalk: Craf-T Products

For years, Allison and her husband had wished and prayed for a baby. They finally received word that a young woman in Hawaii was ready to let them adopt her son. As soon as Ethan Lloyd was placed in Allison's arms, she realized that the courage and generosity of Ethan's birth mother were what had allowed their prayers to be answered at last.

"Because of her extraordinary strength at a very difficult time," says Allison, "that young woman has become my hero. Every single day, I offer a prayer of thanks for the precious gift she has given us."

Allison created this layout to honor the heroism of Ethan's mother and serve as the first page in her son's baby book. "I want him to know his story," says Allison. "I hope he can understand the difficult decision his mother made to give him the life she knew she couldn't offer him on her own."

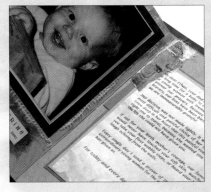

"You Must Do"
by Allison Strine
Atlanta, GA

Photo by Dino Watt;
representation by Shannon Watt

SUPPLIES
Patterned paper: Scrap-Ease
Mulberry paper: PrintWorks
Vellum: Paper Adventures
Computer fonts: Tangerine (title and quote), Lucida Sans (journaling), downloaded from the Internet
Rubber stamps: Above the Mark (profile), ERA Graphics (mermaid), Rubber Stampede (leaves), Stamp Craft (heart), Stampendous!

(texture cube)
Stamping ink: VersaMark, Tsukineko
Mesh: The Paper Company
Pen: Zig Writer, EK Success
Fibers: The Card Ladies
Beads: Beedz, Art Accents
Chalk: Craf-T Products
Mica chips: ArtQuest
Craft wire: JudiKins

Allison didn't have a picture of her baby's birth mother, so she asked a pregnant friend, scrapbooker Shannon Watt, if she could use a photo her husband had taken. Allison made sepia and full-color copies of the picture, trimmed the water from the color version, then adhered it over the water in the sepia-toned version. Note: Picture portion lifts up to reveal journaling and a photo beneath.

Hero Quotes for Tribute Pages

Next time you create a tribute page to a personal or national hero, consider including one of the following quotes. Gathered by assistant editor Lori Fairbanks, they're a fitting addition to help you capture the essence of heroism.

"The ultimate measure of a man is not where he stands in moments of comfort and convenience, but where he stands at times of challenge and controversy."
—*Martin Luther King Jr.*

"Great tragedy has come to us, and we are meeting it with the best that is in our country with courage and concern for others. Because this is America. This is who we are."
—*President George W. Bush*

"You must do the things you think you cannot do."
—*Eleanor Roosevelt*

"Courage is not the absence of fear, but rather the judgment that something else is more important than fear."
—*Ambrose Redmoon*

From *www.quotelady.com*:
"Some people come into our lives and quickly go. Some stay for a while and leave footprints on our hearts. And we are never, ever the same."
—*Anonymous*

"It is said that adversity introduces us to ourselves. This is true of a nation as well. In this trial, we have been reminded, and the world has seen, that our fellow Americans are generous and kind, resourceful and brave. We see our national character in rescuers working past exhaustion; in long lines of blood donors; in thousands of citizens who have asked to work and serve in any way possible."
—*President George W. Bush*

"The bravest are surely those who have the clearest vision of what is before them, glory and danger alike, and yet notwithstanding, go out to meet it."
—*Thucydides*

"Courage is contagious. When a brave man takes a stand, the spines of others are stiffened."
—*Billy Graham*

"Each time a person stands up for an ideal, or acts to improve the lot of others, or strikes out against injustice, he sends forth a tiny ripple of hope, and crossing each other from a million different centers of energy and daring, these ripples build a current that can sweep down the mightiest walls of oppression and resistance."
—*Robert F. Kennedy*

"I believe it is the nature of people to be heroes, given the chance."
—*James A. Autry*

Use an inspiring quote from someone else, or come up with your own. Here, scrapbooker Heather Lancaster penned her own quote, "A random act of kindness is the first whisper of my hero's name." *Page by Heather Lancaster.* **Supplies** *Patterned paper:* Pixie Press (vellum), Scrap in a Snap (black swirls); *Computer font:* PC Pizazz, "For Font Sakes" HugWare CD, Provo Craft; *Swirls template:* Coluzzle, Provo Craft; *Grommets:* Doodlebug Design; *Mirror film:* Gary M. Burlin & Company; *Other:* Studs and chain.

Heather's journaling to note: Look into a mirror and know that inside each and every one of us, inside of you, is a hero! Every individual possesses the ability to give support, friendship, and understanding to the people who enter their lives. A simple act of kindness, compassion or forgiveness has the strength to touch someone else's life in a profound way. Don't for a minute believe that you have not done anything to earn this honor. You are a hero, and like a baby whose smile lightens the darkest day, you are not meant to ponder your abilities or the effect that you have on a person. Instead, go forward and greet each day innocently, proud to be alive and who you are. Embrace the heroes that surround you! Live your life fully and remember to pause frequently to share the strength and the power of love.

The vellum circles include hero examples such as "The man who helped me change a flat tire with stubborn lug nuts," "The little girl who pushed my daughter's wheelchair at the school dance," "The parents who encouraged me," "The teacher who told me I was smart enough to pass his physics class" and more.

Border Ideas: Shadow Boxes
by Lori Houk

My husband, Kent, is the rock of our family. When I saw these rocks at the craft store, I knew instantly that I had to include them on a layout about him. Since the rocks were so big, I didn't know how I was going to use them, but then I came across Heidi Swapp's article on creating shadow boxes on layouts in the April 2002 issue of *Creating Keepsakes*. Here's how you can create this rock border:

❶ Punch large squares out of cardstock. Using a smaller square punch, punch a smaller square out of the large squares you just punched (to create frames).

❷ Punch squares out of a coordinating shade of cardstock to create the backdrop for the frames.

❸ Adhere 3-D foam dots to the frames (you may have to cut them so they don't show through). Attach the frames to the backdrops. You now have shadow boxes.

❹ Adhere the rocks inside the shadow boxes with Glue Dots.

❺ Adhere the shadow boxes to your layout.

This fun rock border is perfect for pages about the qualities you want to instill in your family. *Pages by Lori Houk.* **Supplies** *Computer fonts:* Think Small, downloaded from *twopeasinabucket.com*; Fatty Bombatty, downloaded from the Internet; *3-D foam dots:* Stampa Rosa; *Eyelets:* Dritz; *Other:* Glue Dots by Glue Dots International.

Illustration: Carol Norby

Little Things

Preserve what means the most   *by Mary Larson*

Each time we passed from Missouri to his home state of Kansas, my father would say, "Okay, everyone, roll down your windows." As soon as the sign said that we were entering Kansas, he'd say, "Now, take a big, deep breath!" According to Dad, the air was cleaner, fresher and smelled better in Kansas. My mother, a Missouri girl but a dutiful wife, would roll her eyes as she rolled down her window.

Ever the obedient children, we would do just as Dad told us. Eyes shut tight, I would sniff—and sniff—trying to smell a difference. As I got older, I realized that Dad was just teasing us. Still, his affection for his home state was evident, and I knew he wanted us to feel the same affection.

The "Kansas air" is just one of many little things I remember from my childhood. I would never have thought to scrapbook these items had it not been for an e-mail I received one day. A cyber-friend, Karen Ballentine of San Antonio, Texas, started a thread on an e-mail loop with the question "What are some of the little everyday, odd-ball things that have stuck in your memory?"

Karen told how when she was a child, her mother told her that if she ate bread dough, it would keep rising in her stomach and she would explode! Karen believed her mom and never even tried eating bread dough until she was grown-up and married.

As I considered Karen's question, items began popping into my head. As I wrote them down, I realized that I needed to record the memories. Otherwise, my children wouldn't know several pieces of my childhood that I hadn't thought to share with them. I decided to create an album of "little things" from my childhood. →

Figure 1. Scrapbook a fun family ritual and how your family carried it out. *Page by Mary Larson.* **Supplies** *Lettering template:* Jungle, ScrapPagerz.com; *Computer font:* CK Handprint, "The Best of Creative Lettering" CD Combo, *Creating Keepsakes*; *Plaid vellum:* The Robin's Nest Press; *Colored brads:* HyGlo.

CREATING THE ALBUM

As I considered how best to scrapbook my memories, I faced some hurdles. Because the memories were from my childhood, I didn't have pictures readily available. Plus, the place where I'd experienced these memories was 1,300 miles away! I knew I'd better do some quick planning. Here are four steps I followed to keep the project manageable:

❶ I organized my memories into four categories. These categories included:

Events This category included common holidays, birthdays and events specific to my family. For example, almost every month in the summer, we would have an evening meal of nothing but fruit. My mom called it "Fruit Plate," and she would serve every kind of fruit she could find, plus cinnamon toast.

Rituals This included everyday rituals we did as children. I scrapbooked, for example, how we chose which Kool-Aid to make on a certain day (Figure1). The kids laid out every Kool-Aid flavor we had, then we picked the winner with the verse "One Potato, Two Potato." My children use the same ritual now—it's only right!

People This included memories of people who played a big role in my childhood. One was my father. I remember him calling dandelions "pufferbellies" or saying a shirt was "ring-side-ronk-is" instead of "inside out." I thought his variation was a real word until my future husband heard it and looked at me like I was crazy!

Objects This included simple objects with powerful memories associated with them. A childhood favorite is a set of rosaries that hangs on a custom-made plaque with seven pegs (one for each of us). Just looking at those rosaries brings back the memory of my family kneeling in the living room, in the dark, saying our prayers together, each at our own special spot.

❷ **I went through my list of "little things" and identified which could be captured on film.** Once I'd decided, I called my sister in Missouri, asked her to be my photographer, and gave her a list of items to photograph. All were right in my parents' house or yard. My sister obliged and got me the pictures rather quickly so I could start my project.

❸ **I decided which "little things" needed their own layouts and** **which could be grouped on one layout.** At this point, I realized that crossover existed between the categories and I needed to make some choices. For example, my father liked to wake us up in the mornings by singing "Oh, What a Beautiful Morning" from the musical "Oklahoma." I had to decide whether to include the memory in a layout about my dad or one about family rituals.

❹ **I scrapbooked the memories.** Look at Figure 1 and you'll learn about our Kool-Aid family ritual and the red spatula used to mix up our sweet drink. In Figure 2, I scrapbooked my mother's irises. They'd come up every year, and we'd use the flowers for May Day baskets or teacher gifts.

I have so many recollections of my father that I created an entire layout about him (see Figure 3). I wanted to capture his personality as we saw it as children. One fond memory? When I was very young and my father was sharing a childhood memory, he'd always start his story with the words "When I was a little girl . . ." With my childhood naiveté, I believed he'd once been a little girl just like me. →

Figure 2. Showcase items with a several-year history, plus the memories associated with them. *Page by Mary Larson.* **Supplies** *Lettering template:* Whimsey, Déjà Views, The C-Thru Ruler Co.; *Computer font:* BaaBookHmkBold, Hallmark Card Studio; *Raffia:* Paper Adventures; *Chalk:* Craf-T Products; *Pen:* Zig Writer, EK Success; *Other:* Eyelets and silk flower. *Idea to note:* Mary used a silk flower petal as a guide when cutting out her iris.

Figure 3. Include a host of "little things" in a layout about a certain person or subject. *Pages by Mary Larson.* **Supplies** *Lettering template:* Blockhead Serif, ScrapPagerz.com; *Computer font:* JaneHmk, Hallmark Card Studio; *Colored pencils:* Prismacolor, Sanford; *Pen:* Zig Writer, EK Success; *Chalk:* Craf-T Products; *Other:* Fiber cording.

Figure 4. Create a scrapbook layout that's a random collection of "little things" and their stories. *Page by Mary Larson.* **Supplies** *Lettering template:* Curly-Q, ScrapPagerz.com; *Vellum:* Paper Adventures; *Pen:* Zig Writer, EK Success; *Computer font:* CK Curly, "The Best of Creative Lettering" CD Combo, *Creating Keepsakes.*

Thank goodness I figured out the truth as I got older!

Another layout depicted several objects with stories behind them (see Figure 4). Look carefully and you'll see the ugly popcorn bowl my mom still eats popcorn from, the kangaroo organizer we would borrow nickels from as kids, and the ripped-up shoebox of photos that I still look through every time I go home for a visit.

Take a moment now to ask yourself, "What are the little things I remember from my childhood?" Whether you scrapbook them or not, write the memories down and share them with your loved ones. You could be surprised at how "little things" end up being a big deal to you and everyone else! ♥

Try This Technique: Creating Metal Lid Windows

by Lynne Montgomery

Using metal storage-container lids creates a terrific "window" effect on scrapbook pages. And don't worry about the lids being too bulky; most aren't even as tall as a pop dots. You can attach the lids to a layout in two ways: 1) Find a round craft punch that's the same size as your metal lid, punch a hole, and slip the lid right in, or 2) Hand-sew the lid onto your layout. The metal is fairly soft and thin, so you can punch a needle right through it and tie it to your page with ribbon, fiber or embroidery floss.

Here's how to create a metal lid window using a craft punch:

❶ After finding a craft punch and metal lid with the same diameter, simply punch a hole where you'd like to insert the lid.

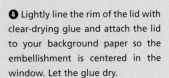

❷ Gently slide the lid up inside the hole. The paper should fit securely in the groove of the lid without any adhesive or glue.

Add a "window scene" to a layout using this unique metal lid technique. *Pages by Lynne Montgomery.* **Supplies** *Computer font:* CK Cursive, "The Best of Creative Lettering" CD Vol. 2, *Creating Keepsakes; Embossing powder:* Suze Weinberg; *Other:* Metal storage container lids, fibers, eyelets, beads and seashells.

❸ Adhere the embellishments that will fill your window to a piece of background paper.

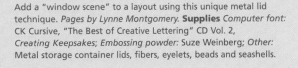

❹ Lightly line the rim of the lid with clear-drying glue and attach the lid to your background paper so the embellishment is centered in the window. Let the glue dry.

❺ Attach the entire embellishment to your page with adhesive, fibers, eyelets or anything else you can imagine!

Heart Talk

It was March 2001, and my friend Denise had less than six months to live. In her own brave way, she said goodbye to her husband, her eight-year-old daughter, and her five-month-old baby girl. She had shared all that was precious to her, and in the end, nothing was left unsaid.

I would lay awake at night thinking about her children. Which memories would her eight year old be able to hold onto forever? Which memories would fade with time? I imagined the questions her baby girl would have about the wonderful mom she couldn't remember.

My thoughts instinctively turned to my kids. They are young. If something were to happen to me tomorrow, what would they remember? Tender moments shared? The silliness? The times I comforted them? Would they truly remember how much I loved them? What a beautiful gift it would be to have those intimate feelings permanently etched on paper.

I decided to take a hard look at the journaling in my scrapbooks. While I had a lot of written information, it wasn't enough of the stuff that really mattered, the things from my heart. My purpose for creating scrapbooks quickly became defined. It is my way of sharing all that is precious to me. I want my children, family, friends and future generations to know my heartfelt thoughts and feelings. I want nothing left unsaid.

How about you? Do your scrapbook pages say what you really need them to say? In years to come, will those who read your scrapbooks need to guess how you felt about the important things in life? Will they know how much you adored your loved ones? Will they feel like they really know you—or simply the events of your life? Let your words speak for you now!

I know it can be intimidating to transfer heartfelt thoughts and feelings to paper. Follow along, and I'll teach you a simple way to move journaling from a surface level to a more intimate level. The secret? Think about onions! (Hey, I'm a visual gal!) →

"Only the heart knows how to find what is precious."

— FYODOR DOSTOEVSKY

BY JULIE SCATTAREGIA

The Onion Skin (On the Surface)
Reveals what is obvious
Journaling example: "The kids were smiling as they posed for a picture in front of the Christmas tree."

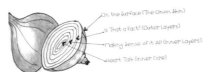

On the Surface (The Onion Skin)
Is That a Fact? (Outer Layers)
Making Sense of it All (Inner Layers)
Heart Talk (Inner Core)

Outer Layers (Is That a Fact?)
Reveals what you know
Journaling example: "Christmas Day 2001. Alexa (4 yrs.) and Aidan (2 yrs.) had so much fun opening their Christmas presents this year."

Inner Layers (Making "Sense" of It All)
Reveals what you experienced
Journaling example: "Christmas Day 2001. Wow, what a morning! At the first sign of light, Alexa was heard yelling, 'Aidan, come here. The carrots are gone. Rudolf was here!' The delicious aroma of homemade cinnamon rolls wafted through the air. Presents were opened in record time, and a whole lot of happy squeals echoed through our home. After catching our breath from all the excitement, we spent the rest of the morning poring over instructions in an attempt to put together those wonderful presents!"

Inner Core
Reveals what you feel
Journaling example: "As I watched you open your Christmas presents this morning, I was reminded of a time when I was a child. I was the one who awoke before dawn, who wondered in amazement how Rudolf knew those were his carrots, who squealed with excitement because Santa brought me just the right toy.

"I was the one who thought Christmas couldn't get any better than this. I was wrong. As only a parent can understand, my joy on Christmas morning has only been magnified as I watch you, my beautiful children, on this very blessed day."

"Thank you for letting me feel the childhood innocence of Christmas morning again. I'm so thankful for all of you and for giving me the best gift of all. You've allowed me to see Christmas through your eyes, and the eyes of a parent."

The kids were smiling as they posed for a picture in front of the Christmas tree.

Figure 1. Journal a photograph at one of four levels: surface, outer, inner and core. *Photo and chart by Julie Scattaregia.*

Discovering Your Journaling "Layers"

Onions? Who'd have guessed it? But think of how the onion consists of several layers. Each time you peel away a layer, you expose more of the inside. The deeper you go, the more aromatic, flavorful and potent it becomes.

Like the onion, your journaling has several layers. *The more outer layers you peel away, the more you expose the inside.* The deeper inside you go, the more intimately we get to know you (the writer) and what you're sharing.

Let's talk about four onion layers as they relate to journaling. We'll start with the onion skin (surface journaling) and end with the inner core (intimate journaling). Again, if the purpose of your scrapbooks is to share your heartfelt thoughts and feelings, we need to get to the core of that onion. Let's get started!

EXERCISE
I strongly encourage you to participate in this exercise. Grab 2–3 photos of the same event or person, a pen and a blank piece of paper. Now you're set!

LAYER 1: ONION SKIN JOURNALING (ON THE SURFACE)
This type of journaling reveals what is *obvious* from your photos. It's the information a total stranger could discern simply by taking a gander at your photos. It's like the skin of an onion. It's topical. It exposes little, if anything, about the subject or the writer.

Take a look at the photo and "onion skin" journaling in Figure 1. From the journaling, did you learn anything new? Did you get to know either the writer or the subject any better? No. All the journaling did was restate what was in the photos.

Look at the 2–3 photographs you grabbed. Take a minute to write down what's obvious. Haven't we all stated the obvious at one time or another? Let's peel away the onion skin and move to the onion's outer layers.

Figure 2. Capture one or more of the five senses through inner layer journaling. *Pages by Julie Scattaregia.* **Supplies** *Vellum:* PaperCuts; *Die cuts:* Creative Memories; *Eyelets, wire, key tag and overlay letter stickers:* Making Memories; *Fibers:* On the Surface; *Beads:* Westrim Crafts; *Pen:* Zig Writer, EK Success; *Computer font:* CK Journaling, "The Best of Creative Lettering" CD Combo, *Creating Keepsakes.*

Journaling to note:
"Is it the fresh air, water, or sunshine that makes you two laugh that deep belly laugh? Whatever it is, we love it! It's hard to believe you were once timid on the boat. That's definitely history!

"How does it feel to be part fish, my little lake lovers? Whether we're playing hard or just soaking up the sun, lake time is awesome family time. I watch you and I know that life is good! June 2002"

LAYER 2: OUTER LAYER JOURNALING (IS THAT A FACT?)

In this layer, your journaling reveals *what you know*. It's the identifying information. It provides answers to who, what, when, where, why and how questions. For example, "Who is in the photo?" "What is the relationship?" "Where is this taking place?" "Why are they there?" and "How old are they?"

The facts given answer the initial questions someone may have when looking at a photo. Consider the "outer layer" journaling from the chart in Figure 1. What did you learn? Factual details. After reading them, you know the event, the year, and the ages of the children. Now, take a minute and look at your own photos. Write down the answers to the "who," "what," "when," "where" and "why" questions.

You have just revealed what you know. Journaling the facts can be important, especially for providing valuable historical information for heritage photos. But factual journaling is usually still at surface level. Let's peel away some more layers.

LAYER 3: INNER LAYER JOURNALING (MAKING "SENSE" OF IT ALL)

Now we're really getting inside the onion! We're into those inner layers. You know, the more aromatic, flavorful and potent ones! We're ready to reveal *what we have experienced.*

We experience life through our five senses (sight, sound, smell, taste and touch). Yet, we often forget to convey the "five senses" details that provide more insight than a photo ever could!

For instance, a photo might show a picture of an apple pie, but unless someone told you, you wouldn't know that the freshly picked, slightly tart orchard apples were smothered in a cinnamon, sugar and caramel glaze that completely filled the room with the aroma of homemade sweetness.

Okay, you get the picture! The things you experience can add so much life to your journaling. Take a look at the "inner layer" journaling in Figure 1. Do you feel like you're there? Can't you almost hear the kids' voices as the kids tear open the gifts? Do you empathize with the parents having to put together the toys?

Take a few minutes and write some inner layer journaling for your photos. You may find that inner layer journaling takes

Figure 3. Choose a photo of a loved one, then journal what that person means in your life. *Page by Julie Scattaregia.* **Supplies** *Patterned paper and stickers:* SEI, Inc.; *Vellum:* PaperCuts; *Eyelets, tags, beads and wire words:* Making Memories; *Fibers:* On the Surface; *Computer font:* CK Journaling, "The Best of Creative Lettering" CD Combo, *Creating Keepsakes. Idea to note:* Julie made her tag tassels with coordinating paper strips.

Journaling to note:
"I love watching you near the water. You're so brave and sure of yourself. Okay, maybe your life jacket has something to do with that. Or the fact that we are usually holding your hand. Even so, I'm overwhelmed by your blind faith and trust. It gives you such freedom. Freedom to play hard. Freedom to believe that you can do anything. Freedom to dream big.
 "All too soon, the time will come when you'll leave your life jacket behind and your hand will gently slip from mine. You may discover there are times when you aren't so brave and sure of yourself. But remember your dreams, Aidan. Protect them. Believe in yourself. For me, I'll hold tight to these tender times. And who knows? Perhaps when I'm older, I'll open my hand and find that a part of you hasn't let go."

Figure 4. Share what you want to say, then choose pictures that illustrate your subject matter. *Page by Julie Scattaregia.*
Supplies *Eyelet charms, eyelets and brads:* Making Memories; *Mesh:* Stampendous!; *Rubber stamps:* Close To My Heart (textured background), Hero Arts (Italian poetry background) and Stampabilities (pocket watch); *Stamping ink:* Close To My Heart; *Rectangle punch for tag:* Fiskars; *Ribbon:* C.M. Offray & Son; *Pen:* Zig MicroPen, EK Success.

Journaling to note:
"It was a special day for me. That's why I wore your work lapel pin to school for my kindergarten photo. It didn't matter to me that it didn't match my dress or that I put it on rather crooked. It was my way of being near you even when we were apart. This week, I helped Alexa get ready for her kindergarten photo. I smiled at the thought of you, Dad.
"I may no longer have your lapel pin, but wherever I go, I always carry a piece of you with me."

more time, but it's certainly worth the effort.

Sensory journaling will evoke emotions and help the reader connect with you. Sharing your experiences this way is good, solid journaling. But we can still take things a step further. Let's get to the inner core of the onion.

LAYER 4: INNER CORE JOURNALING (HEART TALK)
Inner core journaling is intimate journaling at its best. I call it "Heart Talk" because it's just that. It's talk that comes straight from the heart. It's what you think and feel. It's the very essence of who you are, a reflection of you.

"Heart Talk" is about sharing your feelings, hopes, wishes and prayers. It reveals your dreams and desires. At this level, we expose much of ourselves and our subjects. We become more transparent with our feelings.

Don't let this scare you! "Heart Talk" journaling isn't meant to be a confessional, but an opportunity to let others know how much they mean to you. Will they have to guess how you feel, or have you shared it in your journaling? Will they know what is really going on in that heart of yours?

Consider the inner core journaling in Figure 1. Wow! What a distance we've come from simply stating the obvious. Speaking from your heart makes your pages come alive!

Figure 5. Record the perspective of each member of the family. *Pages by Julie Scattaregia.* **Supplies** *Vellum:* PaperCuts; *Eyelets:* Doodlebug Design; *Grommets:* Dritz; *String:* On the Surface; *Ribbon:* C.M. Offray & Son; *Computer font:* Ludica Handwriting, Corel WordPerfect; *Other:* Charms. *Idea to note:* Julie filled her keytags with cardstock and added charms.

Journaling to note:
Julie and her family answered five questions. Sample answers for some of the questions follow.

1. What makes you the happiest? "Knowing my private world is in order" (Steve), "Hearing the words 'I love you, Mommy' " (Julie) and "Wearing dresses" (Alexa)
2. What makes you really laugh?
3. What makes you cry? "When I see an underdog win or someone attain a life's dream" (Steve), "sappy movies" (Julie), "when Mommy leaves for any reason" (Aidan)
4. What do you enjoy doing?
5. If you had one wish, what would it be? "To have all my friends come over and stay forever" (Alexa)

6 Tips For Heart Talk Journaling

"Heart Talk" journaling is extremely powerful. Here are six tips to help you use it on your scrapbook pages:

1 WHEN YOU LOOK AT YOUR PHOTOS, SEE BEYOND THE EVENT. Write what you feel. After looking through a roll of recently developed film, I knew I wanted to create a layout about our special family time at the lake (Figure 2). My goal was to create a layout with inner-layer, meaningful journaling.

At the same time, I purposely set aside one photo for the specific purpose of creating a layout with "Heart Talk" journaling (Figure 3). Why? Because every time I looked at that particular photo, it evoked strong emotions in me about my little boy who won't be little for long. I wanted to share some of my hopes and wishes for my son as he grows.

2 IF YOU HAVE A STORY TO SHARE, TELL IT. THEN FIND THE PHOTOS THAT WILL HELP SUPPORT IT. While getting my daughter ready for her kindergarten photos, I was immediately reminded of picture day when I was in kindergarten. I knew I wanted to create a scrapbook page (Figure 4) that shared this story about how proud I've always been of my dad. I selected pictures of him (my favorite childhood photo of him, and a current one of us) to support this story.

3 WRITE THE WAY YOU SPEAK. How would you verbally share your story with someone? Don't think too much. Feel. Let your words flow from your heart.

4 USE OTHER PEOPLE'S WORDS. Interview your friends and family. Get their perspectives (Figure 5). They can provide valuable insight and their own heart talk!

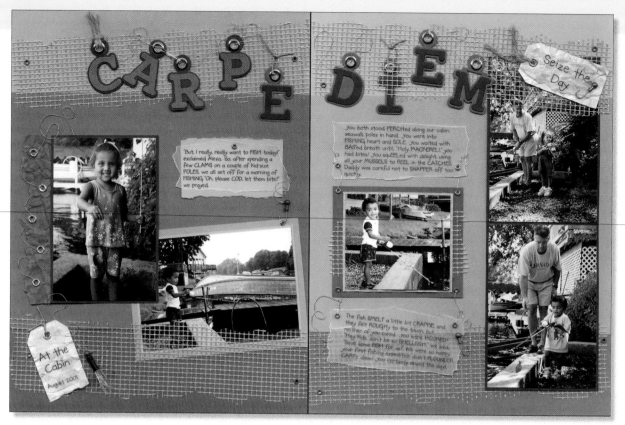

Figure 6. Show your sense of humor with a play on words. *Pages by Julie Scattaregia.* **Supplies** *Vellum:* PaperCuts; *Eyelets:* Stamp Studio; *Grommets:* Dritz; *Craft wire:* Artistic Wire Ltd.; *Letter die cuts:* AlphaDuets, Dandilion; *Creative tags:* DMD Industries; *Mesh:* Magic Mesh, Avant Card; *Chalk:* Craf-T Products; *Computer font:* CK Toggle, "The Best of Creative Lettering" CD Combo, *Creating Keepsakes.*

Journaling to note:
"But I really, really want to FISH today!" exclaimed Alexa. So, after spending a few CLAMS on a couple of kid-size POLES, we all set off for a morning of FISHING. "Oh, please COD, let them bite!" we prayed.

"You both stood PERCHed along our cabin seawall, POLES in hand. You were into FISHING heart and SOLE. You waited with BAITed breath until, "Holy MACKEREL!," you had a bite! You squEELed with delight, using all your MUSSELS to REEL in the CATCHES. Daddy was careful not to SNAPPER off too quickly.

The fish "SMELT" a little bit CRAPPIE, and they felt ROUGHY to the touch, but neither of you cared. You were HOOKED! "Hey kids, don't be so SHELLFISH," we said. "Save some FISH for us!" We were so happy your first fishing expedition didn't FLOUNDER. CARPe diem! You certainly seized the day!"

5 ALLOW YOURSELF TIME.

As hard as it may be, don't worry about the stacks of photos waiting to be scrapbooked. Focus for now on writing down your heartfelt thoughts and feelings.

6 USE HUMOR.

The more onion you peel away, the more your eyes will tear. At the inner layer of journaling, you'll evoke emotions. At the inner core, you'll have yourself and others reaching for tissues during your most tender revelations.

But "Heart Talk" journaling doesn't always need to be serious (Figure 6). Instead of writing "Baby Jake is so cute when he smiles," consider, "You have such a contagious grin! When I see your cheeks disappear behind your toothless grin, I can't help but smile. I hope your cheeks are still disappearing when you're 50!"

Okay, now it's your turn. Look at your photos one more time. See beyond the event. What do you feel? What emotions are evoked? Why? Take a few minutes to write down your thoughts and feelings.

Of course, not every page in your scrapbook needs to contain "Heart Talk" journaling. Yet it all goes back to this: Are your pages saying what you really want them to say? Are you writing enough about what really matters to you?

Perhaps you've discovered that you're satisfied with your journaling. Maybe you've discovered you're ready to go deeper by peeling off the surface layers and exposing more of who you are, what you think, and how you feel.

Have fun with "Heart Talk" journaling. Enjoy yourself. And remember: No one can do a better job of sharing your thoughts and feelings than you! ♥

★ CKU Honor Roll

Katherine's lovely photos and warm palette immediately caught the judges' attention at CKU San Antonio. They were further impressed by her heartfelt journaling and the elegant touches Katherine added to her layout. Note her little letter tiles, the eyelets that hold her fiber borders, and the sweet quotes Katherine added to her journaling tags.

"Whenever I Count My Blessings"

by Katherine Brooks, Gilbert, AZ

SUPPLIES

Patterned paper: Autumn Leaves
Decorative paper: Memory Lane
Corrugated cardstock: DMD Industries
Computer fonts: CK Journaling, "The Best of Creative Lettering" CD Combo, *Creating Keepsakes;* Kayleigh, downloaded from the Internet
Eyelets: Impress Rubber Stamps

Chalk: Craf-T Products
Rubber stamps: PSX Design
Stamping ink: Splendor, Tsukineko
Foam squares: Therm O Web
Fibers: Rubba Dub Dub, Art Sanctum
Punches: Family Treasures
Clay button: Memory Lane
Other: Charm
Tags: Katherine's own designs

Thanks!

What are you thankful for? Hold on—don't skim over that question. Put down the magazine and think for a minute. What are you thankful for?

Whether it's the golden glow of a sunset or your child's laugh, there's gotta be something you're *really* thankful for. In the following pages you'll find layouts from eight talented scrapbookers whose heartfelt journaling will inspire you to create a "What I'm Thankful for" layout as well.

Uh oh, did I just hit a snag? Is there a part of you that's thinking, "Tracy, I'm already so far behind with my scrapbooks. You can't possibly expect me to make a layout on that topic." Well, I'm not *expecting* anything. I'm just *hoping* you'll make a "What I'm Thankful for" layout.

Why? Early this year I faced a bout of depression and, to be honest, I had some days when I struggled to find anything to be grateful for. A dear friend, seeing my pain, challenged me to write down five things I was thankful for every day. Some days this challenge was easy and others, well … you know how depression is.

This simple exercise grounded me in life's simplicities. I learned that I'm grateful for the wind chimes clanging a soft song out my window. And I'm gratified when I hear my cat's rhythmic purr lulling me to sleep.

I'm *hoping* you'll make a "What I'm Thankful for" layout so you, too, can discover the little things that make your life so rich. I promise, your family will thank you for sharing this special part of you with them.

BY TRACY WHITE

ILLUSTRATION BY STEPHANIE WUNDERLICH

Community is an important aspect of life and deserves a place in your album. What do you love about your community? Has it rallied to support you in times of need? Does your community bring purpose to your life? What is your role in your community? Why are you grateful for that role?

Pages by Kelly Anderson. **Supplies** *Mesh:* Magenta; *Alphabet charms and definition:* Making Memories; *Flowers:* Jolee's Boutique, Sticko by EK Success; *Rubber stamps and lock:* Ink It!; *Computer font:* Garamouche, P22 Type Foundry; *Other:* Paper clips and tags.

We're formed by our earliest experiences. What experiences from your childhood are you most grateful for? How have those experiences affected your life today? How do those experiences affect the people around you?

Pages by Christy Gantt. **Supplies** *Patterned paper:* Provo Craft; *Vellum:* The Paper Company; *Brads:* Karen Foster Design; *Embossing powder:* StampCraft; *Metallic rub-ons:* Craf-T Products; *Embroidery floss:* DMC; *Alphabet stamps:* All Night Media; *Computer fonts:* Scriptina (title), downloaded from the Internet; Bradley Hand (journaling), Microsoft Word.

My Smile

A personal story of something I am so thankful for

Most likely you've heard the old "turning lemons into lemonade" cliché, but give it a try. Jot down a list of things you're ungrateful for, then turn them around. How have these challenges blessed or improved you?

Pages by Erin Vandre. **Supplies** *Patterned paper, tags and nails:* Chatterbox; *Computer font:* CK Hustle, "Fresh Fonts" CD, *Creating Keepsakes.*

JOURNALING EXCERPT: "MY SMILE"

In August 2002, I was diagnosed with an acoustic neuroma—a benign brain tumor that grows on the eighth cranial nerve, which controls hearing and balance. Since nerves are close together in your brain, a tumor like this can also affect your seventh nerve, which controls facial function. I had a big tumor—about the size of a small lemon—so keeping hearing in my right ear was out of the question. However, it was unknown before surgery how removing the tumor would affect my facial nerve....

On October 2 2002, after a 13-hour surgery, I was brought to recovery. I don't remember anything, but my mom said the first thing I asked was if could I smile. I could. My face worked perfectly; however, my surgery had not been as successful as the doctors had hoped, and they recommended another surgery to remove more of the tumor. It was extremely hard to do it again since all the same risks were involved, and what if I wasn't as lucky this time? I realized I had no choice, so another surgery was scheduled....

The second surgery and recovery went much better than the first. I healed quickly and was able to return to my normal life sooner than expected. Most of all, I was glad to be able to return to being a mom of a great little boy who I love more than words can express. I hope all people realize what a great blessing it is to be able to smile—I know I will always be grateful.

Pages by Silvia Arizaga Kolksy. **Supplies** *Patterned paper:* Making Memories (scrolls) and Keeping Memories Alive (checked); *Computer font:* Angelina, downloaded from the Internet; *Ribbon:* C.M. Offray & Son; *Other:* Embossed paper.

No doubt you're grateful for the people in your life, but why? Sit down and explore why you love them and how they've affected you, your decisions and your life.

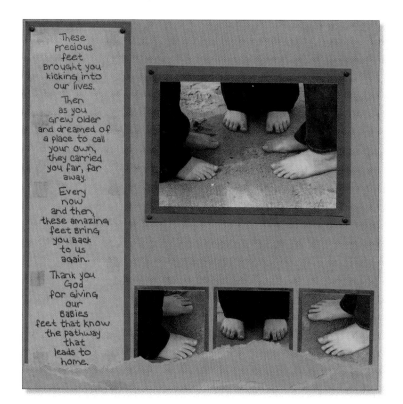

Sit down and ponder what you're thankful for. Oftimes it's the small or "insignificant" items that bring us the most peace.

Page by Cathy Heslop. **Supplies** *Computer font:* Augie, Microsoft Word.

JOURNALING EXCERPT: "YOU"

When we were planning our wedding I had just started working in a very busy practice and didn't have much time off. So there you were, making phone calls, traveling to Napa, helping with invitations, making hair and make-up appointments, choosing the menu.... Our wedding was so beautiful and you planned most of it.

When we found out I was pregnant, there you were again. You read everything there is to know about pregnancy. You bought me a lunch bag and prepared "balanced" meals every day. You came with me to every doctor's appointment. You were by my side when our daughter was born....

You know me very well. You understand my love for music, art and scrapbooking. For my first Mother's Day, you gave me a much-needed Crop-in-Style tote. I was so happy!

You are a wonderful husband and dedicated father. Just the other day, when I came back from the store, I found you with Gigi cinched up tight against your chest and you pulling the carpet washer with one arm. I had to take a picture! You are responsible, dedicated and passionate about your career. So sometimes I wonder, how can you do it all? But you do. And I will be forever thankful.

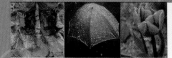

Are you grateful for the comforts of your home, town or country? Look around your environment and identify the items that, if missing, would leave a void. Be sure to include rich details like scents, sounds, textures and the way something looks.

Pages by Christine Brown. **Supplies** *Computer fonts:* Avignon, downloaded from the Internet; Arial Narrow, Microsoft Word.

Does faith in a higher power pull you through life's challenges? How does this faith enrich you, your family and friends? Why are you grateful for the faith you feel?

Page by Jennifer Harris.
Supplies *Patterned paper:* K & Company; *Handmade paper:* Black Ink; *Fibers:* Adornments, EK Success; *Transparency:* Great White; *Computer font:* Euphorigenic, downloaded from the Internet.

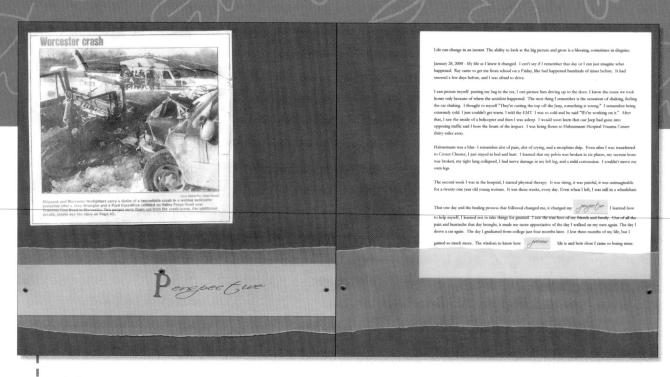

Whether or not you've experienced a life-altering event, you most likely have pinnacle moments that changed your life's direction. What are they? Why are you grateful for them? How have they changed your perspective?

Pages by Deena Hopkins. **Supplies** *Vellum:* The Paper Company; *Eyelet letter and brads:* Making Memories; *Computer fonts:* Scriptina, downloaded from the Internet; Garamouche, Impress Rubber Stamps; *Textured cardstock:* Bazzill Basics. *Photo:* Gene Walsh, *Times Herald* of Norristown, PA.

JOURNALING EXCERPT: "PERSPECTIVE"

January 28, 2000— My life as I knew it changed…. Ray came to get me from school on a Friday, like hundreds of times before. It had snowed a few days before, and I was afraid to drive.

I can picture myself putting my bag in the car. I can picture him driving up to the door. I know the route we took home only because of where the accident happened. The next thing I remember was the sensation of feeling the car shake. I thought to myself, "They're cutting the top off the Jeep; something is wrong." I remember being extremely cold…. I told the EMT I was so cold and he said, "We're working on it." After that, I saw the inside of a helicopter, and then I was asleep. I would soon learn that our Jeep had gone into opposing traffic, and I bore the brunt of the impact. I was flown to Hahnemann Hospital Trauma Center 30 miles away.

Hahnemann was a blur—I remember a lot of pain, a lot of crying and a morphine drip. Even after I was transferred to Crozer-Chester, I just stayed in bed and hurt. I learned that my pelvis was broken in six places, my sacrum bone was broken, my right lung was collapsed, I had nerve damage in my left leg, and I had a mild concussion. I couldn't move my legs.

That day and the healing process that followed changed me—it changed my perspective. I learned how to help myself; I learned not to take things for granted. I saw the true love of my friends and family. Out of all the pain and heartache that day brought, it made me more appreciative of the day I walked on my own again, the day I drove a car again, the day I graduated from college just four months later. I lost three months of my life, but I gained so much more— the wisdom to know how precious life is and how close I came to losing mine. ♥

The Healing Power of Scrapbooking

SHARE HOW YOU MADE IT PAST A PAINFUL EXPERIENCE

Scrapbooking is my favorite way to escape from life's troubles. As I concentrate on solving issues of color and design, I can feel the worries of the day fade into the background. Playing with pictures of beloved family members helps me appreciate my blessings.

At times that's all I want out of scrapbooking, but I've learned that it's possible to explore painful issues on paper, too. For instance, I struggle at times with a poor body image (I know, I'm the only one!), so I created a page about my daughter's

positive reaction to seeing me in a swimming suit. The act of putting words and pictures to paper made me think about an issue I'd been avoiding. I created a layout that demolished my negative thoughts about body image forever. That's the kind of power scrapbooking can have.

While it takes a certain measure of courage to step up to the challenge of scrapbooking a painful memory, the rewards can be extraordinary. Read on for compelling and courageous stories of four women's struggles with, well, life. BY ALLISON STRINE

PINK RIBBON

My sweet Amelia Rose. This photo was taken in November of 2001. You were 3 years old, and 4 months into chemotherapy. Your cheeks were still pink, and the dark purple circles that were to come later had not yet found your eyes. We had just had that terrible moment together, a few days earlier, when you discovered that your hair had almost completely fallen out. I told you gently, to prepare you, and then held you tightly in my arms while you looked in the mirror. I didn't want you to be surprised and alone when you discovered it. I will never ever forget the look on your face when you saw yourself, and when you quickly looked away. Fear, surprise, sadness, and revulsion. I just held you and rocked it away—as much for me as for you I'm afraid.

A few days later, you got dressed and then quietly came to me. Looking up at me with those endlessly blue eyes, you opened up your little fist and showed me the pink ribbon draped across your palm. I had given it to you weeks before to play with. Silently, almost holding my breath with anticipation and happiness, I tied it around your soft little head. We walked into the bathroom together wordlessly, and I scooped you into my arms in front of the mirror. As you turned to look at your beautiful reflection, I saw the smile light across your sweet face. You beamed at the girl in the mirror, and my eyes filled with tears again. You always knew, even when we didn't, just how to make yourself feel better. You could adapt to anything.

Looking back at this picture, your chemo just finished, I still don't know how you managed two and a half years of it, countless pills, injections and needle pokes. Somehow, I think the secret is in this photograph. For weeks, you wore that ribbon like it was a crown, with grace and courage and strength. My brave Amelia Rose, you are simply amazing. 8/2003

 "Courage is not the towering oak that sees storms come and go; it is the fragile blossom that opens in the snow."
–Alice MacKenzie Swaim

Page by Jenna Tomalka. **Supplies** *Patterned cardstock:* Lasting Impressions for Paper; *Ribbon:* C.M. Offray & Son; *Computer fonts:* Marydale (journaling), downloaded from the Internet; CK Peeking Posies (drop caps), "The Best of Creative Lettering" Super Combo CD, *Creating Keepsakes*; *Die-cut alphabet for title:* QuicKutz; *Stickers:* Jolee's Boutique, EK Success.

Pink Ribbon

After the initial shock of learning her daughter Amelia had leukemia, Jenna Tomalka had to force herself to put her emotions aside. During treatment Jenna stayed strong by focusing on daily living, not on the seriousness of the situation.

Two years later, with Amelia in remission, Jenna can finally allow herself the luxury of revisiting the horrifying days of chemotherapy. Notes Jenna, "Each time I let myself go back and consider one of those times—then write the story of it—it feels like I put salve on a burn. It is such a relief to finally spend time thinking about those moments, to finally put them away or share them with others." By creating scrapbook pages about Amelia's illness and treatment, Jenna can heal the painful past and begin to live joyfully in the present.

Pages by Tricia Rubens. **Supplies** *Patterned papers:* Bazzill Basics, Leisure Arts and Making Memories; *Stickers:* Creative Imaginations (poemstone), Making Memories (large page pebbles) and me & my BIG ideas (shabby chic); *Computer fonts:* CK Elegant, "Fresh Fonts" CD, *Creating Keepsakes*; Antique Type, downloaded from the Internet; *Charms:* Making Memories (washers), Jolee's Boutique by EK Success, Michaels (glass heart charms) and Yvonne Albritton Designs; *Tags:* me & my BIG ideas (threads), 7 Gypsies (printed twill), American Tag Co. (price tag) and Dymo Labelmaker (label); *Rubber stamps:* Plaid Enterprises (foam decor); Printer's Alphabet, Hero Arts; Simply Stated, Making Memories; *Circle clips:* Boxer Scrapbook Productions; *Shaped clips, metal screen and metal frame:* Making Memories; *Conchos:* Scrapworks; *Eyelets:* Creative Imaginations; *Rhinestone studs:* Michaels; *Acrylic paint:* Plaid Enterprises; *Quotation:* Elements, Daisy D's; *Fibers:* EK Success (blue) and Timeless Touches (cream); *Other:* Watch parts, old keys, optometrist lens and buttons.

Mommy Sings the Blues

Tricia Rubens spent the first 35 years of her life in a state of sadness and mistrust. After being diagnosed with and treated for depression, Tricia can now look back on her difficult past with kindness and understanding for the person she is.

"Because of misunderstandings about depression," says Tricia, "I didn't talk about it for many years. I was afraid that people would look at me as a nut case. Now I want my family to know about depression and that it is nothing to be ashamed of." By putting her story in writing, Tricia traded her feelings of embarrassment and shame for pride and self-awareness.

Page by Polly McMillan. **Supplies** *Patterned papers:* Paper Adventures (beige background) and The Paper Loft (burlap/tweed); *Tags:* Nostalgiques, Sticko by EK Success (antique), Making Memories (metal rimmed) and Nunn Design (gold framed); *Ribbon:* C.M. Offray & Son; Java Weave; *Stickers:* Nostalgiques, Sticko by EK Success (typewriter keys and cracked-glass letters) and K & Company ("I" letters in title); *Computer font:* CK Script, "The Best of Creative Lettering" CD Combo, *Creating Keepsakes*; *Photo corners:* Dress It Up; *Metal letters and date stamp:* Making Memories; *Other:* Clear vellum, label maker and pens.

What I Didn't Know the Day I Turned 37

After 15 years of marriage, Polly McMillan could best deal with the emotional lows of divorce on paper. Through scrapbooking Polly was able to deal with her overwhelming feelings of sadness and despair.

"I had to force myself to work on this layout so I could face the feelings I was trying to avoid," says Polly. "I would cry as I wrote notes on my yellow pad. Tears would smear the ink, and I'd have to stop and collect myself so I could continue." By completing this difficult and personal layout, Polly feels one step closer to emotional healing.

Page by Miley Johnson. **Supplies** *Patterned papers:* 7 Gypsies (black script), Provo Craft (blue stripe) and Chatterbox (yellow dot); *Eyelets:* Two Busy Moms; *Die cuts and mini-alphabet:* QuicKutz; *Stickers:* Mrs. Grossman's; *Label:* me & my BIG ideas.

The One I Missed

Miley Johnson missed her son's first birthday for an important meeting at work. Immediately regretting her choice, Miley struggled with feelings of guilt and shame until she decided to treat the birthday layout with complete sincerity.

"I knew that the only way for me to move on from this event was to scrap it," says Miley. "It might seem silly that a scrapbook page could heal, but it was the perfect way to get my emotions out and gain peace." In creating this heartfelt page, Miley released her guilty feelings as she openly expressed to her son how much she learned that day.

These brave women show that facing our difficulties is one of the first steps toward healing. If we are willing to explore our feelings on paper, we can help ourselves mend emotional wounds from the past.

I would encourage you to scrapbook a painful memory. Maybe you'll create a layout to be shared with family and friends, or maybe you'll make a page so personal that no one will ever see it. Either way, if you pour your heart and soul onto paper, I guarantee the results will uplift and astound you.

by Lisa Bearnson

Musical memories

Strike a Meaningful Chord with Song Lyrics

Date: October 1976

Occasion: First seventh-grade "mat dance"

Song: "Stairway to Heaven" by Led Zeppelin

Memory: Slow dancing with a boy I didn't even want to be in the same room with. This 11-minute song seemed like an eternity!

Date: April 1980

Occasion: My "first love" broke my heart

Song: "She's Out of My Life" by Michael Jackson

Memory: Crying on my bed, day after day, while listening to this song over and over again

Date: May 1982

Occasion: Slide show during the end-of-year assembly for high-school seniors

Song: "We May Never Pass This Way Again" by Seals & Crofts

Memory: Relieved that my high-school experience was finally over, yet sad that life would never be the same with my friends

Date: July 1989

Occasion: Telling my boyfriend, Steve, that I needed space to figure things out

Song: "Right Here Waiting for You" by Richard Marx

Memory: This song came on a cassette inside a huge balloon. My future husband was giving me my space. He was also telling me that "whatever it takes or how my heart breaks, I will be right here waiting for you."

Outcome: A happy 14-year marriage!

Music is a powerful tool that evokes memories and emotions. We each have special songs tucked away in our minds—songs that remind us of life's experiences, good and bad. Here, talented scrapbookers show how song titles and lyrics play a role in their lives. You'll be motivated to dig deep within and remember the meaningful songs in your life. While some layouts will make you laugh, others will make you cry. Enjoy the musical journey.

Beautiful

Every day is so wonderful
And suddenly, it's hard to breathe
Now and then, I get insecure
From all the fame, I'm so ashamed

I am beautiful no matter what they say
Words can't bring me down
I am beautiful in every single way
Yes, words can't bring me down
So don't you bring me down today

To all your friends, you're delirious
So consumed in all your doom
Trying hard to fill the emptiness
The piece is gone and the puzzle undone
That's the way it is

You are beautiful no matter what they say
Words won't bring you down
You are beautiful in every single way
Yes, words won't bring you down
Don't you bring me down today

No matter what we do
No matter what they say
When the sun is shining through
Then the clouds won't stay

And everywhere we go
The sun won't always shine
But tomorrow will find a way
All the other times

We are beautiful no matter what they say
Yes words won't bring us down
We are beautiful no matter what they say
Yes, words can't bring us down
Don't you bring me down today

Don't you bring me down today
Don't you bring me down today

i am beautiful

Page creator: Anne Heyen,
New Fairfield, CT

Song title: "Beautiful"

Artist: Christina Aguilera

Album: *Stripped*

Genre: Pop

In Anne's words: "Growing up, I was teased about my looks. Comments like 'You'd really be pretty if you got a nose job' still resonate in my head today.

"A few years ago, I knew I was sinking fast. My family had just moved from New York City to the country, and we were having a hard time adjusting. My sons were struggling in school, our budget was tight, and my husband was commuting 140 miles a day to work. I gained weight and became a hermit—my self-esteem was at an all-time low.

"I heard this song then and listened to it over and over again. At the end, I always cried. It became my personal anthem. The words constantly remind me that no matter what anyone else thinks, 'I am beautiful!' I'm a great mother, friend, daughter, aunt and even a scrapper. And, what I think about myself is what's most important."

A song can be your personal anthem.
Pages by Anne Heyen. **Supplies**
Patterned paper: Karen Foster Design;
Vellum: DMD, Inc.; *Computer font:*
2Peas Flea Market, downloaded from
www.twopeasinabucket.com; Beads:
Little Charmers and On The Surface;
Eyelets: Creative Impressions; *Craft wire:*
Artistic Wire Ltd.; *Flower charm:* Making
Memories; *Square punch:* Marvy Uchida;
Tags: Making Memories; *Gesso:* Liquitex;
Embossing powder: Close To My Heart.

Ideas to note: Anne used white Gesso to
paint over the black letters. She cut out
the inside of the metal-rimmed tags.

★

Page creator: Angelia Wigginton, Belmont, MS

Song title: "You Are My Sunshine"

Artist: Jimmie Davis

Genre: Traditional country

In Angelia's words: "I loved this song as a child. When my first child was born, I'd often sing the song's catchy melody to calm, entertain or help her drift off to sleep. When she learned I was expecting another baby, she asked if I would only sing this song to her since the words are 'only sunshine.' We've adapted the song to a plural form so my girls can enjoy it together."

Include an "oldies" song on your layout. *Page by
Angelia Wigginton.* **Supplies** *Vellum:* The Paper Company;
Computer font: 2Peas Chestnuts, downloaded from
www.twopeasinabucket.com; Mini brads: Magic Scraps;
Fibers: Brown Bag Fibers; *Letters, definition and star
eyelet:* FoofaLa; *Other:* Sun charms.

Use chart-topping songs on a layout.
Pages by Shannon Zickel. **Supplies**
Patterned paper: Magnetique, 7
Gypsies; *Computer font:* 2Peas
Flea Market, downloaded from
www.twopeasinabucket.com;
Bookplates: Two Peas in a Bucket;
Mini brads: Lost Treasures; *Other:*
Charms and clock frame. *Ideas to
note:* Shannon copied a sheet of
music onto cardstock. To age it,
she tore, crumpled, ironed, inked,
chalked and sprayed it.

Page creator: Shannon Zickel,
Louisville, KY

Song title: "I Don't Want to Miss
a Thing"

Artist: Aerosmith

Album: Soundtrack from
"Armageddon" movie

Genre: Rock

In Shannon's words: "This song was the
number-one title when my son, Jake, was
born. The song was playing as we drove to
the hospital. The lyrics matched the way
I felt then, and how I feel now about
being Jake's mom. I don't want to miss one
moment of his life. Every time I hear this
song, it makes me cry because my son's
becoming so independent and is growing
up too fast. Every moment with Jake is a
moment I will treasure forever."

Page creator: Terrie McDaniel, League City, TX
Song title: "What If She's an Angel?"
Artist: Tommy Shane Steiner
Album: *Then Came the Night*
Genre: Country

In Terrie's words: "Although the lyrics reference
stories about a homeless man, spousal abuse and
a little girl with cancer, the underlying message is
that these people can be angels. They ensure that
we take the time to help one another.

"As a mom, this song speaks to my heart. It
reminds me that my daughter may be my test in
life and that success relies heavily on my ability to
set aside the responsibilities of the day and be
there for her."

**Use a song as a reminder to always be there for
someone else.** *Page by Terrie McDaniel.* **Supplies**
Patterned papers: Flavia, Colorbök; Karen Foster
Design; *Computer font:* Corabael, downloaded
from the Internet; *Eyelets:* Making Memories;
Other: Fabric and brads.

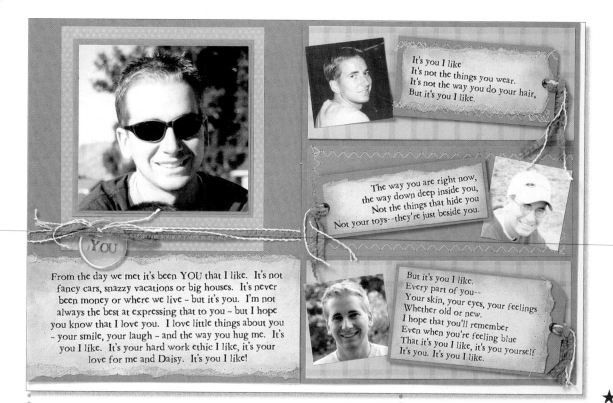

From the day we met it's been YOU that I like. It's not fancy cars, snazzy vacations or big houses. It's never been money or where we live – but it's you. I'm not always the best at expressing that to you – but I hope you know that I love you. I love little things about you – your smile, your laugh – and the way you hug me. It's you I like. It's your hard work ethic I like, it's your love for me and Daisy. It's you I like!

It's you I like
It's not the things you wear.
It's not the way you do your hair,
But it's you I like.

The way you are right now,
the way down deep inside you,
Not the things that hide you
Not your toys--they're just beside you.

But it's you I like.
Every part of you--
Your skin, your eyes, your feelings
Whether old or new.
I hope that you'll remember
Even when you're feeling blue
That it's you I like, it's you yourself
It's you. It's you I like.

Page creator: Joanna Ellis, Rexburg, ID

Song title: "It's You I Like"

Artist: Mr. Fred Rogers

Album: *You Are Special*

Genre: Children

In Joanna's words: "This song was a childhood favorite. It's still one of my favorites because it reminds me of the reasons I love my husband. So often we get caught up in the things of life. This song's lyrics help me remember it's not what my husband wears or how he combs his hair; it's what's inside him that I like."

A popular "Mister Rogers Neighborhood" song enhances the journaling on this adult-themed layout. *Pages by Joanna Ellis.* **Supplies** *Patterned paper:* Lasting Impressions for Paper; *Computer font:* CK Constitution, "Fresh Fonts" CD, *Creating Keepsakes; Tags:* Making Memories; *Eyelets:* Memory Lane; *Alphabet stamps:* PSX Design; *Other:* Fibers and stamping ink.

Page creator: Lee Anne Russell, Brownsville, TN

Song title: "It's a Great Day to Be Alive"

Artist: Travis Tritt

Album: *Down the Road I Go*

Genre: Country

In Lee Anne's words: "It's a rare occurrence for my family to get in the car without someone asking to listen to the Travis Tritt CD. It has 'our song' on it. In fact, we've listened to it so often that we know the words by heart.

"A day doesn't get any better than the day I took these pictures—a newborn colt, a warm spring day, and the smile on Adelaide's face as she watched the colt. This all contributed to the carefree feeling of the day. The title of 'our song' conveyed this perfectly."

A newborn colt, a warm spring day, and a child's smile communicate how great it is to be alive. *Page by Lee Anne Russell.* **Supplies** *Patterned paper:* K & Company; *Speckles:* JudiKins; *Cloisonné:* Stampa Rosa; *Mesh:* Coastal Netting, Magic Scraps; *Eyelets:* Making Memories; *Rubber stamps:* Junque; *Stamping ink:* Adirondack, Ranger Industries; *Chalk:* Craf-T Products; *Mica chips:* USArtQuest; *Other:* Jute. *Idea to note:* Lee Anne glued speckles on the mat, then coated it with clear embossing powder.

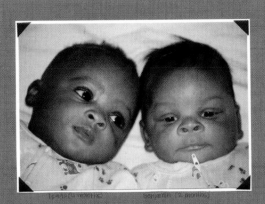

We had great dreams and plans for our family: places to live and see, goals to accomplish, weaknesses to overcome, and traits to develop. We never realized all the jogs and turns that our lives would take, this winding road that could only be walked by faith. Both the hardships and the joys have molded us into the parents we are today. Boys, you have been a marvelous surprise at the end of an uncertain turn. With difficult pregnancies and deliveries, my body could no longer sustain another life. Yet we knew that we had missing family members. Through the Lord's grace and mercy you found us.

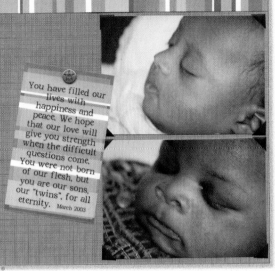

Twin Sons

You have filled our lives with happiness and peace. We hope that our love will give you strength when the difficult questions come. You were not born of our flesh, but you are our sons, our "twins", for all eternity. *March 2003*

When your father and I were first married we spent the summer in Seattle. We had a few tapes that we listened to while making the drive. This album by Dan Fogelberg was one of our listening pleasures. What great memories your father and I shared, singing, driving, dancing and spending our first few months together alone in this beautiful place.

Page creator: Allison Kimball, Salt Lake City, UT
Song title: "Twin Sons of Different Mothers"
Artists: Dan Fogelberg and Tim Weisberg
Album: *Twin Sons of Different Mothers*
Genre: Folk

In Allison's words: "When we got married, my husband and I had lots of hopes and plans for our family. We'd listen to this Dan Fogelberg song and dream about the places we'd go and the goals we'd accomplish. But life took us in another direction. After many difficult pregnancies and miscarriages, my body was in no shape to try again. Through the Lord's grace and mercy, our two boys found us. Our lives are now filled with happiness and peace. These sons were not born of our flesh, but are our 'twins' for all eternity."

Scrapbook how a song helped you through a difficult time. *Pages by Allison Kimball.* **Supplies** *Patterned paper:* Chatterbox; *Vellum:* Paper Adventures; *Computer fonts:* CK Newsprint, "Fresh Fonts" CD, *Creating Keepsakes;* Carpenter ICG, downloaded from the Internet; *Pens:* Gelly Roll, Sakura; *Eyelet:* Making Memories.

Page creator: Angie Cramer, Red Cliff, AB, Canada
Song title: "I'm Gonna Soak Up the Sun"
Artist: Sheryl Crow
Album: *C'mon, C'mon*
Genre: Pop

In Angie's words: "Before we left on a family trip to the Bahamas, my daughter Courtney constantly talked about 'soaking up the sun' and working on her tan. The fact that it was almost winter where we live made it even more important. When I scrapped this photo, I wanted to convey a carefree and fun mood. The lyrics were the perfect inspiration for my page."

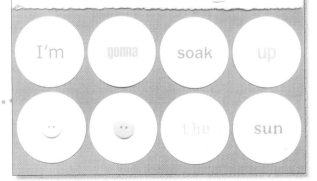

A song title adds a sunny touch to this playful page. *Page by Angie Cramer.* **Supplies** *Computer fonts:* Century Gothic, Verdena, Haettenschweiler, Franklin Gothic Medium, Adjutant and Freebooter, downloaded from the Internet; *Circle punch:* Marvy Uchida; *Other:* Fibers.

LYRICAL MEMORIES BY LISA

You can easily create a themed album using your favorite photos and songs. I created this 6" x 6" album in just a few hours. Simply match up special photos and songs, put the title of the song at the top of the page, copy significant lyrics under the title, and write your journaling at the bottom.

Supplies *Album:* Little Keepers, Cobalt Spring Stripes, We R Memory Keepers; *Tags:* Making Memories; *Computer font:* CK Corral, "Fresh Fonts" CD, *Creating Keepsakes; Word tiles:* Icicles, K•I Memories. *Eyelets:* Making Memories; *Clear paper:* Pockets On A Roll, F & M Enterprises; *Other:* Butterfly.

"In a world of peace and love, music would be the universal language."
— Henry David Thoreau

Song: "Lean on Me"
Artist: Bill Withers

Song: "Angels Among Us"
Artist: Alabama

Song: "Feels Like Home"
Artist: Chantal Kreviazuk
Album: *Dawson's Creek* soundtrack

Song: "How Great Thou Art"
Text: Stuart K. Hine

VICKI LYNN TERRELL

simple pleasures

Do you ever stop in the middle of a moment and think, "Aaah, this is what life's really about"? Today's way of life is so busy, sometimes we forget to pause and enjoy the little things that bring us true happiness. What better way to appreciate those things than with a photograph to capture them forever? Here are a few ideas to help you capture your favorite "simple pleasures" in life:

- ◆ Your favorite place to relax, whether it's the front porch swing, the cozy armchair in the den, or the hot tub on the back patio
- ◆ Your favorite color and where you find it in the world around you
- ◆ Your favorite special indulgences: fresh flowers, trips to the ice cream store, or foot rubs before bedtime
- ◆ Simple games that bring a smile to your face every time
- ◆ Endearing moments with your favorite furry friend
- ◆ A brilliant sunset on your drive home
- ◆ Three things that inspire you every time you see them
- ◆ Your favorite food, and how you like to eat it
- ◆ A bright, blue sky with white, puffy clouds
- ◆ Quiet everyday moments with the people you love
- ◆ Weekend rituals that help you unwind
- ◆ Your favorite place to visit, whether it's in your own home or across town
- ◆ Hobbies that give you a sense of accomplishment without dominating your time
- ◆ Music that puts you in a good mood every time you hear it

ARTICLE BY CATHERINE SCOTT